AppleScript® Programming for the Absolute Beginner

JERRY LEE FORD, JR.

THOMSON

™

COURSE TECHNOLOGY

Professional ■ Technical ■ Reference

To my mother and father for always being there for me. And to my wonderful children Alexander, William, and Molly, and my beautiful wife, Mary.

ACKNOWLEDGMENTS

A book like this is the result of combined efforts of a great many people to whom I owe thanks. For starters, I want to thank the book's acquisitions editor, Mitzi Koontz, for helping to make this book a reality. I also wish to give special thanks to Jenny Davidson for applying her considerable talents and skills to this book. Jenny served as both the book's project editor and copyeditor and worked hard to ensure that everything came together like it was supposed to. Thanks also go out to Brad Miser, who served as the book's technical editor and provided me with his invaluable insight and advice. Finally, I would like to thank everyone else at Thomson Course Technology PTR for their contributions and hard work.

ABOUT THE AUTHOR

Jerry Lee Ford, Jr. is an author, educator, and an IT professional with over 18 years' experience in information technology, including roles as an automation analyst, technical manager, technical support analyst, automation engineer, and security analyst. Jerry has a master's degree in business administration from Virginia Commonwealth University in Richmond, Virginia. He is the author of 21 other books and co-author of 2 additional books. His published works include *AppleScript Studio Programming for the Absolute Beginner, Microsoft Windows Shell Scripting for the Absolute Beginner, Perl Programming for the Absolute Beginner, Beginning REALbasic, Microsoft Windows Shell Scripting and WSH Administrator's Guide, VBScript Professional Projects,* and *Microsoft Visual Basic 2005 Express Edition Programming for the Absolute Beginner.* He has over five years' experience as an adjunct instructor teaching networking courses in Information Technology. Jerry lives in Richmond, Virginia, with his wife, Mary, and their children, William, Alexander, and Molly.

Contents

Part II   LEARNING HOW TO WRITE APPLESCRIPTS................... 77

Chapter 3   WORKING WITH VALUES, VARIABLES, AND CLASSES... 79

Chapter 4   IMPLEMENTING CONDITIONAL LOGIC AND WORKING WITH LOOPS.. 113

Part III   ADVANCED TOPICS...195

Chapter 7 ACCESSING FILES AND FOLDERS..............................197

Chapter 8 AUTOMATING MAC OS X APPLICATIONS.....................227

Chapter 9 **DEBUGGING YOUR APPLESCRIPTS 255**

Chapter 10 **INTRODUCING APPLESCRIPT STUDIO 283**

INTRODUCTION

Welcome to *AppleScript Programming for the Absolute Beginner*. AppleScript is an English-like scripting language that runs on Mac computers. AppleScript offers programmers the ability to interact with and control different parts of the operating system and to control the execution of desktop applications.

AppleScript is an immensely popular scripting language that runs on Mac computers. It comes already installed and is used extensively by the operating system any many of its applications. It is a perfect programming language for first-time Mac programmers and hobbyists. It can be used to increase personal efficiency through the development of workflows that perform predefined tasks that are repetitive or time-consuming. For example, you might develop an AppleScript that automatically prints a copy of any text file added to a particular folder or which renames any file added to a folder to append a date and time stamp to the file. It can also be used to automate tasks that are seldom performed or are complicated and thus subject to human error.

In addition to providing you with everything you need to automate the execution of your favorite applications, AppleScript also provides the ability to interact directly with the user through predefined dialog windows and comes equipped with all the programming structures found in any modern programming language.

This book is dedicated to teaching you how to program using AppleScript. By the time you are finished, you will not only be well prepared to start programming using AppleScript, you will also have built a foundation that will serve you well should you decide to learn other programming languages.

WHY APPLESCRIPT?

AppleScript is a scripting language provided with Mac operating systems dating all the way back to Mac OS 7. With the development of Mac OS X, AppleScript assumed a role as a key Apple technology, having been tightly integrated into the operating system and many Mac OS X applications. AppleScript is an English-like programming language that is easy to learn compared to many other programming languages such as Perl and UNIX shell scripting. As such, it makes for a great first programming language.

AppleScript's overall simplicity and its English-like syntax make it a natural first programming language for Mac users. Yet, AppleScript is robust and powerful enough to meet the needs of professional programmers, allowing programmers to build prototype scripts that might otherwise take more time and effort to build using other programming languages such as C and Objective-C. AppleScript is also the programming language used by AppleScript Studio. AppleScript Studio is a programming language used to develop full-featured desktop applications. As such, learning AppleScript is a prerequisite for anyone interested in becoming an AppleScript Studio programmer.

Anyone who uses a Mac computer can benefit from learning how to program using AppleScript. As this book will demonstrate, learning AppleScript is both useful and fun and makes for a natural first programming language for any Mac user. In addition, AppleScript is an essential second programming language for any professional Mac programmer. So whether you are a hobbyist looking for a personal challenge or a professional programmer looking to add another tool to your arsenal, AppleScript will serve you well.

WHO SHOULD READ THIS BOOK?

When I sat down to write this book, I did so with the goal of teaching you not only how to program with AppleScript but also to help you become an effective programmer. I make no assumptions regarding your previous programming experience or background. The only assumptions I make are that you have access to a Mac computer, you possess a working familiarity with Mac OS X, and you are interested in learning how to use AppleScript to automate certain tasks to make more effective use of your time.

I believe that you will find this book's unique approach to teaching programming through the development of computer games to be both enjoyable and extremely effective. If you are a first-time programmer or a Mac hobbyist, then you should find this book's step-by-step, hands-on approach very helpful. The programming information and knowledge that you learn from this book will help prepare you to tackle a variety of AppleScript programming tasks and will serve you well should you later want to transition over to a different programming language.

If, on the other hand, you are already a professional programmer, you will find this book to be an invaluable quick-start guide, and you'll discover that AppleScript is a great language for writing small scripts that don't justify the effort required to build a full-blown application. In fact, AppleScript can be used to prototype Mac applications and perform proof of concept tests before committing your time and energy to developing full-blown Mac OS X applications.

WHAT YOU NEED TO BEGIN

AppleScript runs on any computer running Mac OS 7.0 or later. When writing this book, I worked on a computer running Mac OS X 10.4. As a result, all of the examples and screen prints that you see will have a Mac OS X look and feel. However, unless otherwise stated, the examples presented in this book should work just fine on any version of Mac OS X and should translate fairly well to Mac Classic as well.

AppleScript is shipped as part of all Mac OS X operating systems. Therefore, you should already have it available to you on your computer. In addition, AppleScript's Script Editor application is also installed by default on Mac OS X. So, as long as you have a computer running some version of Mac OS X, you should be ready to go.

The last chapter in this book covers AppleScript Studio. AppleScript Studio is an advanced Mac OS X programming language that facilitates the development of desktop applications, complete with full graphical user interfaces. If you plan on working with AppleScript Studio, then you will also need to make sure that Xcode is installed on your computer. As of the publishing of this book, the current version of Xcode was version 2.4.1. Xcode may already be present on your computer. To see if it is, look on your computer's startup disk for a folder named Developer. Inside it you should find a folder named Applications, where Xcode can be found. If it is there, then you are good to go, since AppleScript Studio is automatically installed when Xcode is installed. If Xcode is not installed on your computer, you can download it for free at http://developer.apple.com/tools/download/.

HOW THIS BOOK IS ORGANIZED

This book is written with the intention that it be read from beginning to end. However, if you have prior programming experience on the Mac, you may instead want to jump around a bit. However, I recommend that no matter what, you read the first two chapters, which will provide you with essential background information. Unless you are gifted at learning programming languages with minimal instruction, I recommend that you also read Chapters 3 through 6, which provide instruction on basic AppleScript programming, before you try tackling the later chapters.

AppleScript Programming for the Absolute Beginner is organized into four parts. Part I is made up of two chapters that provide you with basic information about AppleScript and the Script Editor. This includes an overview of AppleScript's features and capabilities as well as a review of the steps involved in creating, compiling, and executing AppleScripts.

Part II consists of four chapters that provide you with a complete overview of AppleScript's programming language. You will learn about the language's major programming statements and syntax. This includes learning how to store data in variables, implementing conditional logic, and setting up loops to perform repetitive tasks. You will also learn how to store data using lists and records and to improve the overall organization of your AppleScripts using handlers.

Part III is made up of four chapters that cover advanced topics. These topics include learning how to access files and folders and how to automate a host of Mac OS X applications, like Finder and TextEdit. You will also learn how to debug your Mac OS X applications and work with AppleScript Studio to create desktop applications.

Part IV consists of two appendices and a glossary. The first appendix provides information regarding the materials available to you on the book's companion website, and the second appendix provides a list of resources that you can utilize to continue your AppleScript programming education once you have finished reading this book. Finally, the book's glossary provides you with a list of terms that are used throughout the book.

A high-level overview of each chapter and the topics that are covered are provided here:

- Chapter 1, "AppleScript Basics." This chapter provides a basic overview of AppleScript, including a quick review of the various features that make up and support the scripting language. You will learn about AppleScript's ability to interact with and control Mac applications and the philosophy behind its design. You will also learn how to create your first AppleScript, the AppleScript Humor game.

- Chapter 2, "Getting Comfortable with the AppleScript Script Editor." In this chapter, you will learn about AppleScript's Script Editor. This will include a review of its key features and an explanation of how to use it to create, edit, and execute your AppleScript files. You will also learn how to use the Script Editor to access and view application dictionaries, unlocking the key to learning how to automate Mac applications. In this chapter, you will create the AppleScript Story Teller game.

- Chapter 3, "Working with Values, Variables, and Classes." In this chapter, you will learn how to store and retrieve data using variables. You will learn about the different types of data supported by AppleScript, including numbers, strings, and dates. You will also learn how to convert data from one type to another and how to use arithmetic operators to perform all kinds of calculations. In this chapter, you will create the AppleScript Fortune Teller game.

- Chapter 4, "Implementing Conditional Logic and Working with Loops." In this chapter, you will learn how to apply conditional logic to create AppleScripts that can alter their execution based on the value of the data they are presented with. In addition, you will learn how to set up and execute loops to perform repetitive processes and to process large amounts of data. In this chapter, you will create the AppleScript Typing Test game.

- Chapter 5, "Using Strings, Lists, and Records." In this chapter, you learn how to work with strings, lists, and records. This includes learning how to modify string contents and store groups of related data in lists. You will also learn how to process lists using loops. In addition, you will learn how to format, store, and retrieve data in records. You will create the Godfather Trivia Quiz in this chapter.

- Chapter 6, "Improving Script Organization with Handlers." In this chapter, you will learn how to organize the contents of your scripts into handlers. You will learn how to execute handlers and pass them data for processing. You will see how to set up handlers to pass data back to calling statements and to use handlers as a means of controlling variable scope. You will create the AppleScript Shell game in this chapter.

- Chapter 7, "Accessing Files and Folders." In this chapter, you will learn how to interact with files, folders, and disk drives. You will also learn how to develop AppleScripts that can open and close files and manipulate their contents. This includes learning how to read from and write to files as well as learning how to retrieve file information. You will create the AppleScript Lottery Picker game in this chapter.

- Chapter 8, "Automating Mac OS X Applications." In this chapter, you will learn the fundamental steps involved in accessing and controlling Mac applications. This includes learning how to use application dictionaries to identify commands supported by the applications and to use these commands to develop AppleScripts that automate the operation of applications such as Finder, TextEdit, Safari, iTunes, DVD Player, Address Book, Mail, and the Help Viewer. You will learn how to develop automation workflows that tie together the operations of multiple Mac applications to perform tasks that none of the applications can accomplish alone. You will create the AppleScript Number Guessing game in this chapter.

- Chapter 9, "Debugging Your AppleScripts." In this chapter, you will learn how to identify and eliminate errors that prevent your AppleScripts from running correctly. This includes the identification and removal of syntax, logical, and runtime errors. You will learn how to set up error handlers that can trap and respond to different types of errors. You will develop the Rock, Paper, Scissors game in this chapter.

- Chapter 10, "Introducing AppleScript Studio." In this chapter, you will be introduced to AppleScript Studio and learn how to apply your AppleScript programming skills to the development of AppleScript Studio desktop applications. You will learn about the various components that make up AppleScript Studio. In addition, you will learn how to build applications that include all of the graphical elements, such as buttons and text box controls, that you would expect to find in any Mac OS X application. You will develop the Tic-Tac-Toe game in this chapter.

- Appendix A, "What's on the Companion Website?" This appendix provides an overview of the resources that you will find on this book's companion website. This includes a copy of the source code for each game presented in this book.
- Appendix B, "What Next?" This appendix provides information about resources that you can explore to further your AppleScript education. Here you will find information regarding additional reading material as well as a list of links to AppleScript websites you can visit to learn about the latest happenings in the world of AppleScript programming.
- Glossary. This unit provides a glossary of terms used throughout the book.

Conventions Used in This Book

To help improve the overall presentation and delivery of information in this book and to make it as easy to read and enjoy as possible, I have implemented a number of helpful conventions. These conventions are outlined and described here:

 Hints provide advice on different ways that particular tasks can be accomplished and point out things that you can do to become a more proficient AppleScript programmer.

 Traps point out areas where problems are likely to occur and provide advice on how to avoid those problems, hopefully saving you the pain of learning about them the hard way.

 Tricks provide programming tips and shortcuts designed to help make you a better and more efficient programmer.

Challenges

Each chapter in this book ends with a series of challenges intended to provide you with ideas that you can apply to further improve chapter game projects and further your programming skills.

Part

I

Introducing AppleScript Scripting

AppleScript Basics

A ppleScript is a programming language provided as a built-in operating system component. It has been around since the days of Mac OS 7. Since the introduction of Mac OS X, AppleScript has become an even more important factor in the manner in which both the operating system and your Mac applications work. Apple and third-party application developers use AppleScript to provide additional functionality and convenience to the end user. Millions of people also use AppleScript everyday to develop automation scripts that help make them more productive and efficient. This chapter will introduce you to AppleScript and provide you with an overview of the language and the technology that help make it work. In addition, you will learn how to write your first AppleScript.

Specifically, you will learn about:

- Different ways of saving and distributing AppleScript files
- How to use the Script Editor to create your first AppleScript
- Different ways to set up automated actions using AppleScript

PROJECT PREVIEW: THE APPLESCRIPT HUMOR GAME

In this chapter and in each chapter that follows, you will learn how to develop an AppleScript game. By teaching you how to program through the development of computer games, I hope to provide you with instruction that is both fun and practical. This chapter's game project is the AppleScript Humor game. This game will tell the player a series of jokes. When started, the game will display the dialog window shown in Figure 1.1 and then wait for the player to respond by clicking on one of the two available buttons.

FIGURE 1.1

The AppleScript Humor game waits on the player to click on the Tell Me Some Jokes button. The player is given two choices. Clicking on the Tell Me Some Jokes button initiates game play in which a series of five jokes is displayed. However, if the player instead clicks on the No Thanks button, the dialog window shown in Figure 1.2 is displayed. This window displays a message letting the player know that he is missing out on something good. This window is dismissed when the player clicks on the OK button, at which time the AppleScript stops running.

FIGURE 1.2

A message designed to tempt the player into returning later to play the game.

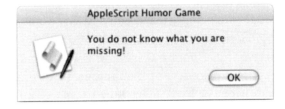

If the player elects to play the game by clicking on the Tell Me Some Jokes button at the opening window, the game will proceed to tell the first of its five jokes, as shown in Figure 1.3.

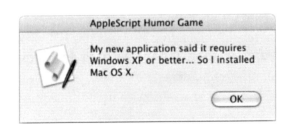
FIGURE 1.3

The first joke told by the AppleScript Humor game.

The player advances from joke to joke by clicking on the OK button that is displayed on each joke's dialog window. Figures 1.4 through 1.7 show the series of jokes told by the game.

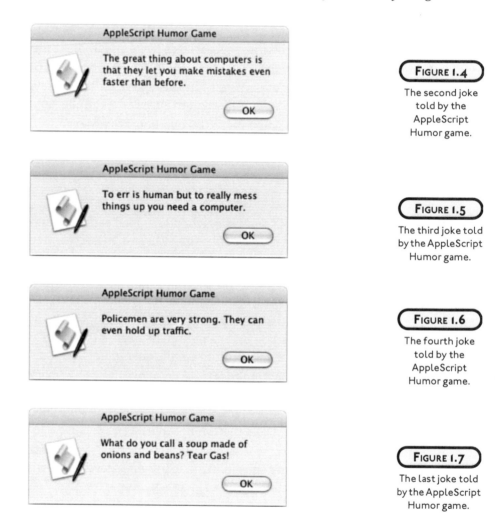

AppleScript Humor Game

The great thing about computers is that they let you make mistakes even faster than before.

OK

FIGURE 1.4

The second joke told by the AppleScript Humor game.

AppleScript Humor Game

To err is human but to really mess things up you need a computer.

OK

FIGURE 1.5

The third joke told by the AppleScript Humor game.

AppleScript Humor Game

Policemen are very strong. They can even hold up traffic.

OK

FIGURE 1.6

The fourth joke told by the AppleScript Humor game.

AppleScript Humor Game

What do you call a soup made of onions and beans? Tear Gas!

OK

FIGURE 1.7

The last joke told by the AppleScript Humor game.

Once the player reads and dismisses the last joke displayed by the game, the AppleScript Humor script stops running, ending the game. By the time you have finished working on the creation and testing of this game, you will have mastered the basic steps involved in developing and executing AppleScripts and will be ready to move on and tackle more complex challenges.

INTRODUCING APPLESCRIPT

AppleScript is a programming language developed and supplied by Apple as a default component in Mac OS X. If you have been a Mac user for any time at all, AppleScript is going to be the easiest programming language for you to get started learning how to program. AppleScript has an English-like syntax that makes it easier to learn and understand than most other programming languages. Its English-like syntax also makes it more intuitive, especially for first-time programmers. AppleScript does not impose as strict a level of syntactic language requirements as do most other programming languages. For example, AppleScript does not force programmers to append a semicolon to the end of every programming statement nor does it mandate the inclusion of parentheses, brackets, and curly braces throughout your program code.

 Although you can develop and run AppleScripts on Mac operating systems beginning with Mac OS 7, this book focuses on the development of AppleScripts designed to run specifically on Mac OS X. Regardless, much of what you will learn from this book can be directly applicable to prior versions of Mac operating systems.

AppleScript first made its debut with the release of the Mac OS 7 operating system. For a number of years, Mac users and programmers paid very little attention to AppleScript. There were even rumors from time to time that Apple might drop its support for the language. However, the release of the Mac OS X operating system gave AppleScript a new lease on life, implementing AppleScript as a core architectural component of the operating system and using it to provide additional functionality for Mac OS X applications. Part of this new functionality included the development of Mac OS X applications that were specifically designed to be scriptable, allowing programmers to develop AppleScripts that could directly interact with and control application operation. As a result, AppleScript has attracted the support of millions of programmers, including third-party Mac software developers who found value in modifying their applications to make them scriptable by AppleScript.

 AppleScript was developed based on an earlier scripting language known as HyperTalk. *HyperTalk* was developed in 1987 by Dan Winkler and was used to develop scripts that were processed by Apple's HyperCard Hypermedia application developed by Bill Atkinson. HyperTalk scripts were used to automate simple tasks.

HyperTalk scripts were written using an English-like syntax that used a logical structure similar to that of the Pascal programming language.

Apple describes AppleScript as an English-like scripting language that is easy to learn. Of course, according to Apple, everything associated with Mac OS X is easy and intuitive. Many of AppleScript's commands and keywords are indeed based on common English words. For example, you can use the `tell` command to submit commands to Mac OS X applications. AppleScript syntax is based on an English-like syntax that references resources like files and folders as nouns and uses verbs like open and close to interact with and control these resources. However, I would be misleading you if I left you with the impression that learning how to become an AppleScript programmer was not a challenging task. To become an effective AppleScript programmer, you must be prepared to invest both your time and energy, as is the case with any other programming language.

The basic purpose of AppleScript is to empower users and programmers with the ability to develop scripts, referred to as AppleScripts, to automate different parts of the operating system and its applications. As such, AppleScripts are a great timesaving tool for automating the execution of repetitive tasks. For example, suppose you were a digital camera buff and you frequently downloaded digital picture files to your computer, and that as a means of organizing your image files, you included the current date as part of every filename. You could of course individually rename each file that you downloaded, appending the current date to the end of each filename. Alternatively, you could develop an AppleScript to perform this task for you and then use this script to rename your image files.

 As with any new technical endeavor, it is important that you begin with a good understanding of the key terminology involved in AppleScript programming. Within this book, the term *AppleScript* is used to refer to both the AppleScript scripting language and to script files created using the AppleScript programming language. A *script file* is a collection of programming statements contained within a file that can be executed as a computer program. The terms script file and script can be used interchangeably. Within this book, the terms AppleScript and script are also used interchangeably.

Although it is the easiest programming language for Mac OS X users and programmers to learn, AppleScript is by no means the only programming language supported by Mac OS X. Other available programming languages include Objective-C, REALbasic, Perl, Ruby, Python, and UNIX Shell Scripting. Each of these programming languages has its own particular set of strengths and weaknesses. What sets AppleScript apart from these programming languages is its ability to interact with and automate Mac OS X and its applications.

No programming language is perfect. AppleScript is no exception. Compared to the other programming languages, AppleScript can sometimes be a little slow and may not perform as well when required to process large amounts of data. In addition, AppleScripts are typically slower when it comes to performing complex mathematic calculations and interacting with the Mac OS X file system.

COMMON TASKS PERFORMED BY APPLESCRIPTS

The main benefit to learning how to program using AppleScript is that you can develop AppleScripts that can save you time and help you to work more efficiently. However, Apple-Scripts can be developed to tackle a host of different challenges and to solve many types of problems. For example, AppleScript can also be used to automate any of the following types of tasks.

- Developing scripts that automate the execution of complex tasks, which are subject to human error when manually executed, or repetitive tasks that while not particularly complex, may be very time consuming.
- Automating the execution and operation of different Mac OS X applications such as Finder and TextEdit.
- Creating automated workflows that automate the operation of two or more applications at a time to perform a task that neither application is independently capable of performing.

Each of these three types of tasks is examined further in the sections that follow.

Automating Complex and Repetitive Tasks

One particularly good use of AppleScript is in the development scripts that perform complex tasks, particularly those that are subject to human error. By developing AppleScripts to perform these types of tasks, you can ensure that they are performed in a precise and predictable manner every time, thus ensuring that tasks are done correctly, no matter how complex they are or how infrequently they may be performed.

Another excellent use of AppleScript is to automate repetitive tasks. As an example of one such task, consider a situation in which you find yourself needing to rename all or some of the files stored in a folder. If the folder contains hundreds of files that need to be renamed, it would take a lot of time to perform this task. After a while, you would probably begin making some typing mistakes, resulting in a number of accidentally misnamed files.

To save yourself the time and tedium of this task, you could instead create an AppleScript to perform the task for you. Any time spent developing the script would be paid back by the time saved in performing the actual file rename task. As an added bonus, you can save the script and reuse it again in the future, thus giving you future benefit from your work as well. Better yet, rather than writing the AppleScript yourself, you may be able to find an AppleScript that somebody else has already written that you can use to perform this task. One of the great things about AppleScript is the number of free scripts that you will find already installed on your computer, just waiting for you to run. In addition, you will have no trouble finding tons of free scripts developed by your fellow AppleScript programmers on the Internet just waiting for you to download.

As it happens, you should already have a script on your computer that you can run to rename any number of files. This script is a Finder script named Replace Text in Item Names and you can find it in /Library/Scripts/Finder Scripts. This AppleScript performs a find and replace operation on every selected file and folder in the active Finder window, allowing you to instantly rename all or parts of file and folder names that match your specified criteria. For example, to use this script to rename one or more files located in a folder, all you have to do is open the folder where the files are stored and then run the script, which you can do by double-clicking on it to open it using the Script Editor application and then clicking on the Script Editor application's Run button. The dialog window shown in Figure 1.8 will be displayed.

 HINT   The Library folder is located at the root level of the computer's startup drive.

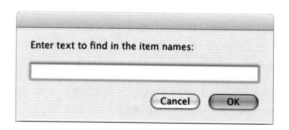

FIGURE 1.8

Using the Replace Text in Item Names script to rename files stored in the active Finder window.

Click on the File Names button and the dialog window shown in Figure 1.9 will be displayed.

FIGURE 1.9

Enter the text that you want to replace in each filename.

Enter the text that you want the script to replace in each filename where a match is found and click on the OK button. The dialog window shown in Figure 1.10 will be displayed.

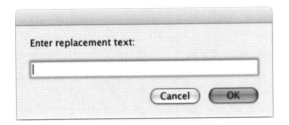

FIGURE 1.10

Enter the
replacement text
for each filename.

After you enter the replacement text, click on the OK button. Next a dialog window similar to the one shown in Figure 1.11 is displayed.

FIGURE 1.11

The script requires
confirmation
before performing
the rename
operation.

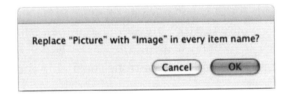

To rename each file whose name contains matching text, click on the OK button. Within a moment, the AppleScript renames all matching files and then ends.

 You will learn more about how to work with the collection of free AppleScripts shipped as part of Mac OS X in Chapter 8, "Automating Mac OS X Applications." This chapter will also identify a number of websites where you can go to download more free AppleScripts. In addition, this chapter will demonstrate how to use AppleScript to develop scripts that interact with and control both the operating systems and its applications.

Automating the Execution and Operation of Mac OS X Applications

AppleScript is a core component of Mac OS X. It facilitates communications between different Mac OS X applications and is designed to provide everything you need to automate the execution of applications. Automated tasks may be as simple as starting Safari and automatically loading a URL or as complex as using Finder to perform a host of different file management tasks.

There is no end of possible examples that you might come up with when developing AppleScripts that automate the execution of Mac OS X applications. The following list identifies just a small percentage of the Mac OS X applications that you can automate using AppleScript.

- Finder
- iPhoto
- Mail
- DVD Player
- iTunes
- iCal
- Terminal
- QuickTime Player

For example, suppose you support a small office of 15–20 users, each of whom has limited experience working with Mac OS X. In this situation, these users may run into all kinds of small problems, potentially running you ragged as you try to answer everybody's questions. One possible solution might be to provide the office staff with instructions on how to access and use the Help Viewer application. Using this application, users can perform keyword searches and retrieve information about particular types of problems.

If you do not have the time or opportunity to teach everyone how to work with the Help Viewer application, you might instead create a small AppleScript that presents the user with a list of common problems. Based on the type of problem selected by the user, the AppleScript could automatically open the Help Viewer application for them and then perform the appropriate search on the user's behalf.

Take a look at the following example. It provides you with a sneak peak of how AppleScript code statements look. In this example, a small AppleScript has been written that opens the Help Viewer and displays a list of help topics based on a predefined search keyword.

```
tell application "Help Viewer"
  activate
  search looking for "printer"
end tell
```

Having not yet covered the fundamentals of AppleScript syntax or reviewed any specific AppleScript keywords or commands, you should not be concerned if this example looks a little strange. Still, given AppleScript's English-like syntax, you can probably figure out what is going on anyway. For starters, the tell command is used to notify the Help Viewer application that a series of commands is going to be sent to it for processing. Next, the activate command is used to start, or activate, the Help Viewer application. The third statement tells the Help Viewer application to perform a search looking for any help topics related to the search keyword printer. Finally, the last statement marks the end of the interaction with the Help Viewer application.

When executed, this example will open the Help Viewer application and display a list of help topics from which the user can select and view, as demonstrated in Figure 1.12, hopefully enabling the user to solve her own problem without having to call upon you for assistance.

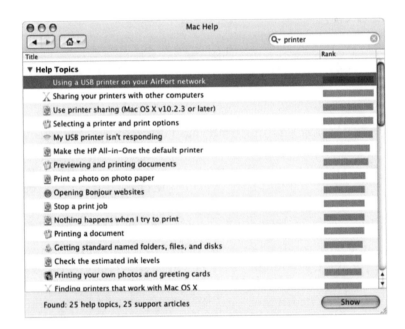

FIGURE 1.12

Provide users with an AppleScript that automates the activation of the Help Viewer application and locates help topics related to printers.

Developing Application Workflows

In addition to automating the operation of individual Mac OS X applications, you can create AppleScripts that can combine and control the actions of two or more applications to create workflows. *Workflows* tie together the operation of two or more applications to perform a task that none of the applications alone are capable of performing. For example, you might want to create an AppleScript that, when executed, copies all of the image files found in a particular folder to a different folder, renames them (using Finder), and then uses iPhoto to display them in a new photo album.

 TRAP   If you create workflows that leverage capabilities provided by third-party applications like Adobe Photoshop and Microsoft Excel, you will have to ensure that these third-party applications are installed on any computer where you want to run your AppleScripts; otherwise, they won't work.

By itself, AppleScript is more limited than most other programming languages in regards to its built-in features and capabilities. AppleScript does not provide built-in support for many programming features. For example, it lacks a large library of built-in functions found in many other programming languages. As such, AppleScript has only limited mathematic capabilities compared to programming languages like Perl and Python. AppleScript also provides limited support for performing string manipulation. However, because of its ability to interact with and control other applications, it can leverage functionality provided by these applications. For example, by automating the Calculator application, you can perform complex mathematic calculations. In addition, by automating the TextEdit application, you can perform all kinds of string manipulation operations. AppleScript is unique in regards to its ability to expend its capabilities well beyond the confines of its own set of built-in features, giving it the ability to perform tasks that other programming languages may not be capable of performing.

So, while you can always use AppleScript as a general-purpose scripting language, its real power comes from its ability to create automated workflows that can leverage the capabilities of the operating system and its applications.

TRICK By leveraging Mac OS X's at or cron command, you can configure the execution of an AppleScript that runs when you are away from your computer, thus allowing you to get work done at anytime. For example, over the years many people have purchased and set up backup programs that they run every night while they sleep to back up any work done on their computer the previous day. Using this same principle, you can configure any script's execution.

OPERATING SYSTEM INTEGRATION

AppleScript is integrated with the operating system at many different points. For starters, you can create, edit, and execute AppleScripts using the Script Editor application. This application is one of many applications automatically installed in Mac OS X. Another particularly useful point of integration is the ability to configure Mac OS X to launch AppleScripts when an assortment of actions occur. For example, you can instruct Mac OS X to run an AppleScript any time a DVD or CD is inserted into the computer's DVD or CD-ROM drive.

Enabling Folder Actions

You can set up scripts that are automatically executed any time the user opens a particular folder by setting up folder actions. A *folder action* is an AppleScript that runs whenever a change occurs in a specified folder. Changes can occur to the contents of a folder for a variety of reasons. For example, you might have an application that runs for hours every day on your computer to generate a report that you are required to review every day as part of your job.

The application might also generate an error report in the event something goes wrong. In either of these two scenarios, it might be very useful to enable folder action for the folder where these files are stored to notify you when a new file has been added.

Alternatively, you might choose to share your ~/Public/Drop Box folder with other people over a network. Using a folder action, you can set up the execution of an AppleScript that notifies you of any addition to your public folder. In fact, you can set this up without writing a single line of code because Apple has already created the necessary AppleScript for you.

> The ~ character represents your home folder. Every user is automatically assigned a home folder that is not shared with other users of the computer, allowing for a private space in which to store personal files.

The first step in setting things up is to enable folder actions on your computer. This is accomplished by control-clicking on the Mac OS X desktop and selecting Enable Folder Actions, as demonstrated in Figure 1.13.

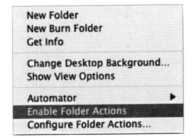

FIGURE 1.13

Enabling Folder
Actions on
Mac OS X.

Next, you need to access your ~/Public folder, control-click on the Drop Box folder, and select Attach a Folder Action, as demonstrated in Figure 1.14.

FIGURE 1.14

Enabling a Folder
Action on the Drop
Box folder.

Next, the Choose a File window will be displayed. Using this window, specify the name and path of the AppleScript that you want to run. As shown in Figure 1.15, in this example the file you will want to set up is /Library/Scripts/Folder Action Scripts/Add-new item alert.scpt. Select that script and click Choose.

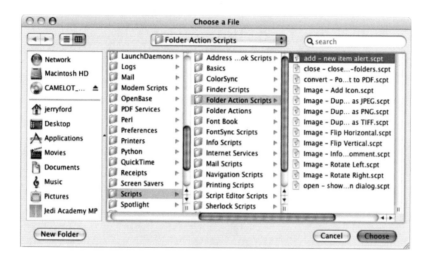

FIGURE 1.15

Using Folder Actions to run an AppleScript that notifies you whenever files are added to a folder.

Now, the next time you are working at your computer and somebody adds a new item to your Drop Box folder, you will see a dialog window like the one shown in Figure 1.16.

FIGURE 1.16

A notification is now generated any time a new file is added to your Drop Box folder.

Accessing AppleScripts through the Script Menu

Another point of integration with AppleScript and the operating system is the script menu. The script menu is an optional button that you can add to the Mac OS X menu bar, which resides in the upper-right corner of the display area. When enabled, clicking on this button displays a menu listing that provides access to hundreds of AppleScripts supplied along with Mac OS X.

By default, the script menu is not enabled. You can enable it by accessing the /Applications/ AppleScript folder and double-clicking on the AppleScript Utility icon. The AppleScript Utility window will appear, as shown in Figure 1.17.

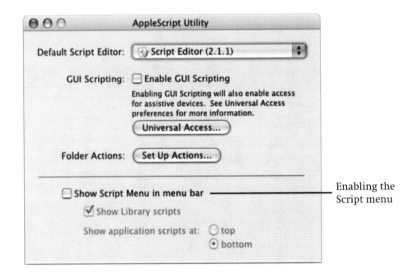

Enabling the Script menu

FIGURE 1.17

Displaying the Script menu on the menu bar.

Select the Show Script menu in the menu bar option located at the bottom of the window and then close the window to enable the display of the Script menu on the menu bar, as shown in Figure 1.18.

FIGURE 1.18

The Script menu provides easy access to any AppleScripts stored in the / Library/Scripts folder as well as any scripts stored in your ⊘/Library/ Scripts folder.

 If you decide later that you no longer need to use the Script menu, you can uninstall it by command-dragging it off of the menu bar. Doing so will remove the Script menu. However, the contents of your ⊘/Library/Scripts folder and the / Library/Scripts folder will remain unchanged.

The Script menu displays lists of scripts stored in two locations, /Library/Scripts and ~/Library/Scripts.

Any AppleScripts you create for your own personal use and which you would like to make available from the Script menu should be stored in the ~/Library/Scripts folder. This folder does not exist by default. You will have to create if yourself. Any AppleScripts that you write that you want to make accessible via the Script menu to all users of the computer should be stored in /Library/Scripts.

The contents of your ~/Library/Scripts folder and the /Library/Scripts folder are organized in folders. Each folder is represented as a submenu on the Script menu. Clicking on a submenu expands its contents, as demonstrated in Figure 1.19.

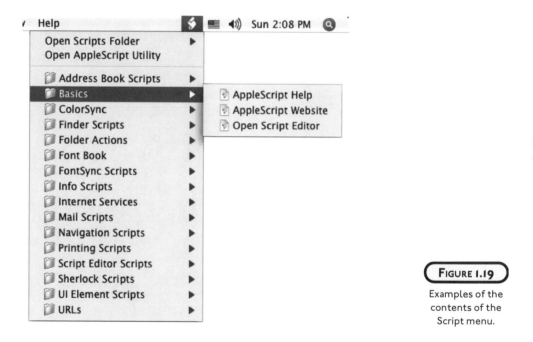

FIGURE 1.19

Examples of the contents of the Script menu.

The Script menu provides you with access to all kinds of AppleScripts, both useful and fun. For example, if you click on the Mail Scripts submenu, you will see a listing of all the scripts stored in the /Library/Scripts/Mail Scripts folder. One such script is the Crazy Message Text script, which generates an e-mail using a variety of different font types, sizes, colors, and other font attributes. To execute this script, just double-click on it and, when prompted, enter a text message of the e-mail you want to generate and then click on the Continue button, as demonstrated in Figure 1.20.

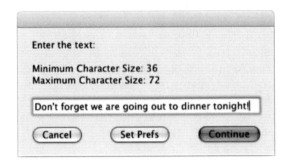

FIGURE 1.20

Generating an
e-mail using the
Crazy Message
Text script.

In response, the script will open the Mail application and generate the text of your e-mail for you, as demonstrated in Figure 1.21.

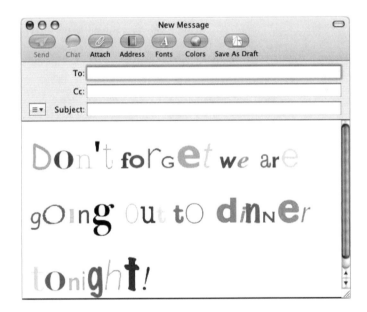

FIGURE 1.21

An example of an
e-mail message
generated using
the Crazy Message
Text script.

 As you know, AppleScript is a powerful scripting language used by programmers to develop automated workflows. However, AppleScript also provides you with access to an assortment of cool features that you can use to work faster and more efficiently. For example, the Script menu can also be used as a mechanism for launching Safari address bar icons as well as files and folders. All that you have to do is drag and drop one of these resources onto your ~/Library/Scripts folders and the next time you open the Script menu, you will be able to double-click on the corresponding new menu entry to launch it.

A QUICK INTRODUCTION TO THE SCRIPT EDITOR

In order to create AppleScripts, you need a text or script editor. One such editor, the Script Editor, is supplied as part of Mac OS X. The Script Editor can be used to write scripts for different programming languages. However, by default it is only pre-configured to support AppleScript programming. The Script Editor provides you with numerous features that facilitate script building, including:

- color code highlighting
- automatic statement indentation
- code compilation and execution

You will find the Script Editor in the /Applications/AppleScript folder. It is started just like any other Mac OS X application by double-clicking on it. Figure 1.22 shows an example of the Script Editor when first started.

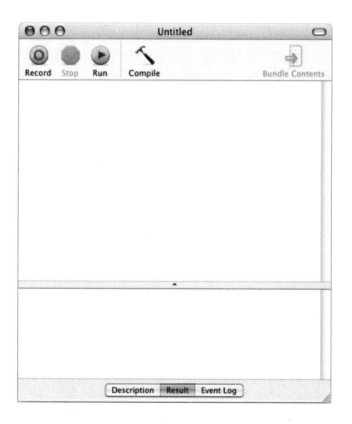

FIGURE 1.22

The Script Editor provides you with the ability to create and execute your AppleScripts.

Creating Your First AppleScript

Once the Script Editor has been started, you can begin creating a new AppleScript. To do so, you must type the code statements that make up the AppleScript into the main text area of the Script Editor. For example, let's create your first AppleScript by typing the following statement into the main text area of the Script Editor, as shown in Figure 1.23.

```
display dialog "Hello World!"
```

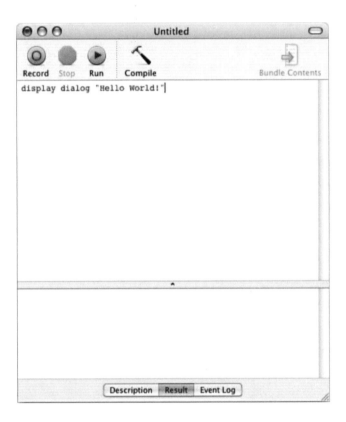

FIGURE 1.23

An example of a small one-line AppleScript.

This statement uses the AppleScript `display dialog` command to display a text string in a dialog window.

Running Your AppleScript

To run your new script and see if it works, click on the green Run button located at the top of the Script Editor in its toolbar. In response, AppleScript will compile your script and convert the text code statement that you just keyed in into a format that the computer can understand and execute.

TIP Computers are only able to run binary programs consisting of different combinations of 0s and 1s. However, humans find this type of communication exceedingly difficult to understand and work with. Modern programming languages like AppleScript allow programmers to key in code statements, which are later converted into machine language through a process known as *compiling*. During the compile process, each code statement that makes up your AppleScript is checked to make sure that it follows AppleScript's syntax rules. If it does not, the compile process is stopped and an error message is displayed.

After a moment, the dialog window shown in Figure 1.24 will be displayed. Note that the dialog window displays not only the specified text string but also two buttons, labeled Cancel and OK.

TRAP If you do not see the dialog window, then you must have made a typo when keying in the code statement. Double-check your typing and try running your AppleScript again.

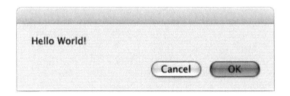

The result of creating and executing your first AppleScript.

When first entered, any text that you type will be displayed in purple. This helps to make any new text stand out from any text that may have already been entered. Once you have finished examining the dialog window that was displayed when you ran your new AppleScript, close the dialog window by clicking on either of its two buttons. Take note of the color that is now used to display the code statement in the Script Editor. The command portion of the statement is shown in blue and the text string portion is displayed in black. The Script Editor does this to help make different parts of your code statements stand out. Note that the bottom pane of the Script Editor window now also displays a message that identifies the button that you clicked when closing the dialog window, as demonstrated in Figure 1.25.

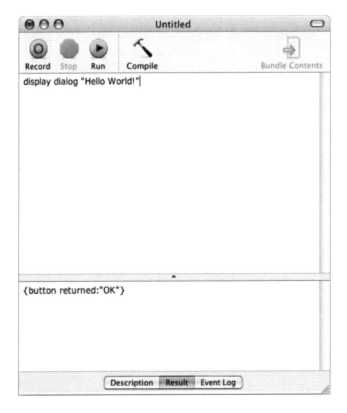

FIGURE 1.25

The Script Editor
provides feedback
in its lower pane
after an
AppleScript has
been run.

Saving Your AppleScript

If you want, you may save your AppleScript so that you can come back later and edit and execute it again. To do so, open the File menu and click on the Save As option. A new sheet window will drop down from the Script Editor's title bar allowing you to enter a name for your new AppleScript, as demonstrated in Figure 1.26. As you can see, the sheet window lets you specify a filename, file format, and the location where you would like to store your AppleScript.

The Script Editor provides you with choices when it comes to selecting the file format of your AppleScript file. Each of these file formats is discussed in detail in the next section.

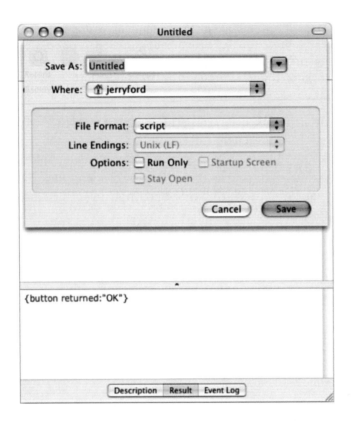

{button returned:"OK"}

FIGURE 1.26

Saving your
AppleScript as a
script file.

Working with Different Types of Script Files

AppleScripts can be saved in several different formats, as outlined here:

- **script.** Generates an AppleScript file with a .scpt file extension and is the default file type for new AppleScripts.

- **application.** Generates a self-contained application, sometimes referred to as an applet, which can be executed like any other Mac OS X application (by double-clicking on it).

- **script bundle.** Generates a distribution package for your script file, allowing you to include any text, image, movie, or other type of files needed by your script. (Supported only on Mac OS X 10.3 and later.)

- **application bundle.** Generates a distribution package for your AppleScript application, allowing you to include any text, image, movie, or other type of files needed by your application script. (Supported only on Mac OS X 10.3 and later.)

- **text.** Saves your AppleScript as a plain text file.

Within the context of AppleScript programming, an *applet* is a term used to refer to AppleScripts set up to run like a regular application. A *bundle* is a folder that has been configured to look like an individual file. Programmers use bundles as a means of packaging resources required by an application or script for execution.

When you double-click on an AppleScript saved using the script format, the script is opened and loaded into the Code Editor. From here you can modify and execute the AppleScript. If you select Application as the format for your AppleScript, a self-contained application will be generated, which can be run by double-clicking on it just like any other application. Of course, you can still edit and modify your AppleScript by first opening the Script Editor and then using it to open your application bundle.

If you choose application bundle or script bundle as the format of your AppleScript file, your AppleScript file will be saved in a folder representing a distribution package. You can store any files needed by your script inside this folder. To do so, just control-click on your script once you have saved it and then select Show Package Contents, as shown in Figure 1.27.

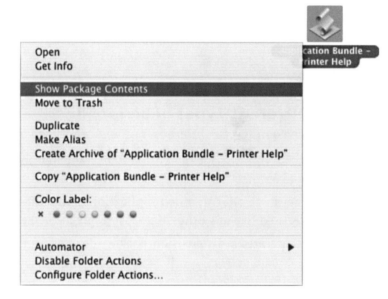

FIGURE 1.27

Packing files needed by your AppleScripts inside a distribution package bundle.

Next, drill down into the /Contents/Resources folders and drag and drop any files needed by your script to execute, as demonstrated in Figure 1.28.

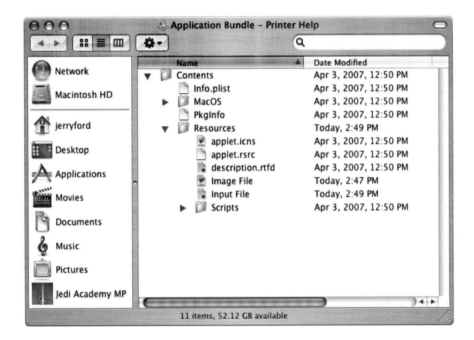

FIGURE I.28

An example of an application bundle to which a number of files have been added.

If you select the text option as the format of your AppleScript, your script will be saved as a plain text file with an .applescript file extension. An advantage of this option is that the resulting file is much smaller, allowing you to e-mail or copy it much more quickly.

You will learn more about how to work with the Script Editor in Chapter 2, "Getting Comfortable with the AppleScript Script Editor."

UNDERSTANDING APPLESCRIPT SYNTAX

Like any programming language, AppleScript consists of a number of keywords and commands. Unlike many programming languages, AppleScript syntax is extremely English-like, using a syntax that is based on nouns and verbs, combined with control commands that control script execution. Within the scope of AppleScript scripting, a *noun* is a resource, such as a file, folder, or disk drive, which is controlled or acted upon. A *verb* is an action that is performed on a noun. Using verbs you can specify that a resource be opened, closed, copied, deleted, etc. Much of the syntax that you follow is mandated by the application with which your AppleScripts will interact and control. This syntax is documented in each application's suite.

A *suite* is a collection of commands and classes provided by a given application that you could incorporate into your AppleScripts. *Classes* are the resources associated with the suite (e.g., the nouns). Using TextEdit again as an example, you will find nouns such as word and paragraph. The *commands* defined inside suites represent the actions (e.g., verbs) that you can use to interact with and control specific resources.

Suites are organized by application. As such, each scriptable application defines the commands that it works with in its suite. The TextEdit application suite, for example, has commands defined within it that are specific to the TextEdit application and thus not supported by other applications. The same is true for the Finder suite and most other application suites.

AppleScript itself defines other suites. For example, there is the standard suite, which defines common commands that are accepted by most applications and the operating system. You can view the contents of suites using the Script Editor's Open Dictionary window, as shown in Figure 1.29.

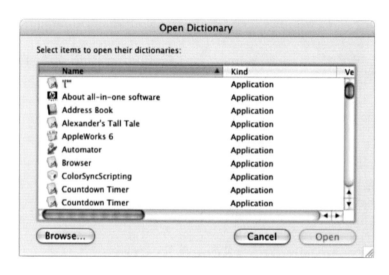

FIGURE 1.29

Using the Open Dictionary window, you can determine which commands are supported by various applications.

HINT

You will learn a lot more about the suites and the Open Dictionary application in Chapters 2 and 8.

A *control* command is used to write statements that control key script operations. For example, control statements are used to implement conditional logic, determining which course of action to take based on the state of a particular resource or the assignment made to a particular value. Other examples of control statements include `tell` blocks, which were demonstrated earlier in the Help Viewer example. `tell` blocks are used to identify the resources to which specific commands are targeted. All programming languages support the implementation of control statements, and much of this book (Chapters 3 through 6) is dedicated to understanding them as implemented by AppleScript.

BACK TO THE APPLESCRIPT HUMOR GAME

All right, that's enough background information on AppleScript programming for now. Let's move on to something a little more fun. It is time to turn your attention back to the development of the AppleScript Humor game. Compared to the game projects that you will be working on later in this book, the AppleScript Humor game is very simple. However, it will provide you with a good starting point.

When going through the steps required to build this script, do not get too caught up in trying to understand what each programming statement does and how it is constructed. It takes time to fully comprehend and understand the various complexities of any programming language, even one as English-like as AppleScript. Understanding the syntax and purpose of AppleScript statements is covered in later chapters. For now, you should focus your attention on the overall mechanics involved in the creation and execution of this AppleScript.

Designing the Game

The development of this AppleScript will follow a specific series of steps, as outlined below. As you work your way through each of these steps, be sure to follow along carefully and not omit any steps. In addition, when keying in code statements, make sure that you type them in exactly as shown. This will help you to avoid errors and will make things go a lot smoother.

1. Open the Script Editor and create a new AppleScript.
2. Add comment statements to the beginning of the script file to document the script and its purpose.
3. Display an opening dialog window and prompt the player for permission to start telling jokes.
4. **Set up the programming** logic required to process the player's response.
5. Add the code statements that will execute if the player decides not to view the game's jokes.
6. Add the code statements that tell the game's first joke.
7. Add the code statements that tell the game's remaining jokes.

Each of these steps is covered in detail in the sections that follow.

Step 1: Creating a New AppleScript File

The first step in the creation of the AppleScript Humor game is to open the Script Editor and create a new AppleScript file named AppleScript Humor.scpt using the following procedure.

1. Start the Script Editor by opening the /Applications/AppleScript folder and double-clicking on the Script Editor icon.
2. With the Script Editor selected, click on the File menu and select the Save As option.

3. In the sheet window that appears, enter **AppleScript Humor** in the Save As field and then specify the location where you want to save your new script file using the Where drop-down menu.

4. Select the Script option from the File Format drop-down menu and then click on the Save button.

 I suggest that you create a new folder to store all your AppleScripts. For example, if you want to be able to access all your scripts from the Script menu, then you will want to create a folder named Scripts inside the library of your home directory (~/Library/Scripts) and store all your AppleScript files there.

Step 2: Documenting the Script and Its Purpose

The next step in the development of the AppleScript Humor game is to add a few comment statements to the beginning of the file to provide some high-level documentation about the script and its author. Within AppleScript comments can be embedded within program code by preceding the comments with a pair of – characters. In the case of the AppleScript Humor game, let's begin by adding the following comment statements to the beginning of the script file.

```
-------------------------------------------------------------------
--
-- Script Name: AppleScript Humor.scpt
-- Version: 1.0
-- Author: Jerry Lee Ford, Jr.
-- Date: August 2007
--
-- Description: This AppleScript tells a series of 5 humorous jokes
--
-------------------------------------------------------------------
```

Script comments have no effect upon the execution or performance of AppleScripts. However, they can be used to provide invaluable information about the contents of AppleScripts.

 To help make things just a little easier on you, I have provided a small AppleScript template on this book's companion website. This template, shown below, can be used as a starting point for all your AppleScripts.

```
-------------------------------------------------------------------
--
-- Script Name:
-- Version:
```

```
-- Author:
-- Date:
--
-- Description:
--
----------------------------------------------------------------------
```

You will find this template, along with the complete source code for all the book's game scripts at www.courseptr.com/downloads.

Step 3: Prompting the Player for Permission to Continue

The next step in the creation of the AppleScript Humor game is to add the code statement responsible for displaying the game's opening dialog window. This statement is shown next and should be added just beneath the comment statements that you just added to the script file.

```
set answer to the button returned of (display dialog ¬
    "Welcome to the AppleScript Humor Game. Click on the " & ¬
    "Tell Me Some Jokes button to " & ¬
    "have a few laughs or click on the No Thanks button to quit." ¬
    buttons {"Tell Me Some Jokes", "No Thanks"} ¬
    with title "AppleScript Humor Game" with icon note)
```

Without getting too deeply involved in a discussion of the syntax involved in formulating this statement, let me just say that what this statement does is display a text message of "Welcome to the AppleScript Humor Game. Click on the Tell Me Some Jokes button to have a few laughs or click on the No Thanks button to quit" inside a dialog window. This window will display two buttons, one labeled Tell Me Some Jokes and the other labeled No Thanks. In addition, a text string of "AppleScript Humor Game" will be displayed in the dialog window's title bar.

As you can see, this single script statement spans a number of lines. By default, any statement that is too long to be displayed on a single line is automatically broken up by the Script Editor and spread over as many lines as required to display the statement. However, if allowed to break up statements in this manner, the Script Editor does not always do so in a manner that is intuitive. As a result, I have elected to instead use AppleScript's continuation character, the ¬ character, to break this statement up into different pieces in a way that is visually clear and easy to understand. In addition, I also used the concatenation operator (&) to create a text string by merging together several smaller strings.

TRICK In order to insert the ¬ into your AppleScript code when working with the Script Editor, you must hold down the Option key and press the l key (that's the letter l and not the number one key).

Step 4: Processing the Player's Response

Now it is time to add the programming logic that will analyze the result returned when the player clicks on one of the dialog window buttons. This is accomplished by adding an if...else statement block to the end of the script file, as shown next.

```
if answer = "Tell Me Some Jokes" then

else

end if
```

The if...else statement is a conditional programming statement. In this example, the if...else statement has been set up to evaluate and determine which button the player clicked on. If the player clicks on the Tell Me Some Jokes button, then code statements that will be embedded within the upper portion of the statement (between the first and second statements) will be executed. Otherwise, if the No Thanks button is clicked, then code statements that will be embedded within the lower portion of the statement (between the second and the third statements) will be executed.

Step 5: Encouraging the Player to Play Again

Now let's add the code statement that is processed in the event the player clicks on the No Thanks button. To do so, type the following statement into the lower half of the if...else statement block (between else and end if) that you just added to the script file.

```
display dialog "You do not know what you are missing!" buttons {"OK"} ¬
  with title "AppleScript Humor Game" with icon note
```

When executed, this statement displays a text string of "You do not know what you are missing!" in a dialog window using the display dialog command.

Step 6: Displaying the First Joke

Now let's begin adding the code statements that are needed to tell the jokes. These statements will be executed when the player clicks on the Tell Me Some Jokes button and should be added to the upper portion of the if...else statement block.

```
display dialog "My new application said it requires Windows XP " & ¬
  "or better... So I installed Mac OS X." ¬
  buttons {"OK"} with title "AppleScript Humor Game" with icon note
```

Although spread out over three lines, only a single statement is shown here. It used the display dialog command to display the game's first joke in a dialog window. This dialog window will display a single button labeled OK, which the player must click on to continue game play.

Step 7: Displaying the Remaining Jokes

All that is left to complete the development of the AppleScript Humor game is to add the statements responsible for telling the game's four remaining jokes. The code statements that tell these jokes are shown here and should be added to the upper portion of the if...else statement block, immediately after the statement responsible for displaying the first joke.

```
display dialog "The great thing about computers is that they " & ¬
  "let you make mistakes even faster than before." ¬
  buttons {"OK"} with title "AppleScript Humor Game" with icon note

display dialog "To err is human but to really mess things up " & ¬
  "you need a computer." buttons {"OK"} ¬
  with title "AppleScript Humor Game" with icon note

display dialog "Policemen are very strong. They can even hold " & ¬
  "up traffic." buttons {"OK"} ¬
  with title "AppleScript Humor Game" with icon note

display dialog "What do you call a soup made of onions and " & ¬
  "beans? Tear Gas!" buttons {"OK"} ¬
  with title "AppleScript Humor Game" with icon note
```

As you can see, these statements are nearly identical. Each uses the display dialog command to display a different text string representing one of the game's jokes.

Running Your New AppleScript Game

Well, that's it. You have finished all of the steps required to create the AppleScript Humor game. Because the development of this game involved a number of different steps, there is plenty of opportunity to get confused when keying in the game's code statements. To help clarify things and to ensure that your copy of the AppleScript is properly written, I have provided a full copy of the game next, showing how it should look after being keyed in. In addition, I took the liberty of adding a number of additional comment statements to the script to further document what is happening at different points within the script file.

```
--------------------------------------------------------------------------------
--
-- Script Name: AppleScript Humor.scpt
-- Version: 1.0
-- Author: Jerry Lee Ford, Jr.
-- Date: August 2007
--
-- Description: This AppleScript tells a series of 5 humorous jokes
--
--------------------------------------------------------------------------------

--Display a welcome message and wait for the player's response
set answer to the button returned of (display dialog ¬
   "Welcome to the AppleScript Humor Game. Click on the " & ¬
   "Tell Me Some Jokes button to " & ¬
   "have a few laughs or click on the Cancel button to quit." ¬
   buttons {"Tell Me Some Jokes", "No Thanks"} ¬
   with title "AppleScript Humor Game" with icon note)

--Determine which button the player clicked and respond accordingly
if answer = "Tell Me Some Jokes" then --The player wants to hear the jokes

   --Display the first joke
   display dialog "My new application said it requires Windows XP " & ¬
   "or better... So I installed Mac OS X." ¬
   buttons {"OK"} with title "AppleScript Humor Game" with icon note

   --Display the second joke
   display dialog "The great thing about computers is that they " & ¬
   "let you make mistakes even faster than before." ¬
   buttons {"OK"} with title "AppleScript Humor Game" with icon note

   --Display the third joke
   display dialog "To err is human but to really mess things up " & ¬
   "you need a computer." buttons {"OK"} ¬
```

```
        with title "AppleScript Humor Game" with icon note

     --Display the fourth joke
     display dialog "Policemen are very strong. They can even hold " & ¬
     "up traffic." buttons {"OK"} ¬
     with title "AppleScript Humor Game" with icon note

     --Display the fifth joke
     display dialog "What do you call a soup made of onions and " & ¬
     "beans? Tear Gas!" buttons {"OK"} ¬
     with title "AppleScript Humor Game" with icon note

else --The player does not want to hear the jokes

     --Display a closing message
     display dialog "You do not know what you are missing!" buttons {"OK"} ¬
        with title "AppleScript Humor Game" with icon note

end if
```

Assuming that your copy of the AppleScript Humor game looks like the copy of the AppleScript shown here, perhaps absent the additional comments that I added, all that remains is for you to compile and run it and see what happens. However, before doing so, you may want to save your script by clicking on the File menu and selecting the Save option.

To run your new AppleScript, click on the green Run button located in the Script Editor's toolbar. Assuming that you did not make any typos when keying in the game's code statements, everything should work as advertised.

SUMMARY

This chapter provided you with a good introduction to AppleScript. You learned about the different types of tasks that can be automated using AppleScript. You learned a little bit about the Script Editor and how to use it to create, save, and execute AppleScripts. You learned about the different options available for saving AppleScripts. You also learned about the different ways of executing AppleScripts, including from the Code Editor, the Script menu, and by setting up folder actions. Finally, you learned how to create your first AppleScript game.

Now, before you move on to Chapter 2, I suggest you take a few extra minutes to see if you can improve the AppleScript Humor game by implementing the following list of challenges.

CHALLENGES

1. As currently written, the AppleScript Humor game currently tells the player five jokes. Make the game more interesting by adding more jokes.
2. As currently written, the opening dialog window displays a somewhat cryptic opening message. Consider rewriting it to make the game more user-friendly.

CHAPTER 2

GETTING COMFORTABLE WITH THE APPLESCRIPT SCRIPT EDITOR

In order to develop AppleScripts you need a script editor. One particularly good script editor, aptly named Script Editor, is a standard Mac OS X application. In this chapter you will learn more about how to work with this exceptional tool. This will include learning how to work with its major features as well as some less obvious but very useful features like the Script Assistant, which assists programmers in completing code statements. In addition, you will learn a little about competing script editors and their advantages and disadvantages. On top of all this, you will learn how to create your next AppleScript game, the AppleScript Story Teller game.

Specifically, you will learn:

- About the layout and operation of the Script Editor application
- About other third-party AppleScript editors
- How to configure the Script Editor application
- How to use the Script Editor application's dictionary browser

PROJECT PREVIEW: THE APPLESCRIPT STORY TELLER GAME

This chapter's game project is the AppleScript Story Teller game. In this game, the player is prompted to answer a number of questions. The answers provided by the player are then used in the generation of a story that is told to the player using the Mac OS X speech synthesizer.

When first started, the game will display a startup screen as shown in Figure 2.1. This screen provides the player with instructions for playing the game. The screen also provides information about the game and its creator.

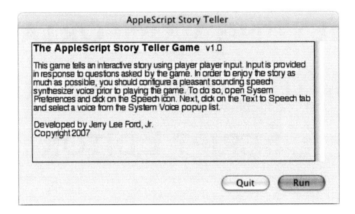

FIGURE 2.1

The startup screen provides instruction on how to play the game.

The startup screen presents the player with two options, Quit or Run. If the player clicks on the Quit button the game ends. If, on the other hand, the player clicks on the Run button, game play begins. A series of five questions is displayed, as demonstrated in Figures 2.2 to 2.6.

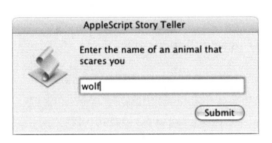

FIGURE 2.2

The first of five questions asked by the game.

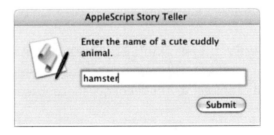

FIGURE 2.3

The second of five questions asked by the game.

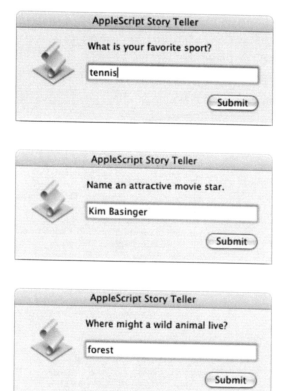

FIGURE 2.4

The third of five questions asked by the game.

FIGURE 2.5

The fourth of five questions asked by the game.

FIGURE 2.6

The final question asked by the game.

Note that the player is asked each question without being provided with the context in which the information will be used, making the resulting story somewhat unpredictable.

Once every question has been answered, the game displays the dialog window shown in Figure 2.7, informing the player that it is ready to begin telling the story.

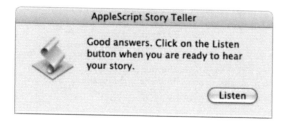

FIGURE 2.7

The game informs the player that it is ready to tell the story.

The player must click on the Listen button to continue. Once the button has been clicked, the game begins telling its story using Mac OS X's built-in voice synthesizer. As the story is told, the input previously collected from the player is inserted at various points in the story. Once the entire story has been told, the text of the story is displayed in the dialog window similar to the one shown in Figure 2.8.

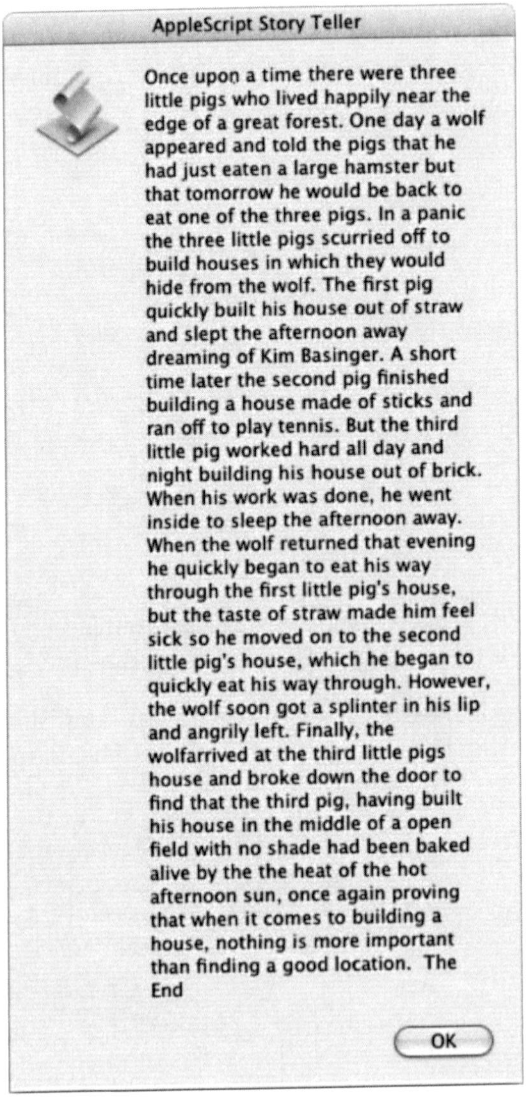

AppleScript Story Teller

Once upon a time there were three little pigs who lived happily near the edge of a great forest. One day a wolf appeared and told the pigs that he had just eaten a large hamster but that tomorrow he would be back to eat one of the three pigs. In a panic the three little pigs scurried off to build houses in which they would hide from the wolf. The first pig quickly built his house out of straw and slept the afternoon away dreaming of Kim Basinger. A short time later the second pig finished building a house made of sticks and ran off to play tennis. But the third little pig worked hard all day and night building his house out of brick. When his work was done, he went inside to sleep the afternoon away. When the wolf returned that evening he quickly began to eat his way through the first little pig's house, but the taste of straw made him feel sick so he moved on to the second little pig's house, which he began to quickly eat his way through. However, the wolf soon got a splinter in his lip and angrily left. Finally, the wolfarrived at the third little pigs house and broke down the door to find that the third pig, having built his house in the middle of a open field with no shade had been baked alive by the the heat of the hot afternoon sun, once again proving that when it comes to building a house, nothing is more important than finding a good location. The End

OK

FIGURE 2.8

The text of the story is displayed.

This gives the player the opportunity to examine the story in detail and assess the different ways her input was used in building the story. When done, the player clicks on the OK button, closing the dialog window and terminating the script's execution.

INTRODUCING THE SCRIPT EDITOR

In order to create and test AppleScripts, you need a script editor. Fortunately, you do not have to look very far because an excellent script editor, conveniently named the Script Editor, is provided as part of the operating system. The Script Editor application runs as a native Mac OS X application and supports a number of features, including:

- Automatic statement color coding
- Automatic statement indentation
- Standard editor features like copy, cut, paste, and undo
- Code completion assistance
- Built-in dictionary browser
- Library palette for quick access to commonly used script application dictionaries
- Result and history tracking of script results and execution
- Find and replace searching
- Navigation bar access to key script elements
- Code snippets that simplify and speed up script development

The primary interface for the Script Editor application consists of two panes divided by a divider bar, as shown in Figure 2.9. The Script Editor application provides access to commonly used commands in a toolbar located at the top of the main editor window. The script pane resides immediately below the toolbar and that is where AppleScript code statements are keyed in. The script pane is separated from the data pane by a divider bar, which can be moved by dragging it to a new location to increase or decrease the space allocated to the two panes. At the bottom of the main editor window is a set of three tabs that control access to the data displayed in the data pane.

The following list outlines the purpose of each of the three tabs.

- **Description.** Stores optional text that can be used to document the script.
- **Result.** Records a record of the result of every script that is run.
- **Event Log.** Keeps a record of outgoing and incoming Apple events (messages sent between Mac OS X applications). Information is written to the Event Log only if the Event Log tab is selected when a script is executed within the Script Editor application.

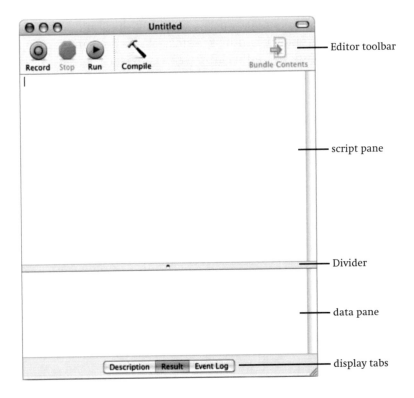

Editor toolbar

script pane

Divider

data pane

display tabs

TRICK

The Script Editor application provides a number of shortcuts that you can use to work more quickly and efficiently. For example, by holding down the Command key and pressing the 1, 2, or 3 keys, you can instruct the Script Editor to switch between the Description, Result, and Event Log tabs. In addition, you can also hold down the Command key and press the R key to run your script, the Command and K keys to compile the current script, or hold down the Command key and press the period key to script the execution of the current script.

Creating and Running Scripts

As you have already seen, you create AppleScripts by keying in code statements into the script pane of the Script Editor application. When initially entered, script statements are shown, by default, in a plain Courier font with no special formatting or color coding, as demonstrated here:

```
tell application "Safari"
activate
open location "http://www.amazon.com"
end tell
```

In this example, the `tell` command is used to instruct AppleScript to submit commands to the Safari Web browser application. Then the `activate` command is executed, starting Safari if it is not already running and bringing it to the front of the desktop. Next the `open` command is used to specify a location or URL for Safari to load. Finally, the end `tell` command is executed, telling AppleScript to stop directing commands to Safari. In Chapters 3–6 you will learn the basic fundamentals and syntax of the AppleScript programming language. So don't worry if the previous examples are a little confusing.

If you click on the Compile button, the Script Editor application will check your AppleScript for syntax errors. The Script Editor application will notify you if it finds an error by displaying a message in a sheet window, as demonstrated in Figure 2.10.

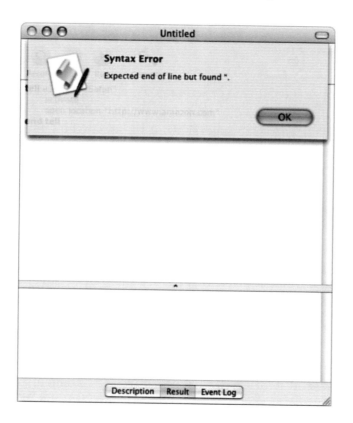

FIGURE 2.10

An example of how the Script Editor application reports on syntax errors.

If, on the other hand, the Script Editor does not find any errors, your code statements will be reformatted as shown next. Note that the Script Editor also indents your code statements to make them more readable. The manner in which the Script Editor reformats code statements is controlled by the application's Preferences settings, which you can change if you want.

Instructions for configuring Script Editor application preferences are provided a little later in this chapter.

```
tell application "Safari"
    activate
    open location "http://www.amazon.com"
end tell
```

Once the Script Editor application determines that your script does not have any syntax errors, you can run it by clicking on the Run button.

TRICK | You do not have to compile your script prior to running it. If you click on the Run button after some changes have been made to your script, the Script Editor application will automatically compile and then run your script (assuming no syntax errors were found).

You can review the result of the last command or action executed by the script by clicking on the Result tab at the bottom of the Script Editor. In addition, if the Event Log was visible at the time the script was run, you'll see log messages showing the actions and results produced by the scripts as it executed.

Recording Scripts

In this book you will learn how to program using AppleScript. The primary method of instruction used is the development of computer games. However, in the real world, the primary use of AppleScript is in the development of automated processes that use Apple events to interact with and control scriptable applications. Not all Mac OS X applications are scriptable. However, you may still be able to use AppleScript to automate them using the Script Editor's Record feature. In order for this feature to work, the application you want to script must be recordable, or to put it another way, it must generate recordable events. Not all Mac OS X applications are recordable but some, such as the Finder, are.

Using the Record feature, the Script Editor application watches for recordable events as you work with other applications, and it writes out equivalent script statements necessary to repeat or play back whatever series of events occur. In other words, it generates code statements that when executed, reproduce whatever series of keystrokes and mouse clicks you may have made when interacting with target applications.

To better understand how the Record feature works, let's look at a quick example. In this example, it is assumed that you have a folder named AccountMgr located at the root of your computer's startup disk and that inside this folder is a file named Log File.rft. It is also assumed that you want to create an AppleScript that when executed, uses Finder to locate and open the file. The first thing that you will want to do is close any Finder windows that may be open. Next, start the Script Editor application and click on the Record icon. Now perform the following series of steps.

1. Double-click on the startup disk icon (by default this is the Macintosh HD icon) to start Finder.
2. Open the AccountMgr folder.
3. Open the Log File.rft file.
4. Close Finder.
5. Click on the Script Editor's Stop button.

At this point, the Script Editor should display the following code statements, representing the recordable events that were generated by Finder as you worked with it.

```
tell application "Finder"
     activate
     select window of desktop
     make new Finder window to startup disk
     select Finder window 1
     set target of Finder window 1 to folder "AccountMgr" of startup disk
     select Finder window 1
     open document file "Log File.rtf" of folder "AccountMgr" of startup disk
     close Finder window 1
end tell
```

 If you try this example, you may find that some duplicate code statements are added to the AppleScript that is generated. There is nothing that you can do to prevent this from happening. However, you can delete any duplicate statements to streamline your AppleScript.

To test out your new AppleScript, click on the Run button. Finder will briefly open, switch to the AccountMgr folder, and then open the Log File.rtf files before closing. As you can see, using the Script editor's Record feature, you can generate entire AppleScript files without writing a single line of code.

Saving Script Files

As you learned in Chapter 1, you can save your AppleScript using a number of different options, including scripts, applications, script bundles, application bundles, and text. The Script Editor supports a number of other options that you may be interested in taking advantage of when saving your AppleScripts, including run-only scripts and scripts that display a startup screen.

Run-Only Scripts

Anyone with whom you choose to share your AppleScripts can, by default, view and examine the code statements that make up your scripts by simply opening the script using the Script Editor application. However, you have the option of selecting the run-only option when saving your AppleScript, as demonstrated in Figure 2.11. In response, the Script Editor will save a run-only version of your application whose code cannot be viewed or modified using the Script Editor applications.

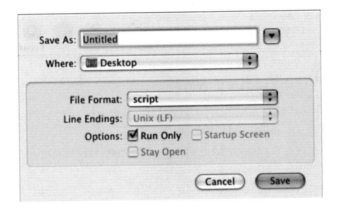

FIGURE 2.11

Saving a run-only
version of your
AppleScript.

TRICK   Although I will not go into how to do it, there are ways of getting your hands on the source code that makes up run-only versions of AppleScripts. However, saving a script using this option is generally enough to keep all but the most determined programmer at bay.

TRAP   Make sure that you save the run-only version of your AppleScript as a copy of the original file so that you will be able to come back later and modify your script file if necessary.

Adding a Startup Screen to Your Scripts

One really useful feature provided by the Script Editor application is its ability to allow you to provide documentation external to the code statements that make up the actual script file. As previously discussed, this is accomplished by clicking on the Description tab located at the bottom of the editor, just beneath the data pane.

If you want, you can also instruct the Script Editor application to display a startup screen for any AppleScript that you save as an application or application bundle. The startup screen is displayed as a dialog window at the beginning of your AppleScript. It displays any text you enter into the Script Editor's Description tab. This provides you with an easy way to display an application splash screen that presents information about your application, company name, website, etc. In addition to displaying whatever text you have specified in the Script Editor application's data pane, the startup screen also displays two buttons on the dialog window, Quit and Run.

To set up a startup screen, all you have to do is select the Startup Screen option when saving your AppleScript file. You can control the appearance of text displayed in the data pane when the Description tab is selected. Using the Font menu, you can make text bold, underlined, and italic. You can also make text bigger or smaller and can even change font type and color. In addition, using the Format menu, you can change the alignment of text, centering it for example.

HINT You will see an example of how to work with the Startup Screen option later in this chapter when you create the AppleScript Story Teller game.

Creating Scripts That Stay Open

The third option available to you when saving an AppleScript is the Stay Open option. Selecting the Stay Open option for an AppleScript that includes an idle handler will result in a script that continues to remain active until the user explicitly terminates its execution. For example, you might develop a script that you want to remain active all the time in order to periodically look for and process certain types of files that you place in a given folder. A script created in this manner displays an icon on the Dock. To terminate the script's execution, you must Control-click or right-click on the script's Dock icon and select the Quit option, as demonstrated in Figure 2.12.

Keep In Dock
Open at Login
Show In Finder
Hide
Quit

FIGURE 2.12

Terminating an
AppleScript
created using the
Stay Open option.

A *handler* is a group of program statements that are called on to execute in response to an event. AppleScript supports numerous types of handlers, including the idle hander. You will learn all about working with handlers in Chapter 6, "Improving Script Organization with Handlers."

CONFIGURING SCRIPT EDITOR PREFERENCES

The Script Editor application is highly customizable, providing programmers with an assortment of configuration options that allows them to set up the application to suit their personal preferences and working style. As is the case with most Mac OS X applications, Script Editor preferences are configured by accessing the Script Editor menu and then selecting the Preferences menu. In response, the Script Editor's Preferences window is displayed. This window consists of five separate views, which are selected by clicking on icons representing each view in the window's toolbar.

General Preferences

The Preferences window's General view contains a single configuration setting, as shown in Figure 2.13. This is the Default Language setting, which by default is AppleScript. This setting can be changed by clicking on the associated popup menu and selecting any of the OSA compliance scripting languages that are listed. By default, the only option available is AppleScript. Other scripting language options will only be available if they have been installed on the computer. OSA stands for *Open Scripting Architecture*, and it is a framework that allows OSA-compliant scripting languages developed by third-party developers to be substituted for AppleScript. OSA scripting languages have access to Apple events and can be used as a substitute scripting language for programmers who have previous experience with or a personal preference for another programming language.

The default OSA scripting language is set from the General preferences.

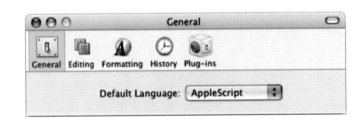

 Currently, the only major OSA scripting language available besides AppleScript is JavaScript OSA. JavaScript OSA is a special version of the JavaScript programming language that has been modified to execute directly on the operating system. It does not execute within the context of an Internet browser. In fact, JavaScript OSA does not support browser- based programming at all. You can learn more about JavaScript OSA and download a free copy of it by visiting http://latenightsw.com/freeware/JavaScriptOSA. It should also be noted that other scripting languages, such as Perl and Python, have been developed that provide alternative ways of accessing and interacting with Apple events (outside of the OSA framework).

Editing Preferences

The Preferences window's Editing view provides access to configuration options that affect line wrapping, tab control, and the availability of the Script Editor application's Script Assistant, as shown in Figure 2.14.

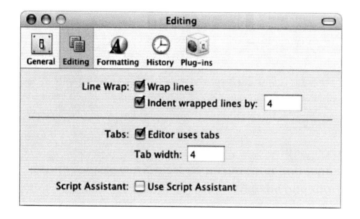

FIGURE 2.14

Configuration settings related to the Editor's behavior are located on the Editing preferences view of the Preferences window.

The Wrap Line option controls where and how the Script Editor application wraps code statements that are too long to fit on a single line. By default the Wrap Lines option is enabled and the Indent Wrapped Lines By option is set to 4 characters. The Tabs section controls tab behavior within the Editor. By default, the Editor Uses Tabs option is selected and Tab width is set equal to 4 characters. Script Assistant is a code completion feature that when enabled, configures the Script Editor application to monitor your code statements as you are keying them in and suggests different ways of completing terms as you are typing them in. If you want, you can accept the suggestion that is provided, thus saving yourself the time and effort of keying them in yourself.

HINT

The Script Assistant can be used to save you both time and keystrokes as you key in code statements. In addition, it can also be used to reduce typos that often occur as you type lengthy statement keywords. You will learn how to work with and take advantage of the Script Assistant a little later in this chapter.

Formatting Preferences

The Preferences window's Formatting view, shown in Figure 2.15, provides access to configuration options that control the type of fonts used to represent the different words that make up code statements. In addition, you can specify other text formatting options, including font size and color.

FIGURE 2.15

You can configure
the font type, size,
and color used to
represent the
words that make
up code
statements.

To change the font type or size for a given category, double-click on the desired font name. In response, the Font window is displayed, allowing you to modify font type and size. To change font color, double-click on the desired color swatch. In response, the Color Picker is displayed, allowing you to select a new color. Any font changes that you make will take effect the next time you compile your AppleScripts.

> **HINT** Any changes made to Formatting preferences also affect the format setting displayed by the Xcode code editor. Xcode's code editor is discussed later in this chapter. Xcode is a key component of AppleScript Studio, which you will learn about later in this chapter.

History Preferences

The Preferences window's History view, shown in Figure 2.16, provides access to settings that control whether the Script Editor application retains information regarding script results and execution history. By default, Result and Event Log history are automatically enabled. However, you can disable these features by clearing the appropriate checkbox controls. In addition, you can configure the number of entries that both the Result and Event Log files can store. Also, the Log Only When Visible option can be set or cleared, controlling whether history log data is recorded when the Event Log tab is not selected.

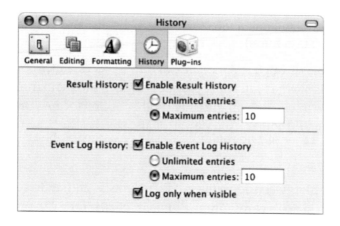

FIGURE 2.16

Configuring Result and Event Log settings.

Plug-ins Preferences

The Preferences window's Plug-ins view, shown in Figure 2.17, displays a list of plug-ins installed on the computer. A plug-in is an extension that adds new features to the Script Editor.

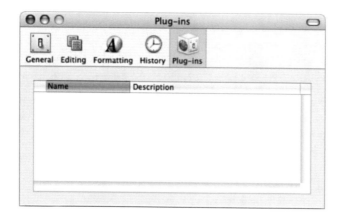

FIGURE 2.17

AppleScript is highly extensible.

CONFIGURING THE SCRIPT EDITOR TOOLBAR

By default, the Script Editor's toolbar displays the following icons.

- **Record.** Initiates building a script by translating user actions into script statements.
- **Stop.** Stops script recording or execution.

- **Run.** Runs or compiles and runs the script currently being edited.
- **Compile.** Prepares a script for execution by creating a version of the script that can be executed.
- **Bundle Contents.** Displays a drawer window showing the contents of a bundle (enabled only for script and application bundles).

Every command made available through the toolbar can also be accessed through the Script Editor application's menus. As such, if you want you may remove the toolbar to make more room inside the editor window by clicking on the Hide Toolbar option located under the View menu. In addition to removing the toolbar from view, this also toggles the Hide Toolbar menu item off and replaces it with the Show Toolbar menu item, allowing you to redisplay the toolbar any time you want.

The Script Editor's toolbar is highly configurable, allowing you to add and remove toolbar icons and to configure toolbar size. To configure the toolbar, click on the Customize Toolbar option located under the View menu. In response, a sheet window is displayed that provides easy access to additional toolbar content, as shown in Figure 2.18.

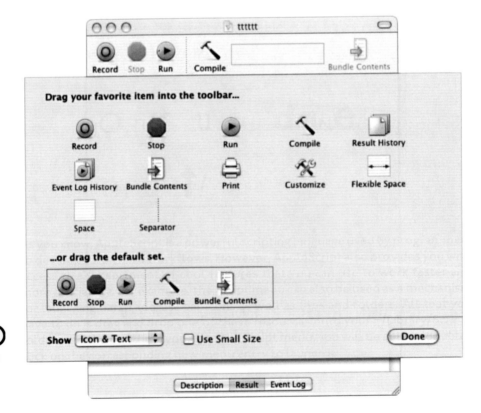

FIGURE 2.18

Configuring the
Script Editor
application's
Toolbar.

To add an icon to the toolbar, simply drag and drop it to the desired location on the toolbar. Other toolbar icons will automatically adjust their location to make the necessary room. To remove a toolbar icon, just drag and drop it onto the sheet window. You can also configure the layout of the toolbar by adding icons representing blank space and separator bars. If you prefer, you can reset the toolbar back to its default layout at any time by dragging and dropping the collection of icons displayed at the bottom of the toolbar configuration sheet onto the toolbar.

You can also control toolbar icon appearances by selecting any of the following three options displayed in the Show popup control located at the bottom-left corner of the screen.

- Icon & Text
- Icon Only
- Text Only

Lastly, you can increase or decrease the size of the toolbar by selecting or clearing the Use Small Size checkbox.

Using Advanced Script Editor Features

The Script Editor application supports a host of advanced options that, although they're not immediately apparent, you should know about. By taking advantage of these options you will be able to work more efficiently with fewer errors—the end result being better AppleScripts that take less time to write.

Working with the Navigation Bar

Although not enabled by default, the Script Editor provides a Navigation Bar control that you can use to locate different script elements, including subroutines, global variables, and properties. To enable this feature and begin working with it, click on the Show Navigation Bar option located on the View menu. In response, the Navigation Bar is added to the Script Editor application's display, just under the toolbar, as shown in Figure 2.19.

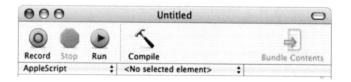

Figure 2.19

The Navigation Bar is displayed just under the toolbar.

The Navigation Bar is made up of two parts. The first part is a Language popup that when clicked displays a list of scripting languages that are currently available for use, as demonstrated in Figure 2.20.

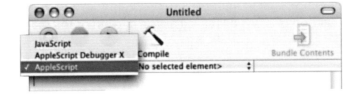

The second part of the Navigation Bar is the Elements popup, which displays the name of the currently selected element (subroutine, property, or variable) and displays a listing of all script elements when clicked, as demonstrated in Figure 2.21. Clicking on one of the elements in the popup list instructs the Script Editor application to jump to and display it in the script pane.

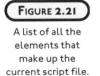

Using Context Generated Code Snippets

If you want, you can get the Script Editor application to help you write portions of your code statement. This is accomplished by either placing the cursor at the location in a script file where you want to have new code inserted or by selecting one or more code statements that you want to embed inside code statements that will be generated by the Script Editor application.

The Script Editor application provides access to code snippets via a context menu that is accessed by holding down the Control button while using the mouse to click on an area inside the script pane. To really understand how this works, take a look at the following example.

For starters, open a new Script Editor application window by clicking on File and selecting the New menu item. Next click inside the script pane and press the Enter key a couple times to advance the cursor down the display area. Then type the following statements.

```
activate
open location "www.tech-publishing.com"
```

Now, select both of these statements and then press and hold down the Control key and click on the left mouse button. In response, a context menu like the one shown in Figure 2.22 will be displayed.

FIGURE 2.22

Adding contextual menu script statements to your AppleScripts.

The lower half of the contextual menu contains the following collections of script snippets.

- Action Clauses
- Conditionals
- Dialogs
- Error handlers
- Folder Actions Handlers
- Image Manipulation
- Iterate Items
- Repeat Routines
- String Comparison
- Tell Blocks

Each of these categories provides access to specific script snippets, which you can access by clicking on an entry's disclosure triangle. For example, in Figure 2.22, the code snippets for Tell Blocks have been displayed. From this list, select the Tell Application snippet. In response, the following statements will wrap around the AppleScript statements that you have already typed in.

```
tell application ""
activate
open location "http://www.tech-publishing.com"
end tell
```

All that remains to get this example working is to enter the word Safari inside the empty pair of double quotes on the opening statement and compile your script as shown here.

```
tell application "Safari"
    activate
    open location "http://www.tech-publishing.com"
end tell
```

You now have a working example of an AppleScript that will start the Safari web browser and open a specified web page.

 The remainder of this book is dedicated to teaching you the fundamentals of AppleScript programming and will cover topics such as conditional logic, error handling, repeat routines and string comparison operations. As you work your way through the book, just remember that as you learn how to work with each of the different programming constructs shown in Figure 2.22, you have easy access to script snippets that can help you write equivalent code statements.

Leveraging the Power of the Script Assistant

Another very helpful scripting feature provided by the Script Editor application is the Script Assistant. The Script Assistant is an optional feature that by default is turned off. When enabled, the Script Assistant monitors you as you key in script statements and offers up suggestions for completing keywords and statements. By accepting these suggestions, you can not only work faster by reducing the number of keystrokes required to write out statements, but you also eliminate typos, thus creating more error-free program code.

The first step in working with the Script Assistant is to enable it, which you can do by selecting the Use Script Assistance option located on the Editing view of the Preferences window.

 TRAP   Depending on your version of Mac OS X, you may need to close or restart the Script Editor application for the Script Assistant feature to take effect.

Once the Script Assistant is operational, you can begin entering code. As soon as the Script Assistant sees an opportunity to complete a given keyword or statement, it will display an ellipsis in light gray text next to the cursor. This lets you know that it has suggestions for completing the current keyword or statement, as demonstrated in Figure 2.23.

FIGURE 2.23

The Script Assistant has suggestions for completing the current keyword or statement.

To view the Script Assistant's suggestions, press the F5 key. In response, a list appears that you can navigate using the up and down arrow keys, as demonstrated in Figure 2.24. To select an entry, press the Enter key.

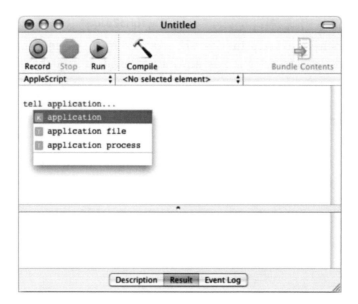

FIGURE 2.24

To pick a
suggestion, simply
select it and press
the Enter key.

RESEARCHING APPLICATION DICTIONARIES

AppleScript is a relatively small programming language. It depends on other applications to extend its capabilities. This is made possible through the exchange of messages between AppleScript and applications in the form of Apple events. In order to interact with and respond to AppleScripts, an application must be scriptable.

A big part of AppleScript programming is knowing which applications are and are not scriptable. Scriptable applications publish lists of Apple events that they are capable of responding to in the form of dictionaries. In order to automate and control applications, you will find yourself spending a lot of time reading through application dictionaries to determine which types of resources and features the application exposes and which types of commands it recognizes and will respond to.

Since each application defines its own terminology, learning how to develop scripts that automate a new application may make you feel like you are learning a new programming language all over again. To help make things as easy on you as possible, the Script Editor application supplies you with access to a dictionary browser that you can use to search application dictionaries.

Working with the Dictionary Browser

To open the dictionary browser, click on the File menu and select the Open Dictionary menu item. In response, the Open Dictionary window appears, as shown in Figure 2.25.

FIGURE 2.25

The Open Dictionary window provides quick access to application dictionaries.

To open an application's dictionary, scroll up or down to find it, select it, and then click on the Open button. In response, the Script Editor extracts information from the selected application's dictionary and displays it in the dictionary browser window, as demonstrated in Figure 2.26.

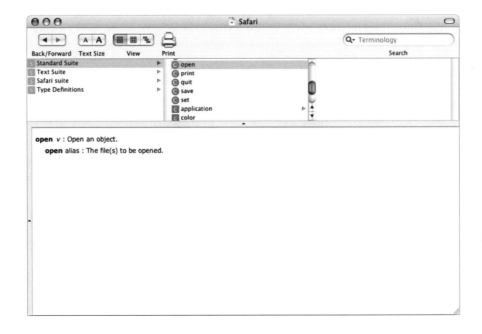

FIGURE 2.26

Using the dictionary browser to look up application commands.

The dictionary browser organizes application dictionaries into suites. A *suite* is a collection of related classes and commands defined in application dictionaries. *Classes* are scriptable objects (nouns) that you can programmatically interact with in the application. *Commands* are the verbs that you can use to interact with and control scriptable objects.

TRICK Most of the time you will find what you are looking for in the Standard Suite. So always begin looking there first when searching for a particular class or command.

As you can see in Figure 2.26, disclosure triangles are used to drill down into suites and classes to view their contents. In addition, information about the selected class or command is displayed in the bottom half of the window.

HINT You will learn more about application dictionaries later in Chapter 8, "Automating Mac OS X Applications."

Taking Advantage of the Library Palette

Another quick way of assessing application dictionaries is to use the Library Palette. The Library Palette provides access to commonly used dictionaries. To open the Library Palette, open the Window menu and click on the Library menu item. In response, the Library Palette, shown in Figure 2.27, is displayed.

FIGURE 2.27

Using the Library Palette to access commonly used dictionaries.

The Library Palette displays a list of commonly used application dictionaries. To access a given application's dictionary, just locate it in the list and double-click on it. If you find that you often need to work with an application dictionary that is not listed in the Library Palette, you can add an entry for it by clicking on the Add icon in the Library Palette's toolbar and then specifying the name and location of the associated application. Similarly, if there are application dictionaries in the list that you do not plan on working with, you can remove them by selecting each dictionary and clicking on the Remove icon.

ALTERNATE SCRIPT EDITORS

The Script Editor application is by no means your only option for developing and executing AppleScripts. In this section, you will learn about several different script editors that you might want to consider using as an alternative to the Script Editor application. These script editors include:

- Smile
- Script Debugger
- Xcode

 Each of these alternative script editors has its own particular sets of strengths and weaknesses. However, for the sake of simplicity, I will stick with the Script Editor application. It is universally available and provides all of the features needed to develop AppleScripts.

Smile

Smile is a free AppleScript editor developed by Satimage and is advertised as a Macintosh computer programming and working environment that is based on AppleScript. You can download a free copy of it from http://www.satimage.fr/software/en/downloads_smile.html. Smile provides you with a full-featured script editor. As Figure 2.28 shows, Smile creates text windows, into which you add the code statements that make up your AppleScript files.

Like the Script Editor Application, you can open as many text windows as you want, thus you can work on as many scripts as you want at the same time. This feature is especially useful when you want to copy and paste code between scripts. Rather than displaying script results in a pane at the bottom of the text window, Smile displays the results in a console window, as demonstrated in Figure 2.29. If you are working with multiple scripts at the same time, the results of all scripts that are executed will be written to the same console window, helping to reduce desktop clutter.

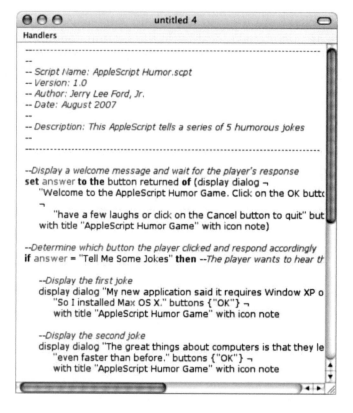

FIGURE 2.28

Smile provides you with access to an easy-to-use editor that includes color-coding and statement indentation.

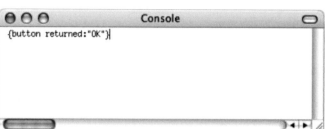

FIGURE 2.29

Smile records a history of results generated by your AppleScripts in a console window.

Smile also provides easy access to its own dictionary browser, as demonstrated in Figure 2.30.

One area where Smile falls a little short is it does not yet support the generation of script or application bundles. If you need to work with either of these two file types, you will probably be better off using a different code editor. In addition, Smile's dictionary browser is not as robust as that of the Script Editor application or the other third-party code editors covered in this chapter. Still, as far as script editors go, Smile has all of the basic features covered and does provide a viable alternative to the Script Editor application.

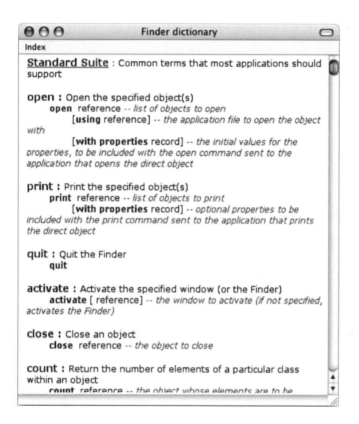

FIGURE 2.30

Smile's dictionary
browser.

Script Debugger

Script Debugger, shown in Figure 2.31, is an AppleScript editor developed by Late Night Software. Although not free, you can download and try it out for a free period before deciding whether you want to purchase it. To download the Script Debugger, visit http://www.latenightsw.com/sd4/index.html.

HINT As of the writing of this book, Script Debugger was available for a free 20-day trial and could be purchased online for $199.

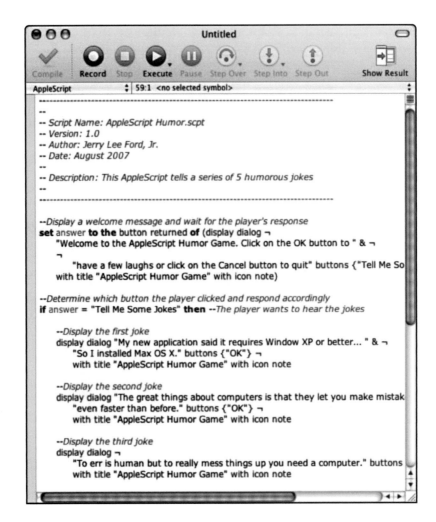

FIGURE 2.31

The Script
Debugger
AppleScript code
editor.

Like Smile, the Script Debugger lets you work with multiple scripts at the same time and provides a result, if available, that keeps you informed of how the script ended. Instead of displaying the result at the bottom of the code editor or in a separate console window, Script Debugger displays it in a drawer window attached to the editor's main window, as demonstrated in Figure 2.32. This keeps result information close at hand without reducing the amount of space available for viewing code or increasing desktop clutter with additional windows.

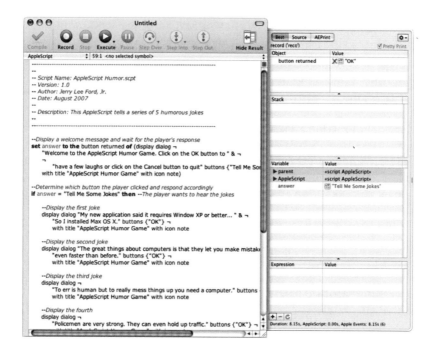

FIGURE 2.32

The results window can be viewed and dismissed at any time by clicking on the toolbar's Show Result and Hide Result icons.

One area in which Script Debugger really shines is in its support for dictionary browsing. This includes the ability to view dictionary information in different formats, including a graphical diagram showing the overall structure of application dictionaries, as demonstrated in Figure 2.33.

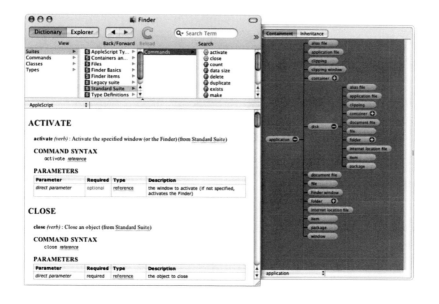

FIGURE 2.33

The Script Debugger's dictionary browser feature provides programmers with the ability to view dictionary information using several different views.

Unlike Smile, the Script Debugger does provide support for working with script and application bundles. In addition, the Script Debugger provides you with a full-featured scripting environment that includes integrated debugging features not found in Apple's Script Editor application. For example, the Script Debugger lets you set breakpoints and use options like Step Over, Step Into, and Step Out to control statement execution.

A *breakpoint* is a marker that identifies a point within a script file where script execution is temporarily halted. By temporarily halting a script's execution, programmers can check on the value of script variables. In addition, once paused, the programmer can execute commands that provide detailed line-by-line control over the execution of the code statements that make up the rest of the script.

Perhaps the Script Debugger's biggest drawback is its cost. It is the only script editor covered in this chapter that is not available for free. However, for any AppleScript programmer intent on developing professional quality AppleScripts, this editor's advanced features and capabilities may very well be worth the extra cost.

Xcode

Another editor that you may want to investigate is the Xcode project editor. This editor comes as part of Xcode. Xcode is a program editor that provides advanced editing and script debugging features. *Xcode* is the default editor for AppleScript Studio, which is covered later in this book in Chapter 10, "Introducing AppleScript Studio." AppleScript Studio is automatically installed when you download and install Xcode. Xcode provides programmers with a number of advanced features including code completion and a script debugger. If it is not already installed on your computer, you can download and install Xcode for free at http://developer.apple.com/tools/download/.

Be sure to read Chapter 10 to learn more about Xcode and AppleScript Studio. In addition, you may want to read *AppleScript Studio Programming for the Absolute Beginner*, from Course Technology.

Xcode assists you in the creation of new AppleScripts through the execution of an Assistant, as demonstrated in Figure 2.34.

FIGURE 2.34

Using Xcode's New project wizard to create a new AppleScript application.

Once you have selected the type of AppleScript file you want to create, the Assistant prompts you to supply a name and folder for your new script, as demonstrated in Figure 2.35.

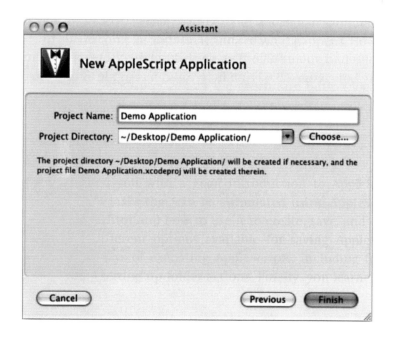

FIGURE 2.35

Assigning a name to your new AppleScript file.

After clicking on Finish, the Assistant terminates, and you will be presented with the Xcode project window, as demonstrated in Figure 2.36.

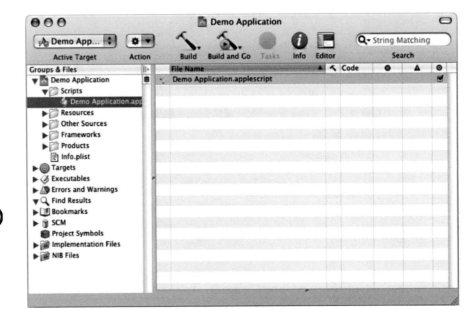

Xcode's project window is the central point for managing any development project.

On the left-hand side of the project window, you will see a hierarchical display of all the components that make up the new project. Clicking on the Script icon reveals the script file for the AppleScript application. If you double-click on this file, it will be opened in Xcode's code editor, as demonstrated in Figure 2.37. From here you can compile (Build) or run (Build and Go) your new AppleScript.

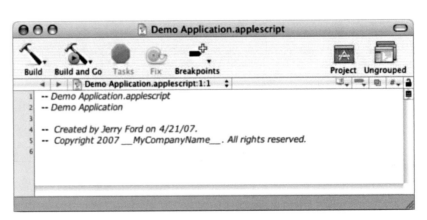

FIGURE 2.37

Xcode's code editor looks and operates in a manner very similar to the way the Script Editor application runs.

Xcode also provides you with access to its dictionary browser, which, as you can see in Figure 2.38, looks and operates much like the dictionary browser supplied with the Script Editor application.

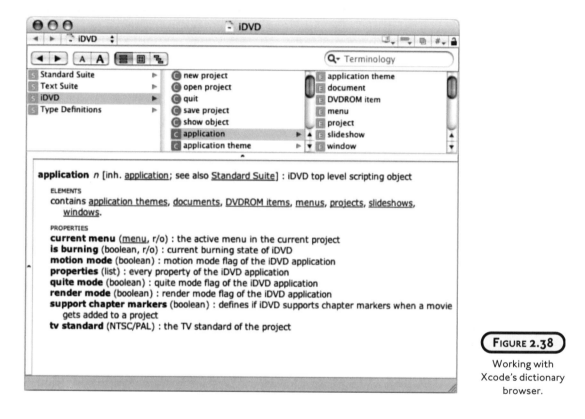

FIGURE 2.38

Working with Xcode's dictionary browser.

Perhaps Xcode's biggest drawback, from a purely AppleScript point of view, is that it was not developed exclusively with AppleScript in mind. As such, Xcode is packed with features that you do not need, making it a little harder to learn and work with. Still, if you plan on leveraging your AppleScript programming skills and learning how to develop AppleScript Studio applications, you will have to learn how to work with Xcode anyway. As such, you may find it preferable to work with just the one editor rather than using the Script Editor application for developing AppleScripts and Xcode for developing AppleScript Studio applications.

BACK TO THE APPLESCRIPT STORY TELLER GAME

All right, it is time to turn your attention back to the development of the AppleScript Story Teller game. In this game, you will learn how to tell a mad-lib-style story that incorporates user input, which is collected through a series of questions. To tell this story, you will use the operating system's built-in voice synthesizer to tell the story out loud.

As with the last chapter's game project, continue to keep your focus on the overall mechanics involved in developing the game. Chapters 3–6 will teach you what you need to know about AppleScript syntax and programming techniques. Once you have completed these chapters, you may want to return and review this game again.

Designing the Game

The development of the AppleScript Story Teller game will follow these eight steps:

1. Open the Script Editor, create a new AppleScript, and save it as an application with a name of AppleScript Story Teller.
2. Add statements to the script file that document the script and its purpose.
3. Define a variable containing the name of the game.
4. Prompt the player to supply required input.
5. Let the player know the game is ready to assemble its story.
6. Create the story.
7. Tell the story.
8. Display the story.

As you work your way through each step, make sure that you follow along carefully and do not skip any steps. Also, make sure that you type in everything exactly as shown. This way you will avoid making any unnecessary errors and things will go a lot smoother.

Step 1: Creating a New AppleScript File

The first step in the creation of the AppleScript Story Teller game is to open the Script Editor application and save a new AppleScript file named AppleScript Story Teller as a standalone application (applet) by following the steps outlined here:

1. Start the Script Editor application.
2. Click on the File menu and select the Save As option.
3. In the sheet window that appears, enter **AppleScript Story Teller** in the Save As field and then specify the location where you want to save your new script file using the Where drop-down list.
4. Select the Application option from the File Format drop-down list.

5. Select the Startup Screen option.
6. Click on the Save button.

 By selecting the Startup Screen option, you configure your AppleScript to display a small startup screen window at runtime that will display any text that is entered into the Script Editor's data pane when the Description tab is selected.

Step 2: Documenting the Script and Its Purpose

The next step in the creation of the AppleScript Story Teller game is to begin documenting the script file. This will be accomplished in two ways. First, you will add text to the Description tab view of the Script Editor application's data pane. Second, you will add a few comment statements documenting the script and its program code.

Adding Descriptive Text

One really useful feature provided by the Script Editor application is its ability to allow you to provide documentation external to the code statements that make up the actual script file. As previously discussed, this is accomplished by clicking on the Description tab located at the bottom of the editor, just beneath the data pane. To set this up for the AppleScript Story Teller game, make sure that the Script Editor's Description tab is selected and type the following text into the data pane.

```
The AppleScript Story Teller Game  v1.0


This game tells an interactive story using player input. Input is provided in response
to questions asked by the game. In order to enjoy the story as much as possible, you
should configure a pleasant sounding speech synthesizer voice prior to playing the
game. To do so, open System Preferences and click on the  Speech icon. Next, click on
the Text to Speech tab and select a voice from the System Voice popup list.


Developed by Jerry Lee Ford, Jr.
Copyright 2007
```

To make the name of the game stand out, select it and then click on the Font menu and select the Bold menu item. In response, the Script Editor application will display this text in a bold font, as demonstrated in Figure 2.39.

FIGURE 2.39

Documenting an
AppleScript by
adding descriptive
text to the
Description tab.

Embedding Comments into the Code File

Now that you have added descriptive text to the Description tab view in the Script Editor
application's data pane, let's embed a number of comment statements at the beginning of
the script code file to provide additional information about the script and its author. The
statements to add are shown here:

```
--------------------------------------------------------------------------

--

-- Script Name: AppleScript Story Teller.scpt

-- Version: 1.0

-- Author: Jerry Lee Ford, Jr.

-- Date: August 2007

--

-- Description: This AppleScript tells a story using the Mac OS X

-- voice synthesizer

--

--------------------------------------------------------------------------
```

To make the comment statements that you've added to the beginning of the script file even more useful, you may want to consider expanding them to include the following types of information.

- Last revision date
- Your company name, address, and contact information
- Your home page's URL
- Your e-mail address

Step 3: Making a Variable Assignment

The AppleScript Story Teller game will communicate with the player using a series of dialog windows. Each of these windows will display a title bar that displays a text string. In the AppleScript Story Teller game, the name of the game will be displayed as the text in the title bar.

Rather than hardcode a string of "AppleScript Story Teller" as the title bar string each time a new popup dialog is defined (using the display dialog command), a variable named NameOfGame will be defined and assigned a value of "AppleScript Story Teller". This is accomplished by adding the following statements to the end of the code file:

```
--Assign the name of the story to a variable
set NameOfGame to "AppleScript Story Teller"
```

 A *variable* is a pointer to a location in memory where a piece of data is stored. You will learn more about variables and their construction in Chapter 3, "Working with Values, Variables, and Classes."

Step 4: Collecting Player Input

The next step in the development of the AppleScript Story Teller game is to add the code statements responsible for the generation of the dialog windows that collect input from the player. These statements are shown next and should be added to the end of the script file.

```
-- Ask the first question
set creature to the text returned of (display dialog ¬
    "Enter the name of an animal that scares you" default answer ¬
    "" buttons {"Submit"} with title NameOfGame with icon note)


-- Ask the second question
set critter to the text returned of (display dialog ¬
    "Enter the name of a cute cuddly animal." default answer ¬
```

```
        "" buttons {"Submit"} with title NameOfGame with icon note)

-- Ask the third question
set sport to the text returned of (display dialog ¬
      "What is your favorite sport?" default answer ¬
      "" buttons {"Submit"} with title NameOfGame with icon note)

-- Ask the fourth question
set dream to the text returned of (display dialog ¬
      "Name an attractive movie star." default answer ¬
      "" buttons {"Submit"} with title NameOfGame with icon note)

-- Ask the fifth question
set location to the text returned of (display dialog ¬
      "Where might a wild animal live?" default answer ¬
      "" buttons {"Submit"} with title NameOfGame with icon note)
```

Each of these five sets of statements uses the `display dialog` command to display a message in a dialog window. The player's response is captured and assigned to a unique variable name, allowing each piece of data to be referenced again later in the script.

Step 5: Notifying the Player when the Game Is Ready to Build the Story

The next step in the development of the game is to add statements that display a message (again using the `display dialog` command) that informs the player that the game is ready to tell its story.

```
--Notify the player the story is ready to be told
display dialog ¬
      "Good answers. Click on the Listen button when you are ready " & ¬
      "to hear your story." buttons {"Listen"} ¬
      with title NameOfGame with icon note
```

Step 6: Creating the Story

The text that makes up the game's story is written out as a series of strings that are concatenated together using the & concatenation operator in conjunction with the ¬ continuation operator. The end result is one long string, which is then assigned to a variable named StoryText. The statements that accomplish this task are shown next and should be added to the end of the script file.

```
--Build the story by inserting player input
set StoryText to "Once upon a time there were three little pigs who " & ¬
    "lived happily near the edge of a great " & location & ". One " & ¬
    "day a " & creature & " appeared and told the pigs that he had " & ¬
    "just eaten a large " & critter & " but that tomorrow he would " & ¬
    "be back to eat one of the three pigs. In a panic the three " & ¬
    "little pigs scurried off to build houses in which they would " & ¬
    "hide from the " & creature & ". The first pig quickly built his " & ¬
    "house out of straw and slept the afternoon away dreaming of " & ¬
    dream & ". A short time later the second pig finished building a " & ¬
    "house made of sticks and ran off to play " & sport & ". But the " & ¬
    "third little pig worked hard all day and night building his house " & ¬
    "out of brick.  When his work was done, he went inside to sleep " & ¬
    "the afternoon away. When the " & creature & " returned that " & ¬
    "evening he quickly began to eat his way through the first " & ¬
    "little pig's house, but the taste of straw made him " & ¬
    "feel sick so he moved on to the second little pig's " & ¬
    "house, which he began to quickly eat his way through. " & ¬
    "However, the " & creature & " soon got a splinter in his lip and " & ¬
    "angrily left. Finally, the " & creature & ¬
    "arrived at the third little pig's house and " & ¬
    "broke down the door to find that the third pig, having " & ¬
    "built his house in the middle of an open field with no " & ¬
    "shade had been baked alive by the " & ¬
    " heat of the hot afternoon sun, once again proving " & ¬
    "that when it comes to building a house, nothing is more " & ¬
    "important than finding a good location."
```

Note that all the words shown in bold are variable names. Each instance of a variable name is automatically replaced with its assigned value when the story is assembled.

Step 7: Telling the Story

Now that the game's story has been assembled, it is time to begin telling the story. To do so you will use the say command to call on the Mac OS X speech synthesizer and pass it the StoryText variable containing the story to be read out loud. The statement that performs this task is shown next and should be added to the end of the script file.

```
--Use the say command to tell the story using the computer's
--built-in voice synthesizer
say StoryText
```

Step 8: Displaying the Story

The last step in the development of the AppleScript Story Teller game is to add the following statement to the end of the script file. This statement uses the `display dialog` command to display the text for the entire story in a dialog window.

```
--Display the text of the story
display dialog StoryText & "  The End" buttons {"OK"} ¬
     with title NameOfGame with icon note
```

The dialog window will remain displayed until the player clicks on its OK button, closing the window and terminating the AppleScript's execution.

Running Your New AppleScript Game

Well, that's it. As long as you have not made any typing mistakes when keying in the code statements that make up the AppleScript Story Teller game, everything should be ready to go. So go ahead and compile and run your script. If you run into any syntax errors during compilation, read the resulting error messages carefully and then go back and double-check your typing and look for any mistakes that you may have inadvertently made.

SUMMARY

In this chapter you learned the ins and outs of how to work with the Script Editor application. This included learning how to create run-only versions of your AppleScripts as well as how to add startup screens to them. You also learned how to configure Script Editor preferences and how to add and remove icons from the Script Editor application's toolbar. This chapter also provided you with information on how to work with the Script Editor application's dictionary browser and Library Palette. Now, before you move on to Chapter 3, I suggest you take a few extra minutes to see if you can improve the AppleScript Story Teller game by implementing the following list of challenges.

CHALLENGES

1. As currently written, the story produced by the AppleScript Story Teller game makes limited use of player input. Consider rewriting the story to make more frequent use of player input, thus increasing the player's contribution to the story.

2. Consider reworking the text that is stored in the data pane when the Description tab is selected to provide the player with better instructions. In addition, you might also want to add your website address, company address, or whatever contact information you may have.

Part

II

CHAPTER

WORKING WITH VALUES, VARIABLES, AND CLASSES

So far, the focus of this book has been on providing you with background information about AppleScript and getting you comfortable with the basic mechanics involved in creating and executing AppleScripts. This included an in-depth review of the Script Editor. Now it is time to start digging into the AppleScript programming language. This is the first of four chapters dedicated to this task. In this chapter, you will learn how to work with different types or classes of values and how to store and retrieve values using variables. You will also learn the basics of statement and code block syntax. On top of all this, the chapter will guide you through the development of your next computer game, the AppleScript Fortune Teller.

Specifically, you will learn:

- How to formulate AppleScript statements and code blocks
- How to store and retrieve values using variables
- The rules for naming variables
- How to work with different data classes

PROJECT PREVIEW: THE APPLESCRIPT FORTUNE TELLER GAME

This chapter's game project is the AppleScript Fortune Teller. This game is designed to respond to questions asked by the player. To play, the player must ask questions that can be answered with Yes/No answers. When first started, the game displays a popup window that provides the player with instructions on how to formulate questions, as shown in Figure 3.1.

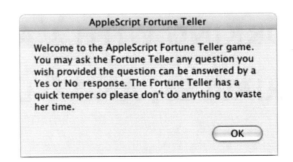

FIGURE 3.1

The player is forewarned that the Fortune Teller has a quick temper.

Once this window is dismissed, the game displays another dialog window that prompts the player to type in a question for the Fortune Teller to answer, as shown in Figure 3.2.

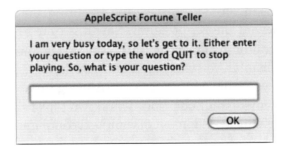

FIGURE 3.2

The player can enter the word QUIT at any time to stop playing the game.

If the player clicks on the dialog window's OK button without entering anything in the window's text field, the game responds by displaying the dialog window shown in Figure 3.3.

FIGURE 3.3

Clicking on OK without asking a question brings out the Fortune Teller's wrath.

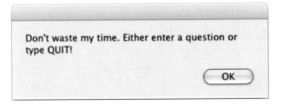

The game is designed to provide any of six randomly selected answers when responding to player questions. Sometimes the Fortune Teller responds with a specific answer, as demonstrated in Figure 3.4.

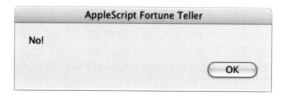

FIGURE 3.4

An example of one of the Fortune Teller's more friendly responses.

As Figure 3.5 demonstrates, sometimes the Fortune Teller refuses to answer the question asked by the player.

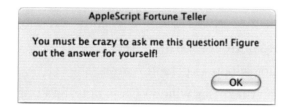

FIGURE 3.5

The Fortune Teller's quick temper sometimes results in less than friendly responses.

The player may pose as many questions as desired to the Fortune Teller. When done, the player must enter the word QUIT to stop playing. In response, the game displays the dialog window shown in Figure 3.6. The game ends when the player dismisses this window.

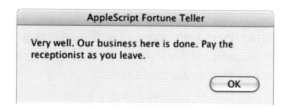

FIGURE 3.6

The ill-tempered Fortune Teller insists on being paid for her services.

COMMUNICATING WITH THE USER

One feature not provided by AppleScript is the ability to create robust graphical user interfaces. However, the language does provide support for generating a number of dialog windows as discussed in the sections that follow.

> **HINT** Although AppleScript does not support the development of windows with complex user interfaces made up of graphical elements such as buttons, slider controls, and popup lists controls, AppleScript Studio does. AppleScript Studio is discussed in Chapter 10, "Introducing AppleScript Studio."

Collecting User Input

You have already seen many instances of how to work with the `display dialog` command in order to display dialog windows. The `display dialog` command is very versatile. In its simplest form, it will display a text message and two buttons, OK and Cancel. For example, the following statement will generate a dialog window that displays a text message and two default buttons (OK and Cancel).

```
display dialog "In the end there can be only one."
```

However, you can supply any of the following optional arguments in order to modify the dialog window generated by the `display dialog` command.

- `buttons`. Defines a list of 1 to 3 buttons to be displayed.
- `default button`. Sets the dialog window's default button.
- `with icon`. Displays an icon on the dialog window (stop, note, and caution).
- `giving up after`. Closes the dialog window after a specified period of time.
- `with title`. Displays a text string in the dialog window's title bar.

Using these optional arguments, you can construct a wide variety of different dialog windows. For example, you've already seen the optional `buttons` parameter used numerous times in this book, as demonstrated here:

```
display dialog "In the end there can be only one." Buttons {"Yes", "No"}
```

Here, the default OK and Cancel buttons have been replaced with two buttons labeled Yes and No. By adding the optional `default button` parameter, you can specify which button is set up as the dialog window's default button, as demonstrated here:

```
display dialog "In the end there can be only one." Buttons {"Yes", "No"} ¬
    default button 2
```

Dialog buttons are positional, with the first button assigned a position of 1, the second button a position of 2, and the third button a position of 3. You can add an optional `with icon` parameter to display an icon on the dialog window, as demonstrated here:

```
display dialog "In the end there can be only one." with icon stop
```

Using the `giving up after` parameter, you can set a period of time after which the popup dialog will automatically be closed, should the user not respond to it, as demonstrated here:

```
display dialog "In the end there can be only one." giving up after 15
```

Here, the dialog window has been set up to wait 15 seconds before disappearing. The `display dialog` command also allows you to display a text string in the popup dialog's title bar by specifying the optional `with title` parameter, as demonstrated here:

```
display dialog "In the end there can be only one." with title "Demo"
```

AppleScript allows you to mix and match different combinations of parameters or to use them all at the same time, as demonstrated here:

```
display dialog "In the end there can be only one." ¬
    buttons {"Yes", "No"} default button 2 with icon stop ¬
    giving up after 15 with title "Demo"
```

When executed, this example generates the dialog window shown in Figure 3.7.

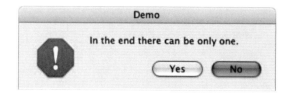

FIGURE 3.7

Using the `display dialog` command to display a dialog window loaded with optional features.

You can do a lot more with the `display dialog` command than just display text messages in dialog windows. You can also set up programming statements that can determine which button the user clicked on when responding to dialog windows. This is accomplished by embedding the `display dialog` command inside a `set` statement, as demonstrated here:

```
set answer to the button returned of (display dialog ¬
    "Click on OK to continue or Cancel to quit." ¬
    buttons {"OK", "Cancel"})
```

You can then examine the value assigned to the `answer` variable to determine which button the user clicked. In addition to displaying a text message and prompting the user to respond by clicking on a button, you can also set up the `display dialog` command to display a text field in order to prompt the user to enter text input, as shown here:

```
set answer to the text returned of (display dialog ¬
        "What is your name?" default answer "" ¬
        buttons {"OK"})
```

Here, instead of specifying that the set statement should set the value of the answer variable to the button returned, the statement has been set up to set the value of the answer variable to the text returned by the display dialog command. Note that in the case of the preceding example, an empty string (default answer "") is specified. If you want, you could specify a default answer in place of the empty string. In which case the user would have the option of accepting the default response or overtyping it with a new response, as demonstrated here:

```
set answer to the text returned of (display dialog ¬
        "What is your name?" default answer "John Doe" ¬
        buttons {"OK"})
```

When executed, this example displays the dialog window shown in Figure 3.8.

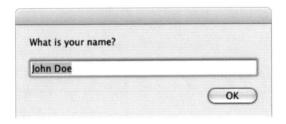

FIGURE 3.8

Providing a default answer when prompting the user to provide input.

Displaying Alert Messages

Another option for communicating with users is to use the display alert command to display a text string in a dialog window. Unlike the display dialog command, the display alert command is limited to displaying text and buttons. You can use this command to display up to three buttons. In addition, you can display both a header and a message string, as demonstrated here:

```
display alert "Listen up!" message "Something has gone wrong."
        buttons {"Quit", "Try again", "Cancel"}
```

When executed, this statement displays the dialog window shown in Figure 3.9.

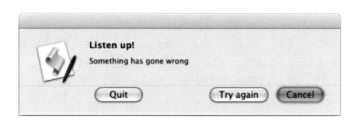

FIGURE 3.9

Displaying a
warning message
using the display
alert command.

Like the display dialog command, you can also use the display alert command in conjunction with the set command to ascertain which button the user clicks.

Letting the User Select from a List

Another handy command that you may want to use in order to interact with the user is the choose from list command, which provides you with the ability to display a list of strings or numbers from which the user can make a selection.

To effectively use this command, you should embed it within a set statement, as shown next. This will allow you to programmatically determine which item the user has selected from the list.

```
set answer ¬
    to choose from list {"Apples", "Oranges", "Grapes", "Pears", "Other"} ¬
    with prompt "Pick a Fruit:"
```

HINT A *list* is a collection of two or more items enclosed within { } characters.

Here, a list made up of five items is displayed, as demonstrated in Figure 3.10. The user must select an item and then click on the OK button. The selected value is then returned as a list and stored in the variable specified by the set statement.

FIGURE 3.10

Prompting the
user to select
from a list of
options.

Other Dialog Windows

In addition to the `display dialog`, `display alert`, and `choose from list` commands, Apple-Script provides you with access to a number of additional commands that you can use to interact with the user using various predefined dialog windows. A list of these commands is provided here:

- `choose color`. Displays the Color Picker dialog window, allowing the user to select a color.
- `choose file`. Displays the Open File dialog window, allowing the user to specify the location and name of a file.
- `choose folder`. Displays the Choose Folder dialog window, allowing the user to specify the location and name of a folder.
- `choose file name`. Displays the Save File dialog window, allowing the user to specify the location where a file should be saved.
- `choose application`. Displays the Choose Application dialog window, allowing the user to select an application.
- `choose URL`. Displays the Choose URL dialog window, allowing the user to specify the name of a network server.
- `choose remote application`. Displays the Choose Remote Application dialog window, allowing the user to specify the IP address of the computer where an application can be selected.

APPLESCRIPT COMMANDS AND STATEMENTS

As you have already seen, AppleScript's programming language provides programmers with access to many commands. Commands are instructions that perform tasks. Commands are one of the building blocks used in the formulation of statements. A *statement* is a line of program code. You have already seen numerous commands in action in this book. Examples include:

- `display dialog`
- `tell`
- `say`
- `set`

Some commands like the `display dialog` command are capable of returning a result that can then be used as input. Other commands like `beep`, discussed later in this chapter, simply perform a specified action without returning a result. Many commands are built into

AppleScript. Other commands are provided by third-party applications. In order to take advantage of commands, you must understand their syntax. When it comes to third-party commands, this may mean spending a lot of time using the Dictionary browser to determine which commands are available and how to use them.

Language-Like Syntax

AppleScript is an English-like programming language. As such, many of its commands and their syntax closely mimic the syntax of the English language. For example, the `tell` command is used to direct commands to other applications in order to tell them what to do.

AppleScript's programming language is filled with transitional words like `the`, `as`, `is`, and `of`. These words are used in the formulation of English-like expressions. An *expression* is a set of words that is evaluated in order to generate a value. For example, the following statement checks to see if the value assigned to a variable named `x` is equal to 10.

```
if x is equal to 10
```

This statement reads in a manner that is very similar to spoken English. This language-like syntax helps to set AppleScript apart from many other programming languages. For example, in most other programming languages, the previous statement would be written like this:

```
if x = y
```

Since flexibility and ease of use is a hallmark of AppleScript programming, AppleScript will allow you to use either form of syntax that you want. However, sometimes AppleScript's devotion to English-like syntax can be a little long winded. For example, most programming languages will allow you to assign a value to a variable, like so:

```
x = 100
```

However, AppleScript only permits you to assign values to variables using the `set` command, as shown here:

```
set x to 100
```

Improving Statement Readability with Optional Words

AppleScript lets you be as cryptic or as robustly linguistic as you want to be. By this I mean that AppleScript provides programmers with all kinds of optional words that you can add to program statements to make them more linguistically English-like. However, in the spirit of flexibility, you do not have to use any of these optional words. For example, consider `the`. You can use `the` whenever it sounds and feels right. For example, the following statement assigns the current date to a variable named `MyBirthday`.

```
set MyBirthday to current date
```

While this statement is fairly straightforward, you can make it a little more understandable by inserting the, as demonstrated here:

```
set MyBirthday to the current date
```

the has no impact on any statements in which it is used. Its only purpose is aesthetic. As such, even though it does not provide any added value, you could use it as demonstrated below, and the result would be exactly the same as for the two previous examples.

```
set MyBirthday to the the the the the the current date
```

Using English Words and Phrases

AppleScript also lets you substitute English words and phrases in place of different operators to improve the overall readability of your AppleScripts. For example, the following statement checks to see if the value assigned to a variable named x is equal to 10.

```
if x = 10 then
```

This statement should look very familiar to any programmers for many other programming languages. It uses the equal operator to compare the value of one value against another. In this case, the comparison is between a variable and a numeric value. If you prefer, you can rewrite this statement using many different English words and phrases. For example, the following statement uses the is keyword in place of the = operator.

```
if x is 10 then
```

If you prefer, you can use the equals keyword in place of the is keyword and achieve the same result, as shown here:

```
if x equals 10 then
```

Alternatively, you can use the is equal to phrase, as shown here.

```
if x is equal to 10
```

Singular and Plural Words

Many AppleScript keywords come in both singular and plural forms. For example, Finder allows you to work with both a file and files, as well as a folder or folders. As such, you could generate a list of all the files located in your documents folder using the singular form of the folder noun, as demonstrated here using the singular form:

```
tell application "Finder"
```

```
    list folder (path to documents folder)
end tell
```

Similarly, you could use files (the plural of file) to retrieve a list of all the files located in your home folder.

```
tell application "Finder"
    get files of home
end tell
```

 To determine whether an application accepts a plural form for a given noun, reference that application's dictionary.

Abbreviating Keywords

AppleScript also allows you to abbreviate many different words. For example, instead of typing out the word application, you can type app and AppleScript will know what you mean. Likewise, you can type prop in place of the word property. When you compile your AppleScript, the Script Editor will replace these abbreviations with the complete spelling of its associated word.

Statement Continuation

As you have already seen, unless explicitly extended using the ¬ (continuation) character, AppleScript statements must be written on a single line. However, using the ¬ character, you can spread a statement over as many lines as necessary. Once used, you cannot include anything else following the ¬ character without generating an error. In addition, if you need to continue a string over two or more lines then you must break the string up into smaller strings and use the & concatenation character in addition to the ¬ character, as demonstrated here:

```
display dialog "To spread this statement out over more than one line " & ¬
    "you must concatenate and continue it as demonstrated here."
```

Building Code Blocks

In addition to single-line statements and the use of the ¬ character to spread a statement out over more than one line, AppleScript also lets you define code blocks. A *code block* is a group of statements that are executed as a unit. A code block begins with an opening statement and ends with a closing statement that includes the end keyword, as demonstrated here:

```
on open
    (*Insert Code here*)
end open
```

Here a code block has been used to define an `open` event handler.

 The above event handler is based on the `open` event and is used as the basis for creating droplets. An *event* is an action, such as the starting of an AppleScript or the dropping of a file or folder onto an AppleScript that can be used as the trigger for initiating the execution of statements that respond to the event. A *droplet* is an AppleScript that executes whenever a file or folder is dropped onto it, allowing the file or the contents of the folder to be processed in some way. You will learn about events and droplets later in Chapter 6, "Improving Script Organization with Handlers."

You can include any number of code statements inside a code block. Once compiled, any statements included inside the code block are automatically indented to make the code block easier to read. Another example of a code block involves the use of the `tell` command. When used this way, the `tell` command has the following syntax.

```
tell target
    statements
end tell
```

The `tell` command is used to identify the target to which embedded code block statements are focused. For example, the following statements use the `tell` command to direct commands that automate the TextEdit application.

```
tell application "TextEdit"
    activate
    set text of document 1 to "Once upon a time..."
end tell
```

Here, a `tell` code block has been set up to start the TextEdit application (if it is not already running) and then to write out a line of text in a new document. Note the use of the `of` keyword in this example to identify the object attribute (document) that is to be manipulated.

 The `tell` command can also be used to formulate single line statements using the following syntax.

```
tell Target to Command
```

Target is a placeholder representing the application to which the *Command* is directed. For example, the following statement starts the TextEdit application, if it is not already running and brings it to the front of the desktop.

```
tell application "TextEdit" to activate
```

KEEPING TRACK OF DATA

All but the most simple and basic AppleScripts are designed to accept, process, and manipulate data in some manner. The data may be collected from the operating system or be provided by the user. In AppleScript, variables are used to manage the storage and retrieval of data. A *variable* is a pointer to a location in memory where data is stored. Variables provide a means for storing data input that can be referenced and modified as necessary during script execution.

Assigning Data to Variables

The most common way of assigning a value to a variable is to use the `set` command. This command has the following syntax.

```
set VariableName to Value
```

VariableName is a placeholder representing the name of the variable to which *Value* is assigned. For example, the following statement demonstrates how to assign a value of 10 to a variable named `PlayerScore`.

```
set PlayerScore to 10
```

You can modify the value assigned to a variable by simply executing another `set` command, as demonstrated here:

```
set PlayerScore to PlayerScore + 1
```

 TRICK   The previous statement modified the value assigned to the `PlayerScore` variable by taking its current value and adding one to it. Therefore, if the value of `PlayerScore` were set to 10, the previous statement would modify it by incrementing its value by 1, resulting in a new assignment value of 11.

Instead of assigning values to variables one at a time, AppleScript provides programmers with the ability to assign data to groups of variables using lists. As has been previously stated, a list is a collection of two or more values enclosed within {} characters, as shown here:

```
set {FirstName, MiddleName, LastName, Suffix} to ¬
    {"Jerry", "Lee", "Ford", "Jr."}
```

Here, the variable `FirstName` is assigned a value of `"Jerry"`. The variable `MiddleName` is assigned a value of `"Lee"`. The variable `LastName` is assigned a value of `"Ford "`. And the variable suffix is assigned a value of `"Jr."`.

If you want, you can also use the `copy` command to assign values to variables. The syntax of the `copy` command is outlined here:

```
copy value to VariableName
```

VariableName is a placeholder representing the name of the variable to which `value` is assigned. For example, the following statement demonstrates how to use the `copy` command to assign a value of 10 to a variable named `PlayerScore`.

```
copy 10 to PlayerScore
```

Retrieving Data from Variables

There are two ways to retrieve the values assigned to variables. The first option is to use the `get` command, which has the following syntax.

```
get VariableName
```

VariableName is a placeholder representing the variables whose value is to be retrieved. For example, the following statement uses the `get` command to retrieve the value assigned to a variable named `PlayerScore`.

```
set CurrentValue to get PlayerScore
```

In this example, the value of `PlayerScore` is retrieved and assigned to a variable named `CurrentValue`.

The second option for retrieving data stored in variables allows programmers to omit the use of the `get` command and instead access a variable's value by simply referencing its name, as demonstrated here:

```
set CurrentValue to PlayerScore
```

Property Variables

In AppleScript, a *property* is a special type of variable. Once assigned, a property's value remains accessible during and after script execution. This allows you to create AppleScripts that can save, modify, and access values across different executions of a script. This might come in handy in a situation where you need to develop a game script that keeps track of the game's highest score. Using a property, you can initially set the value representing the game's high score to zero and then update it as necessary during game play to reflect the player's highest score. The value assigned to the property will still be available later on, should the player stop playing and come back later to play more.

The syntax used to declare a property is outlined here:

```
property VariableVame : AssignedValue
```

VariableName is a placeholder for the name assigned to the property and *AssignedValue* is a placeholder for the value to be assigned to the property. The following example demonstrates how a property's value is retained over multiple executions.

```
property x : 0
set x to x + 1
display dialog x
```

Key in this example as an AppleScript and then run it. At the end of the first execution, a popup dialog will appear displaying a value of 1. Run the script again and a value of 2 will be displayed.

AppleScript's Rules for Naming Variables

Like other programming languages, AppleScript imposes a number of very specific rules on the naming of variables. AppleScript variable names cannot consist of language keywords such as `tell`, `beep` or `if`, `then`, `else`, and so on. In addition to these rules, you need to avoid using dictionary terms that are defined by the different applications that you may want to automate. Although AppleScript allows programmers to create very long and descriptive variable names, it does impose a 251 character limit. Though I cannot imagine a need to create a variable name greater than 251 characters, if you try to do so the Script Editor will display the error message shown in Figure 3.11.

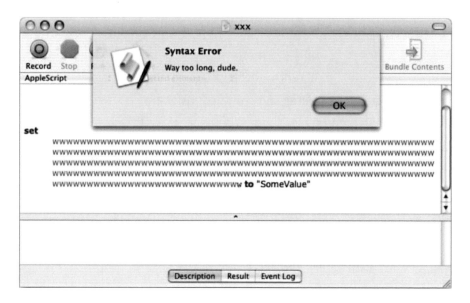

FIGURE 3.11

Don't let it be said that the developers of AppleScript lack a sense of humor.

Avoiding dictionary words that may be defined by Apple and third-party applications can pose a real challenge. One way of dealing with this challenge is to develop your own variable naming scheme. For example, consider creating variable names that consist of multiple words like UserName or HighScore. Alternatively, you might want to prefix your variable name with a three character string that describes its data type. For example, a variable that will be used to store string data might be assigned a variable name that begins with the characters str, as demonstrated here:

```
set strHostCountry to "USA"
```

AppleScript variable names must begin with a letter or the underscore character. The rest of the characters that make up a variable name are limited to the list of characters outlined in Table 3.1.

TABLE 3.1 APPLESCRIPT VARIABLE NAMING RULES

Characters	Description
a–z	Lowercase letters
A–Z	Uppercase letters
0–9	Numeric digits
	The underscore character

To get a better feel for the types of variable names that AppleScript considers valid, take a look at the following list.

- User_ID —Uppercase, lowercase characters and the underscore character
- x2007 —Begins with a lowercase character and contains numbers
- strUserName —Mixed case characters
- strusername —All lowercase characters
- STRUSERNAME —All uppercase characters

On the other hand, AppleScript will flag each of the following examples as invalid if you try to compile an AppleScript that contains them.

- beep —Variable names cannot be made up of AppleScript keywords
- 1stDayOfTheWeek —Cannot begin with a number
- Custmer@EmailAddress —Cannot contain special characters

TRICK

If you feel compelled to assign a variable a name that does not follow the previously defined rules, AppleScript will let you do so provided that you enclose the variable name inside a matching set of || characters using the following syntax.

```
set |VariableName| to Value
```

Using this syntax, you can assign any name you want to AppleScript variables. For example, the following statement defines a variable named |tell| and assigns it a value of 5.

```
set |tell| to 5
```

To refer to this variable later in an AppleScript, you must remember to include vertical bars, as demonstrated here:

```
if |tell| = 5 then
    ...
end if
```

Variable Names and Case-Sensitivity

AppleScript does not differentiate between different uses of case when referencing variable names. As long as you spell a variable name the same way each time you want to reference it, AppleScript does not care what case you use. For example, as far as AppleScript is concerned, all of the following variable names are identical.

- HIGHSCORE
- highscore
- HighScore

HINT

Do not be alarmed if you find that AppleScript has retyped the spelling of your variable names after compiling your script. Any time AppleScript determines that a variable name has been entered more than once using different cases, it automatically takes the case that was used for the first stance of the variable name and then reapplies that case to all instances that follow. This has no impact on your AppleScript and will help make things easier to read and understand by keeping things consistent.

Beware of Undefined Variables

Unlike many other programming languages, AppleScript does not assign default values to variables. As a result, you cannot reference a variable until you have assigned a value to it. If you attempt to do so, your script will not compile and the Script Editor will display an error message, as demonstrated in Figure 3.12.

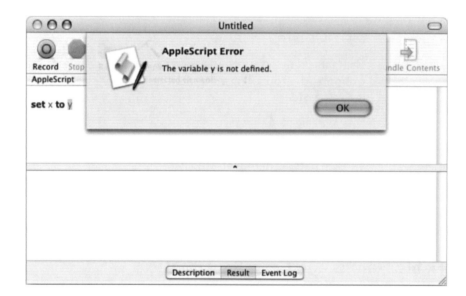

UNDERSTANDING APPLESCRIPT VARIABLE CLASSES

Many programming languages require that you specify or declare a value's data type when assigning it to a variable. AppleScript does not have this requirement. Instead, AppleScript variables are implicitly declared upon their initial reference. In other words, if you want a variable named UserScore, just start using it.

All AppleScript variables are assigned a *data type* or *class* that classifies the type of data that is being stored and identifies the type of operations that can be performed on the data. For example, a variable of the class string can be appended to another string to create a larger string. Numeric classes, on the other hand, support a range of numeric operations such as addition, subtraction, multiplication, and division. You do not have to worry about how to specify a variable value's data type. AppleScript will take care of this for you based on the type of value you assign to it.

The Boolean Class

One type of data supported by AppleScript is the Boolean class. Boolean data is limited to either of two values, true or false. The Boolean class is very important to AppleScript because so many operations within scripts involve the generation of a result that yields either a true or false value. For example, the if statement, which forms the cornerstone of conditional logic within modern computer programming, facilitates this very type of operation. Based on the value of expressions that are analyzed, if statements evaluate the true or false status of expressions in order to control the logical flow of statement execution with AppleScripts.

 HINT Although you have already seen examples of conditional logic in action, I have not explained yet how it all works. You will learn all about conditional logic in Chapter 4, "Implementing Conditional Logic and Working with Loops."

The String Class

You have already seen strings used many times in this book. A string is formulated by enclosing one or more characters inside a pair of matching double quotation marks. For example, the following statements assign a string to a variable named Title.

```
set Title to "Absolute Beginner's Guide to AppleScript Programming"
```

By assigning a string to a variable, you implicitly tell AppleScript the type of data that it is working with. Some commands and operations only work with strings. For example, the display dialog command is only capable of displaying text. Fortunately, as will be discussed a little later in this chapter, if you pass the display dialog command a non-string value, it will convert that value to a string and display it. Other operations are less forgiving. For example, using the & operator, you can combine or concatenate two strings together to form a new string, as demonstrated here:

```
set x to "AB" & "C"    --x is set equal to "ABC"
```

If you attempt to use the & operator to work with a string and a number as demonstrated here, AppleScript will implicitly convert the numeric value to a string and then add the two strings together.

```
set x to "4" & 10    --x is set equal to "410"
```

In this example, AppleScript looked at the first value and the & operator and determined that based on this information, it could only complete the processing of the statement if it converted the numeric value of 10 to a string. However, if you flipped the order in which the two values were presented, as demonstrated here, you end up with a completely different result.

```
set x to 10 & "4"    --x is set equal to {10, "4"}
```

This time AppleScript sees that the first value that it is presented with is a numeric value of 10. This value is not compatible with the & concatenation operator that follows. Rather than produce an error and quit, AppleScript instead takes the two specified values and adds them to a list.

You will learn how to work with strings later in Chapter 5, "Using Strings, Lists, and Records."

The Integer Class

In AppleScript, an integer is a numeric value in the range of −536870911 to 536870911. Integers are whole numbers. They cannot contain a decimal point. Unlike real numbers, discussed in the next section, integers more efficiently store whole numbers that fit within its range.

If your AppleScript has an integer value that is later modified, resulting in either a real number (a numeric value that includes a decimal point) or a value that exceeds AppleScript's range for integers, that value will automatically be converted to a real number.

Because AppleScript does not allow programmers to explicitly declare a variable class, you do not have to worry about whether you are setting up a variable to store an integer or a real number. AppleScript will make the correct assignment for you.

The Real Class

AppleScript stores numbers that contain a decimal point or that exceed the range supported by integers as real numbers. AppleScript real numbers have a range of −1.797693e308 to 1.797693e308. Like integers, real numbers are used for storing and manipulating numeric data. Examples of real numbers would include 99.99 and 99999999999. AppleScript also supports the representation of real numbers using scientific notation. For example, if you want you could set the value of a variable named UserScore as shown here:

```
set UserScore to 2e2
```

When you compile this example, the Script Editor will often automatically translate the value represented by the scientific notation to a different format shown here:

```
set UserScore to 200.0
```

It can be difficult to predict exactly how real numbers written using scientific notation will be represented in your scripts once they have been compiled. To demonstrate what I mean, create a new AppleScript and add the following statement to it.

```
set x to 97e23
```

When you compile your script, the Script Editor will modify and redisplay the code statement as shown here:

```
set x to 9.7E+24
```

The Date Class

AppleScript also provides programmers with access to a date class, which is used to store and access date and time related data. AppleScript stores date and time data in the following format.

```
weekday, month day, year hh:mm:ss ampm
```

AppleScript supports a range of different values that can be accessed when working with the date class. Table 3.2 provides a list of these values.

TABLE 3.2 DATE CLASS PARAMETERS	
Parameter	**Range**
ss	A two-character number representing seconds
mm	A two-character number representing minutes
hh	A two-character number representing hours
day	1–31
weekday	Monday, Tuesday, Wednesday, Thursday, Friday, Saturday, Sunday
month	January, February, March, April, May, June, July, August, September, October, November, December
year	A four-character year
ampm	am or pm

Working with the date class is relatively straightforward. For example, the following statement demonstrates how to retrieve the current date.

```
set TodaysDate to current date
```

Here, the current date command is used to retrieve the current date, which is then assigned to a variable named TodaysDate. When executed, this statement will assign a value like the one shown below to the variable TodaysDate.

```
Saturday, August 12, 2007 5:22:34 PM
```

To make the date class easy to work with, AppleScript provides programmers with access to a number of properties. Each of these properties provides access to date and time information in various formats. Table 3.3 provides a listing of these properties and provides a description of their values.

TABLE 3.3	DATE CLASS PROPERTIES
Property	**Description**
year	Returns a four-character year
month	Returns a value of January, February, March, April, May, June, July, August, September, October, November, or December
day	Returns an integer in the range of 1–31
hours	Returns an integer representing the number of hours since midnight
minutes	Returns an integer in the range of 1–60
seconds	Returns an integer in the range of 1–60
time	Returns an integer representing the number of seconds since midnight
weekday	Returns a value of Monday, Tuesday, Wednesday, Thursday, Friday, Saturday, or Sunday
date string	Returns a string formatted as weekday, month day, year
short date string	Returns a string formatted as mm:dd:yyyy
time string	Returns a string formatted as hh:mm:ss AM/PM

In order to better understand how to take advantage of the properties listed in Table 3.3, let's take a look at the following example.

```
set TodaysDate to current date

if weekday of TodaysDate = Sunday then
     display dialog "Remember to cut the grass."
else
     display dialog "Today is " & (weekday of TodaysDate) & ¬
          " so relax." as string
end if
```

Here, the weekday property is examined to determine if it is equal to Sunday. If it is, a message is displayed reminding the user to cut the grass. If, however, this example is executed on any day of the week other than Sunday, a different message is displayed.

Determining a Value's Class

Every variable used in an AppleScript is automatically assigned a class based on the type of data assigned to it as a value. Using the class command, you can programmatically determine a value's class. The following example demonstrates how to work with this command.

```
set GameOver to true
set PunchLine to "What's up doc?"
set InitialScore to 100
set VarianceLevel to 1.0
set MyBirthday to current date

display dialog (class of GameOver) as string      -- Displays Boolean
display dialog (class of PunchLine) as string     -- Displays string
display dialog (class of InitialScore) as string  -- Displays integer
display dialog (class of VarianceLevel) as string -- Displays real
display dialog (class of MyBirthday) as string    -- Displays date
```

Note the use of the parentheses in each of the display dialog statements shown above. The use of the parentheses is optional. You can remove them and it will not have any effect on the way the script runs. I added them to make the code statements easier to read. This is a good example of AppleScript's flexibility and programmer-friendly coding style.

DATA COERCION

AppleScript automatically recognizes a value's data type based on how you use it. For instance, any value enclosed inside a pair of matching double quotation marks is treated by AppleScript as a string type.

```
set x to "Alexander Ford"
```

On the other hand, assigning a numeric value as shown next results in a numeric assignment. Note that numeric values are not enclosed within double quotation marks.

```
set x to 10
```

If, however, you enclose a number within double quotation marks as shown next, AppleScript will assign the value a string data type.

```
set x to "10"
```

AppleScript also lets you make an explicit data type assignment using an as clause, as demonstrated here:

```
set x to 10 as string
```

This is an example of *explicit coercion*. It is often unnecessary to explicitly convert data from one type to another. In many cases, AppleScript will *implicitly coerce* data from one type to another, when the situation appears to call for it. For example, the following statements assign a numeric value of 10 to a variable named x and a string of "5" to a variable named y.

```
set x to 10
set y to "5"
```

 HINT AppleScript variables are not tightly associated with data types. As such, AppleScript will allow programmers to store any type of data they want in a variable and reassign a different value with a totally different data type to that variable.

If you then attempt to add these two values together as shown next, AppleScript will realize that it is working with two incompatible data types and resolve the situation by converting the string of "5" to its numeric equivalent, resulting in a numeric value of 15 being assigned to the z variable.

```
set z to x + y
```

However, this type of automatic data type conversion is not always appropriate, as shown here:

```
set x to 10
set y to "Molly"
set z to x + y
```

If you attempt to run this example, AppleScript will generate an error message that states that it cannot make "Molly" into a type of number.

TAKING ADVANTAGE OF CONSTANTS

In addition to providing you with the ability to dynamically store and retrieve data stored in variables, AppleScript also lets you work with constants. A *constant* is a value that is known at development time and does not change. AppleScript provides programmers with access to a number of constants. For example, the mathematical value of pi can be referenced using the pi constant, as demonstrated here:

```
set x to 10 + pi
```

When executed, this example assigned a result of 13.14159265359 to a variable named x. AppleScript supports a number of different types of constants. Other examples of constants provided by AppleScript include the Boolean values of true and false and values representing both the days of the weeks and the months of the year (Sunday, Monday, Tuesday, Wednesday, Thursday, Friday, Saturday, January, February, March, April, May, June, July, August, September, October, November, December).

BACK TO THE APPLESCRIPT FORTUNE TELLER GAME

Okay, now it is time to turn your attention back to the development of this chapter's game project, the AppleScript Fortune Teller game. This game will provide you with an opportunity to apply your newly developed understanding of variables. In addition, this game will also demonstrate how to create random numbers, which in the world of game development is an important tool for any programmer to know how to use.

Designing the Game

As with all the AppleScripts that you will create as you work your way through this book, the AppleScript Fortune Teller game will be created in a series of steps. In the case of the AppleScript Fortune Teller game, eight steps will be followed.

1. Create a new AppleScript and save it with a name of AppleScript Fortune Teller.
2. Add statements to the script file that document the script and its purpose.
3. Define a variable that will be used to control game play.
4. Display instructions for playing the game.
5. Set up a loop allowing repeated statement execution.
6. Prompt the player to enter a question.
7. Terminate game play when instructed by the player.
8. Generate answers to player questions.

As you work your way through this AppleScript, pay special attention to how and where variables are used to store and retrieve data. This applies to data storage and the analysis of data keyed in by the user, the generation and use of the game's randomly generated number, and the assignment and display of Fortune Teller responses.

Step 1: Creating an AppleScript File

The first step in the creation of the AppleScript Fortune Teller game is to start up the Script Editor application and create a new AppleScript file named AppleScript Fortune Teller by following these steps:

1. Start the Script Editor application.
2. Click on the File menu and select the Save As option.
3. In the sheet window that appears, enter **AppleScript Fortune Teller** in the Save As field and specify the location where the script should be saved using the Where drop-down menu.
4. Click on the Save button.

Step 2: Providing High-Level Script Documentation

Let's continue the development of the AppleScript Fortune Teller game by providing a little documentation about the game that provides a brief explanation of its purpose and identifies its author and copyright information. This documentation will be provided in two places. First, you will add text to the Description tab view of the Script Editor application's data pane. Second, you will embed comment statements alongside script statements.

Adding External Descriptive Text

To add the first set of script documentation, click on the Description tab located at the bottom of the Script Editor application, just beneath the data pane, and then enter the text shown here:

```
The AppleScript Fortune Teller Game  v1.0


This game imitates a session with a somewhat rude and cranky Fortune Teller. Players
may ask as many questions as they want. Game play is terminated when the player enters
the word QUIT.


Developed by Jerry Lee Ford, Jr.
Copyright 2007
```

To make this information more visually appealing, highlight the name of the game and then click on the Font menu and select the Bold menu item. In response, the Script Editor application will display this text in a bold font, as demonstrated in Figure 3.13.

 If the name of the game does not appear to be highlighted after making it bold, try selecting a different font.

FIGURE 3.13

Providing
additional
information about
the game in the
Description view
of the Script
Editor's data pane.

Embedding Comments Inside the Script

Now let's add the following comment statements to the beginning of the AppleScript. These statements identify the name and purpose of the script as well as its author and creation date.

```
--------------------------------------------------------------------------
--
-- Script Name: AppleScript Fortune Teller.scpt
-- Version: 1.0
-- Author: Jerry Lee Ford, Jr.
-- Date: August 2007
--
-- Description: This AppleScript provides randomly selected answers
-- to player questions in a manner that imitates a virtual fortune
-- teller.
--------------------------------------------------------------------------
```

Step 3: Defining a Variable to Control Game Play

A loop will be set up later in the script that controls the interaction between the player and the fortune teller, allowing the player to ask as many questions as she wants. The loop will be set up to execute based on the value assigned to a Boolean variable named EndOfGame. Initially, this variable will be assigned a value of false and will remain that way until the player decides to quit playing the game, at which time the value will be assigned a value of true.

The following statement defines the EndOfGame variable and sets its initial value. Add this statement to the script, immediately following the comment statements that you added in the previous step.

```
set EndOfGame to False
```

> **HINT** A *loop* is a collection of code statements that are repeatedly executed, providing an efficient means of automating repetitive tasks. Loops can also be used to process collections of data and the contents of files. You will learn all about loops in Chapter 4, "Implementing Conditional Logic and Working with Loops."

Step 4: Providing Instruction for Playing the Game

The next step in the development of the AppleScript Fortune Teller game is to display a dialog window that provides the player with instructions for playing the game. This is accomplished by adding the following statements to the end of your AppleScript.

```
-- Display a welcome screen that introduces the game to the
-- player and explains how questions must be formatted
display dialog "Welcome to the AppleScript Fortune Teller game. " & ¬
      "You may ask the Fortune Teller any question you wish " & ¬
      "provided the question can be answered by a Yes or No  " & ¬
      "response. The Fortune Teller has a quick temper so " & ¬
      "please don't do anything to waste her time." buttons {"OK"} ¬
      with title "AppleScript Fortune Teller"
```

As you can see, these statements consist of comments and a display dialog command that displays a text string containing the game's instructions. In addition, a single OK button is displayed on the dialog window and the text string "AppleScript Fortune Teller" is displayed in the window's title bar.

Step 5: Adding a Loop to Control Player Interaction

The next step in the development of the AppleScript Fortune Teller game is to add a loop to the script that will be responsible for managing the interaction between the player and the Fortune Teller. This is accomplished by adding the following statements to the end of the AppleScript.

```
repeat until EndOfGame = True


end repeat
```

These two statements set up a `repeat` loop code block that will execute until the value assigned to the `EndOfGame` variable is set equal to a Boolean value of `true`. You will learn how to work with loops later in Chapter 4.

Step 6: Prompting the Player for Input

The next step in the development of the AppleScript Fortune Teller game is to add the program code that is responsible for prompting the player to enter her question. This is accomplished by embedding the following statements inside the `repeat` loop code block that you set up in the previous step.

```
-- Prompt the player to ask the Fortune Teller a question
set question to text returned of (display dialog ¬
    "I am very busy today, so let's get to it. Either enter " & ¬
    "your question or type the word QUIT to stop playing. " & ¬
    "So, what is your question?" default answer ¬
    "" buttons {"OK"} with title "AppleScript Fortune Teller")
```

As you can see, these two statements consist of a comment followed by a `set` statement that takes the text input returned by a `display dialog` command and assigns it to a variable named `question`.

Step 7: Managing Game Termination

Next, you need to add code statements that examine the input keyed in by the player to determine whether the player has decided to quit playing the game. The player does this by entering the word QUIT into the dialog window and then clicking on the window's OK button.

```
-- Check to see if the player has decided to quit playing
if question = "quit" then

    --Display the game's final window
    display dialog "Very well. Our business here is done. " & ¬
        "Pay the receptionist as you leave." buttons {"OK"} ¬
        with title "AppleScript Fortune Teller"
    set EndOfGame to True
    return
end if
```

Because AppleScript treats variable names in a case-insensitive manner by default, you do not need to worry about the case used by the player when keying in the word QUIT. The AppleScript will accept any case used (QUIT, quit, Quit, QuIT, etc). When the player types in the word QUIT, these statements display a humorous message in a dialog window and then change the value assigned to the EndOfGame variable to true. This will result in the termination of the repeat loop the next time it iterates. Next, the return command is executed. The return command causes an immediate termination of the current iteration of the repeat loop. As a result, the loop will begin a new iteration and since the value assigned to EndOfGame is now equal to true, the loop will stop executing and the script will end.

Step 8: Generating Answers to Questions

If the player does not enter the QUIT command when responding to the dialog window, then either of two things has happened. Either the player clicked on the OK button without typing or the player has entered some text, which the game will assume is a valid question (although this might not be the case).

The last set of code statements that you need to add to this script will handle both of these situations. These statements are shown next and should be embedded into the repeat loop immediately following the previous set of statements (but before the closing end repeat statement).

```
-- Display an error message in the event the player fails to
-- enter any text before clicking on the OK button
if question = "" then
    display dialog "Don't waste my time. Either enter a " & ¬
        "question or type QUIT!" buttons {"OK"}
else

        -- Generate a number between 1 and 6
    set RandomNumber to random number from 1 to 6

        -- Assign answers based on the randomly assigned value
    if RandomNumber = 1 then
        set reply to "Yes!"
    end if

    if RandomNumber = 2 then
        set reply to "No!"
```

```
        end if

        if RandomNumber = 3 then
            set reply to "Maybe!"
        end if

        if RandomNumber = 4 then
            set reply to "You must be crazy to ask me this " & ¬
                "question! Figure out the answer for yourself!"
        end if

        if RandomNumber = 5 then
            set reply to "How should I know? Flip a coin!"
        end if

        if RandomNumber = 6 then
            set reply to "I most sincerely doubt it!"
        end if

        -- Play a beep sound to let the player know the
        -- Fortune Teller has conjured up an answer
        beep

        -- Display the game's randomly generated answer
        display dialog reply buttons {"OK"} ¬
            with title "AppleScript Fortune Teller"

end if
```

These statements consist of a series of embedded `if` statements that analyze the value assigned to the `question` variable. If `question` is set equal to "" then this indicates that the player clicked on the OK button without entering any text, in which case a dialog window is displayed that warns the player not to waste the fortune teller's time and the rest of the statements that follow are skipped. If on the other hand, the player did enter something in the dialog window's text field before clicking on the OK button, a random number is generated and assigned to a variable named `RandomNumber`.

The `random number` command generates a number. By default a random real number between 0 and 1 is generated. However, by specifying a lower and an upper bound using the `from` and `to` keywords, you can control the range of numbers that will be used. In addition, if you specify both the lower and upper bounds as integers, AppleScript will only return randomly generated integer values. In the AppleScript Fortune Teller game, a range of 1 to 6 is specified.

A series of six `if` statement code blocks are then set up in order to analyze the value of the randomly generated number and determine which text string should be assigned to the `reply` variable. Next, the `beep` command is executed and then the value assigned to `reply` is displayed in a dialog window, answering the player's question.

The `beep` command plays the default system sound and is typically used to get the user's attention.

Testing the Execution of the AppleScript Fortune Teller Game

Okay, assuming that you did not accidentally skip any steps or mistype any code statements, your new AppleScript game should be ready to run. Go ahead and compile and execute it. If the Script Editor displays any syntax error messages, use the information provided to track down the statement(s) where the errors exist and check to see what you may have mistyped or left out and then try compiling and running your AppleScript again.

SUMMARY

In this chapter you learned about the different classes of data types supported by AppleScript. You learned how to assign data to and retrieve data from variables. You learned the rules that AppleScript requires you to follow when naming variables. You also learned how to use lists to populate groups of variables. This chapter also demonstrated how to explicitly coerce variable values from one data type to another and explained how to work with properties. On top of all this, you learned about statement and code block syntax.

Now, before you move on to Chapter 4, consider setting aside a little more time to improve the AppleScript Fortune Teller game by addressing the following list of challenges.

CHALLENGES

1. Consider modifying the game to prompt the player to enter her name at the beginning of the game and then modify the game so that the Fortune Teller addresses the player by name.

2. As currently written, the AppleScript Fortune Teller game provides only a limited set of answers to the player. Consider expanding the pool of available answers from 6 to 10 or 12 in order make the game less predictable.

Implementing Conditional Logic and Working with Loops

Two core features provided by all modern programming languages are the ability to execute conditional logic and the ability to perform repetitive tasks using loops. Conditional logic involves the examination of data and execution of different sets of programming statements based on the value of that data. Using conditional logic you can develop AppleScripts that alter their execution based on the data that they are presented with. In AppleScript, conditional logic is implemented using variations of the if statement. Loops are sets of programming statements that are repeatedly executed in order to process large amounts of data or to perform a repetitive process over and over again. Loops are set up using different variations of the repeat statement. This chapter will teach you how to work with each form of the if and repeat statement supported by AppleScript. In addition, you will learn how to create your next computer game, the AppleScript Typing Test.

Specifically, you will learn how to:

- Use different forms of the if statement to set up conditional logic that controls the execution of different sets of programming statements
- Nest if statements within one another to build more complex programming logic

- Use relational operators to perform different types of comparisons
- Use compound operators to combine different logical tests
- Use arithmetic operators to perform mathematic operations
- Use the different forms of the `repeat` statement to set up loops that perform repetitive tasks

PROJECT PREVIEW: THE APPLESCRIPT TYPING TEST GAME

In this chapter's game project, the AppleScript Typing Test, you will develop an electronic typing test that challenges the player to type increasingly complex sentences without making any typos in less than 20 seconds per sentence. At the end of the test the player's performance is graded and the player is informed of her passing or failing score. The game begins by displaying a startup screen that tells the player the rules of the game, as demonstrated in Figure 4.1.

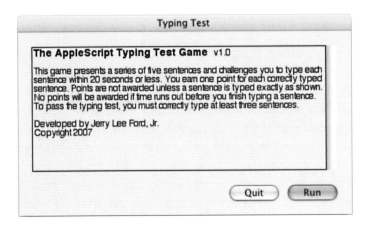

FIGURE 4.1

The startup screen for the AppleScript Typing Test game.

The player can click on the Quit button to terminate the game or click on the Run button to begin the game. The game's first typing challenge is relatively easy, as shown in Figure 4.2.

FIGURE 4.2

The first typing challenge presented by the AppleScript Typing Test game.

The second typing challenge presented by the game is a little more complex, as shown in Figure 4.3.

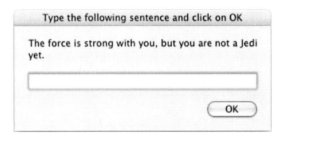

Type the following sentence and click on OK

The force is strong with you, but you are not a Jedi yet.

OK

FIGURE 4.3

The second typing challenge presented by the AppleScript Typing Test game.

Figure 4.4 shows the third sentence displayed by the game. As with all the typing challenges, the player has 20 seconds in which to type the sentence before the dialog window disappears. The player will not receive credit for a sentence that has not been typed within the allowed time.

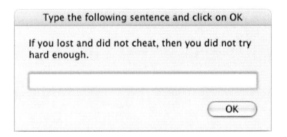

Type the following sentence and click on OK

If you lost and did not cheat, then you did not try hard enough.

OK

FIGURE 4.4

The third typing challenge presented by the AppleScript Typing Test game.

Figure 4.5 shows the fourth sentence displayed by the game. The sentence is too long to be displayed all at once in the text field where the player is required to type it. Therefore, the player must finish typing the sentence quickly enough to allow time to use the arrow keys to scroll back and review her input or type carefully enough to feel comfortable submitting her sentence without proofreading it.

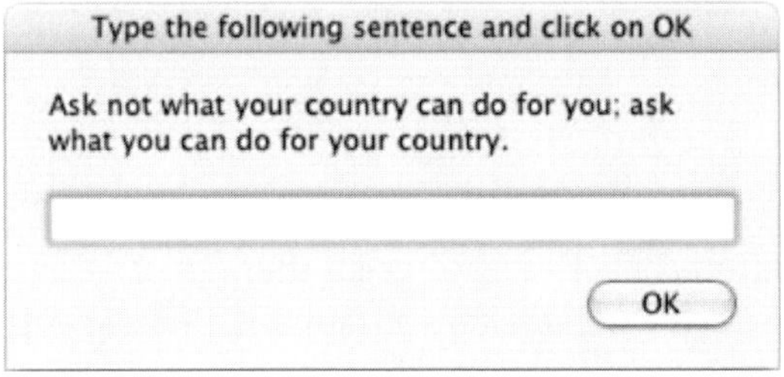

Type the following sentence and click on OK

Ask not what your country can do for you; ask what you can do for your country.

OK

FIGURE 4.5

The fourth typing challenge presented by the AppleScript Typing Test game.

Figure 4.6 shows the last typing challenge presented by the game. As with all previous sentences, the slightest deviation will result in an error. This means that the player must not only avoid making any typos but also avoid accidentally inserting any extra spaces and ensure that the appropriate closing punctuation is supplied.

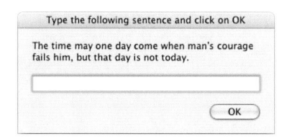

FIGURE 4.6

The fifth typing challenge presented by the AppleScript Typing Test game.

Each time the player finishes typing in a sentence and clicks on the OK button, the game immediately checks the player's work for errors. If the player successfully typed the sentence exactly as shown in the allotted amount of time, the dialog window shown in Figure 4.7 is displayed, providing the player with immediate positive feedback.

FIGURE 4.7

The game provides immediate feedback for every sentence the player types.

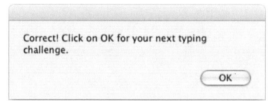

If the player makes a mistake in typing a sentence, the dialog window shown in Figure 4.8 displays.

FIGURE 4.8

The game notifies the player whenever an error is made.

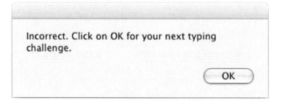

Finally, once the player has completed all five typing challenges, the game tabulates the player's final score and lets her know if she passed or failed (see Figure 4.9).

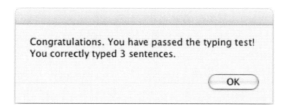

FIGURE 4.9

To pass the test, the player must successfully type at least three sentences.

FUNDAMENTALS OF CONDITIONAL LOGIC

By implementing conditional programming logic, you can develop AppleScripts that are capable of adapting their execution based on different conditions. To put it another way, using conditional logic, your AppleScripts can be set up to execute different sets of programming statements based on the value of the data they are presented with. This data may be collected from the operating system. Data may also come from files stored on the computer or it may be provided directly by the user.

Regardless of where the data originates, you can set up your AppleScript to analyze it using the `if` statement. To get a feel for how to work with the `if` statement, take a look at the following code block.

```
if the temperature is less than 85 degrees then
    pack lunch
    drive to the park
    Feed the ducks
end if
```

A *code block* is a collection of one or more program statements that execute as a unit. Code blocks can be created using both the `if` and the `repeat` statements.

Pseudocode is an English-like outline that identifies the logical steps used to accomplish a particular task. Pseudo statements focus on defining the logic required to perform a given task without worrying about the programming statements required to actually accomplish the task. By using pseudocode to outline the overall logic required to create all or part of a program or script, you get the chance to organize your thoughts. At the same time you give yourself the chance to map out the overall logic that needs to be followed when developing the code required to create an actual script file. By taking the time to outline your thoughts in this manner, you are less likely to make logical mistakes when programming, and as a result, you will be able to produce better and more efficient script files.

The previous example is a pseudocode outline that uses a rough English outline to identify a series of tasks to be performed in the event a tested condition evaluates as being `true`. In this example the condition being evaluated is whether the temperature is less than 85 degrees. If the condition is true, the three actions outlined inside the `if` statement code block are executed. If the conditional turns out to be false, these three statements are not processed and the entire `if` statement code block is skipped. Processing resumes with the first code statement that follows the code block. As the previous example demonstrates, an `if` statement code block begins with the `if` keyword and ends with the `end if` keywords.

Implementing Conditional Logic Using the if Statement

As has been stated, the `if` statement provides you with a means of applying conditional logic within AppleScripts. AppleScript lets you apply the `if` statement in two different ways. For starters, you can use it to develop conditional statements that are small enough to be written on a single line. When used in this manner, the `if` statement has the following syntax.

```
if Expression then Statement
```

Here, *Expression* represents any valid expression and *Statement* represents an AppleScript statement that will be executed if, and only if, the value of *Expression* evaluates as being `true`. To better understand how to work with this form of the `if` statement, consider the following example.

```
if UserName = "Molly" then display dialog "Hello Mighty One!"
```

Here, the value assigned to a variable named `UserName` is evaluated to determine if it is equal to `Molly`. If it is equal, then the value of the result of the tested expression will evaluate as being `true`. If this is the case, the `display dialog` statement that follows is then executed. Otherwise, the `display dialog` command is skipped.

The nice thing about this form of the `if` statement is that it lets you set up simple conditional tests using a minimum of space. However, in most cases you will find that it is insufficient for all but the simplest conditional tests. More often than not, you will need to use the `if` statement to create a code block in which you can embed any number of code statements that are executed only in the event the tested expression evaluates as being `true`. The syntax used by the `if` statement when used to create a code block is outlined here:

```
if Expression then
    Statements
end if
```

Using this syntax, you can rewrite the previous example as demonstrated here:

```
if UserName = "Molly" then
    display dialog "Hello Mighty One!"
end if
```

When written as a code block, you can embed as many code statements as you want inside the if statement code block. For example, if you wanted, you could modify the preceding example as shown here:

```
if UserName = "Molly" then
    display dialog "Hello Mighty One!"
    display dialog "How are you today?"
end if
```

In this example, two separate display dialog commands are executed when the value of UserName is found to be equal to Molly.

TRAP   One programming concept that has not been covered yet in this book is that of variable scope. A variable's *scope* represents the location within an AppleScript where the variable and its value can be accessed. Any variables defined within if statement code blocks are local to those code blocks, meaning that the variables will cease to exist when the code blocks stop executing, thus preventing their values from being accessed from other locations within their scripts. You will learn more about variable scope later in Chapter 6, "Improving Script Organization with Handlers".

Providing for an Alternative Course of Action

The expression contained in every if statement is analyzed, resulting in a value of either true or false. In the preceding section you learned how to develop an if statement code block that executed when the value returned by the if statement was true. The if statement is extremely flexible, providing you with a number of variations that you can use to execute alternate courses of action should the expression being evaluated result in a value of false.

To implement this form of programming logic, you need to include the else keyword as part of your if statement code block, using the syntax outlined here:

```
if Expression then
    Statements
else
    Statements
end if
```

Here, if the result of the if statement's expression evaluates as being true, the statements that follow it are executed. On the other hand, if the value of the expression evaluates as being false, these statements are skipped and the statements that follow the else keyword are processed instead. Thus one set of statements, but never both sets of statements, is always executed.

To get a better feel for how this works, take a look at the following example.

```
if UserName = "Molly" then
    display dialog "Hello Mighty One!"
    display dialog "How are you today?"
else
    display dialog "Hello!"
    display dialog "It is nice to meet you."
end if
```

Here, the value assigned to a variable named UserName is evaluated; if it is equal to "Molly", then two display dialog statements are executed that address the user in a personal manner. However, if the value of UserName is not equal to "Molly", then a more generic set of messages is displayed.

Examining Multiple Conditions

The if statement can also be used to set up code blocks that can evaluate numerous alternative conditions by adding the else if keywords. As a result, you can create more complex and comprehensive programming logic. The syntax for this form of the if statement code block is shown here:

```
if Expression then
    Statements
else if Expression then
    Statements
else if Expression then
    Statements
  .
  .
  .
else
    Statements
end if
```

Here, an *expression* is defined by the opening `if` statement. If this statement evaluates as being `true`, the statements that immediately follow are executed. If, on the other hand, it evaluates as being `false`, the expression specified by the first `else if` statement is evaluated and if this expression evaluates as being `true`, the statements associated with that statement are executed. Otherwise the expression associated with the next `else if` statement is executed. The statements associated with the first expression to result in a value of `true` are processed and all remaining statements within the `if` statement code block are skipped. If none of the expressions evaluate as being `true`, then the statements associated with the optional `else` statement, if present, are executed.

To get a better feel for how this works, take a look at the following example.

```
if UserName = "Molly" then
    display dialog "Hello Mighty One!"
    display dialog "How are you today?"
else if UserName = "William" then
    display dialog "Hey champ!"
    display dialog "How is it going?"
else if UserName = "Alexander" then
    display dialog "Hey bud!"
    display dialog "It is good to see you."
else
    display dialog "Hello!"
    display dialog "It is nice to meet you."
end if
```

Here, the value of `UserName` is checked to see if it is equal to `"Molly"`. If it does equal `"Molly"`, a pair of `display dialog` statements are executed. If it is not equal to `"Molly"`, the `else if` statement that follows checks to see if it is equal to `"William"`. If it is, a pair of `display dialog` statements are executed. If it is not equal to `"William"`, the `else if` statement that follows checks to see if it is equal to `"Alexander"`. If it is, a pair of `display dialog` statements are executed. If it is not, the `else` statement that follows displays a more generic set of messages.

Implementing Complex Logic By Nesting If Statements

One of the things that make `if` statement code blocks really powerful is that you can *nest* or *embed* them within one another. As a result, you can implement more complex and powerful conditional logic, as demonstrated here:

```
set DateString to the current date
set ToDay to weekday of DateString
```

```
set ThisDate to day of DateString
set TheHour to hours of DateString

if ToDay = Friday then
    if ThisDate = 13 then
        if TheHour is less than or equal to 20 then
            display dialog "Be careful! Today is Friday the 13th" & ¬
                " and the day is young." buttons {"OK"}
        else
            display dialog "Whew! It looks like we are safe!"
        end if
    end if
end if
```

Here, a variable named DateString is assigned the current date and time using the current date command. Next, three additional variables are defined and assigned values using different properties belonging to the Date class. ToDay is assigned a string representing the current day of the week (Monday, Tuesday, Wednesday, Thursday, Friday, Saturday, or Sunday). ThisDate is assigned a numeric integer value representing the day of the month (1–31) and TheHour is assigned a numeric integer value representing the hour of the day since midnight.

Next, a series of three if statement code blocks are embedded within one another. The outermost if statement code block analyzes the value of ToDay to see if it is equal to Friday. If it is not Friday, the example is done and the script results in no action. If it is Friday then the first embedded if statement executes, checking to see if the value assigned to ThisDate is equal to 13. If it is not, then the example is done and the script results in no action. Otherwise another embedded if statement code block is executed. This code block includes an else condition. As a result, one of two sets of statements embedded within the if statement will be executed. If the value assigned to TheHour is less than 20 (e.g., 8 o'clock) the first set of statements executes. Otherwise, the statements associated with the else keyword are executed.

HINT   The Date class was discussed in detail in Chapter 3, "Working with Values, Variables, and Classes."

PERFORMING DIFFERENT COMPARISON OPERATIONS

Up to this point, all of the comparison operations that you have seen in this chapter have used the equals (=) operator to determine whether two values were equal. AppleScript provides programmers with a range of relational operators that allow you to test for different types of value relationships. For example, you can use the > operator to check and see whether one value is greater than another value and the < operator to see if one value is less than another value. Table 4.1 provides you with a list of these relational operators supported by AppleScript.

TABLE 4.1	RELATIONAL OPERATORS
Operator	**English Equivalent**
=	equals
	is
	is equal to
≠	is not
	is not equal to
>	is greater than
<	is less than
≥	is greater than or equal to
≤	is less than or equal to

 TRICK You will not find any keys on your keyboard that correspond to ≠, ≤, or ≥. To type these characters, hold down the Option key and press the =, <, or > keys.

Each of these relational operators works by comparing two different values and returns a value of true or false based on that evaluation. For example, to see if the value assigned to a variable is greater than another value, you could use the > operator, as demonstrated here:

```
if x > 10 then
    display dialog "X is bigger than 10!"
end if
```

Because of its support for English-like syntax, AppleScript will allow you to use either a relational operator or its English equivalent when formulating expressions. To see what I mean, consider the following example.

```
if UserName = "Molly" then
```

Here, the value of UserName is analyzed to see if it is equal to Molly. If you prefer, you could rewrite this statement using one of the available English equivalents, as shown here:

```
if UserName is equal to "Molly" then
```

Both this and the previous statement are functionally identical, as is this statement:

```
if UserName is "Molly" then
```

The choice of using relational operators or their English equivalents is entirely up to you. However, to keep things simple and for the sake of consistency, I recommend you pick one or the other and stick with it throughout your AppleScripts.

ANALYZING MATHEMATICAL EXPRESSIONS

AppleScript provides a range of arithmetic operators that you can use to build mathematical expressions, whose results you can then analyze and use to control the logical execution of statements within your AppleScripts. The arithmetic operators supported by AppleScript are demonstrated in Table 4.2.

TABLE 4.2 ARITHMETIC OPERATORS

Operator	Description Example		Result
+	Addition	x = 5 + 5	10
−	Subtraction	x = 10 − 5	5
*	Multiplication	x = 10 * 5	50
/	Division (Option /)	x = 10 / 1.05	9.52380952381
^	Exponentiation	x = 5 ^ 2	25
div	Integer division with the result returned as a non-rounded integer	x = 10 div 1.05	9
mod	Integer division with the remainder returned as an integer	x = 10 mod 1.05	.55

 If you prefer, you may substitute ÷ for the / character when performing a division operation. You will not find a ÷ key anywhere on your keyboard. To enter this character, press and hold down the Option key while pressing the / key. However, the next time you compile your script, the Script Editor will automatically replace any ÷ characters with the / character.

USING COMPOUND OPERATORS TO BUILD COMPLEX CONDITIONAL LOGIC

In addition to relational and arithmetic operators, AppleScript also provides programmers with access to a set of compound operators, which you can use in place of embedded if statements to develop complex conditional logic. Table 4.3 lists AppleScript's compound operators and outlines their purposes.

TABLE 4.3	**COMPOUND OPERATORS**	

Operator	Description
and	Returns a value of true only if both expressions return values of true.
or	Returns a value of true if either expression returns a value of true.
not	Reverses or negates the value returned by an expression.

To see an example of how to use a compound operator, take a look at the following example.

```
set DateString to the current date
set ToDay to weekday of DateString
set ThisDate to day of DateString

if ToDay = Friday and ThisDate = 13 then
    display dialog "Be careful. It is Friday the 13th!"
end if
```

Here, the and operator is used set up a complex conditional test that requires that ToDay is equal to Friday and ThisDate is equal to 13. In order for the embedded statement to execute, both of these conditional checks must evaluate as being true. This example is functionally equal to the following set of statements, which rely on embedded conditional statements to perform an equivalent set of logical checks.

```
if ToDay = Friday then
    if ThisDate = 13 then
        display dialog "Be careful. It is Friday the 13th!"
    end if
end if
```

As you can see, using the and compound operator you can develop complex conditional logic using fewer code statements with no loss in readability. The or operators work in very much the same manner, as demonstrated here:

```
if ToDay = Friday or Today = Saturday then
    display dialog "No work today!"
end if
```

Here, the value of ToDay is analyzed twice and if either analysis results in a value of true, a text message is displayed. Unlike the and and the or compound operators, the not operator does not perform any comparison operation. Instead, the `not` operator is used to reverse or negate the value of an expression, as demonstrated here:

```
set ToDay to weekday of the (current date)

if not ToDay = Saturday or Today = Sunday then
    display dialog "Better shave! Today is a work day."
end if
```

Here, a text message is displayed only in the event that the current day of the week is not Saturday or Sunday.

TRICK If you prefer, you can enclose the pair of expressions being evaluated inside parentheses to help make things a little more readable, like so:

```
if not (ToDay = Saturday or Today = Sunday) then
    display dialog "Better shave! Today is a work day."
end if
```

Beyond making the code a little easier to read and follow along, the addition of the parentheses has no impact on evaluation of the two expressions or on the operation of the `if` statement.

Using Loops to Perform Repetitive Actions

Another critical programming tool that is fundamental to the development of AppleScripts is the use of repetitive programming logic. AppleScript repetitive processing, commonly referred to as looping, relies on the `repeat` statement. A *loop* is a set of statements that are executed over and over again to process large amounts of data or to repeat a series of actions. For example, you might set up a loop to process the contents of a text file, starting at the beginning of the text file and processing each line until the last line is reached. Alternatively, you might set up a loop to control the execution of a computer game, repeatedly prompting the player for input and processing that input to produce some sort of output.

As is the case with the `if` statement, AppleScript supports multiple variations of the `repeat` statement, as listed here:

- `repeat`
- `repeat x times`
- `repeat while`
- `repeat until`

- `repeat with`

- `repeat with...in`

 TRICK Like `if` code blocks, any variables defined within a `repeat` code block are local to that code block. Therefore, the variables cease to exist when the code block stops executing, preventing their values from being accessed from other locations within the script. You will learn more about variable scope later in Chapter 6, "Improving Script Organization with Handlers."

Looping Forever

The most basic form of the `repeat` statement is used to set up loops that process forever. As such, it is up to the programmer to include additional programming logic that determines when the loop should stop processing. Like the `if` statement, the `repeat` statement is used to set up code blocks. The syntax for this form of the `repeat` statement code block is shown here:

```
repeat
     Statements
end repeat
```

This form of loop begins with the `repeat` keyword followed by one or more embedded statements that will be executed each time the loop repeats. The loop ends with the `end repeat` statement. To get a feel for how to work with this type of loop, consider the following example.

```
set Counter to 1
set DisplayString to ""

repeat

     set DisplayString to DisplayString & Counter & " "

     if Counter ≥ 10 then
          exit repeat
     end if

     set Counter to Counter + 1

end repeat

display dialog "I can count: " & DisplayString buttons {"OK"} ¬
     with title "Counting Demo"
```

Here, two variables have been defined. `Counter` is used to keep track of a numeric integer value that is incremented by the loop at the end of each iteration. `DisplayString` is used to store a list of numbers appended to it as the loop runs. When the loop first starts executing, the value assigned to `Count` is 1 and the value assigned to `DisplayString` is an empty string (`""`). The first statement inside the loop appends the current value of `Counter` to the current value of `DisplayString`. AppleScript automatically implicitly coerces the value of `Counter` into a string to perform the append (concatenation) operation. Next, an `if` statement code block is executed. Its job is to terminate the execution of the loop using the `exit repeat` statement once the value of `Counter` exceeds 10. The last statement in the loop increments the value assigned to `Counter` by 1 each time it executes. When executed, this example displays the dialog window shown in Figure 4.10.

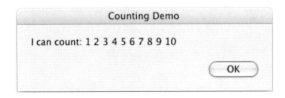

FIGURE 4.10

Setting up a loop
to count from
1 to 10.

HINT You can use the `exit repeat` statement to terminate any loop. When executed, an `exit` statement stops the loop's execution and processing control is passed to the next statement that follows the loop.

Simple repeat loops are sometimes used to set up a script that waits for a particular event to occur. For example, you might want to create an AppleScript that processes a file that is automatically created on your computer everyday. If the file is not available when the script starts running, you might set up a loop that pauses and rechecks for the availability of the file every few minutes until it becomes available.

HINT You can pause a script's execution for a specified number of seconds using the `delay` command. To use this command you only need to pass it a number as an argument representing the number of seconds you want your script to pause, as demonstrated here.

```
delay 5   --Pauses script execution for 5 seconds
```

Rather than using the `delay` command inside a loop to continually pause a long running AppleScript, you may want to instead set up an `idle` handler to allow AppleScript to more efficiently take care of things. In this scenario, all you would have to do is insert any code statements you want to be repeatedly executed inside the `idle` handler. You will learn about event handlers later in Chapter 6.

Looping a Specific Number of Times

If you know in advance how many times you want a loop to repeat, then you can use the following form of the `repeat` statement. Using this syntax, you relieve yourself of the responsibility of having to use a variable to keep track of loop iteration and eliminate altogether the need to use the `exit repeat` statement.

```
repeat X times
     Statements
end repeat
```

Here, the loop is repeated a specific number of times as specified by the value assigned to X. To see how this loops works, take a look at the following example.

```
set DisplayString to return & return

set counter to 1

repeat 10 times

     set DisplayString to DisplayString & counter & " " & return

     set counter to counter + 1

end repeat

display dialog "I can count: " & DisplayString buttons {"OK"} "Counting Demo"
     with title "Counting Demo"
```

Here, a loop has been set up that will execute 10 times, as demonstrated in Figure 4.11. As with the preceding example, statements have been added to the loop to display a listing of 10 numbers.

TRICK

Take note of the use of the `return` keyword in the preceding example. Return is a global property whose value is predefined by AppleScript. This particular global property translates into a link break character, allowing you to insert physical line breaks inside strings.

AppleScript provides you with access to other global properties including `tab` and `space`, which are used to insert a tab and a blank space into strings. AppleScript provides programmers with access to numeric global properties, like the numeric value of `pi`. You can also access the number of seconds in a minute, hour, day, or week by referencing the `minutes`, `hours`, `days`, and `weeks` global properties.

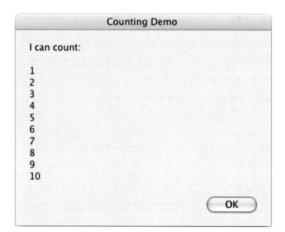

FIGURE 4.11

Looping a
predefined
number of times.

Looping as Long as a Condition Is True

Another way that you can use the repeat statement to set up a loop is to define loops that
iterate as long as a specific value remains true. This form of the repeat loop adds the while
keyword to the beginning of the loop and specifies an expression whose value is checked at
the beginning of each iteration of the loop. The syntax for this form of the repeat code block
is shown here:

```
repeat while Expression
      Statements
end repeat
```

If the value of the expression evaluates as being true, the loop is executed. Otherwise, it is
skipped. To see this type of loop in action, check out the following example.

```
set answer to ""

repeat while answer is not equal to "Quit"

      set answer to text returned of ¬
            (display dialog "Enter a name or click on OK to quit" ¬
                  default answer "Quit" buttons {"OK"})

      display dialog "You entered : " & answer buttons {"OK"}

end repeat
```

Here, a loop has been set up to iterate until the user enters a value of Quit into a dialog window. The instructions on the dialog window, shown in Figure 4.12, tell the user to either type in a name (overtyping the default value of Quit) or to just click on the OK button. Each name typed in by the user is displayed in a new dialog window. This continues until the user submits a value of Quit by clicking on the OK button (without typing in a name).

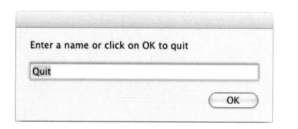

FIGURE 4.12

Controlling user input using a loop.

Looping as Long as a Condition Is False

Instead of using the `while` keyword to set up a loop that iterates while a tested condition remains true, you can use the `until` keyword to set up a loop to iterate until a tested condition becomes `true`. In other words, the loop will repeat itself as long as the tested condition remains `false`. The syntax for this form of the `repeat` code block is shown here:

```
repeat until Expression
     Statements
end repeat
```

To see an example of how to work with this form of the repeat loop, take a look at the following example.

```
set answer to ""

repeat until answer is equal to "Quit"

    set answer to text returned of (display dialog ¬
        "Enter a name or click on OK to quit" ¬
        default answer "Quit" buttons {"OK"})

    display dialog "You entered : " & answer buttons {"OK"}

end repeat
```

As you can see, this example performs the same task as the preceding example. The only difference is that the keyword `until` has been substituted for the `while` keyword and the `is not equal` English equivalent operator has been change to `is equal to`.

Using a Counter to Control a Loop's Execution

You can also set up a version of the `repeat` loop whose execution is controlled by a variable that is defined within the loop. The advantage of this form of the `repeat` loop is that you can execute detailed control over the value of the variable by assigning its starting and ending values as well as the value used to increment the variable. The syntax for this form of loop is shown here:

```
repeat with CounterVariable from Start to End [by Counter]
        Statements
end repeat
```

CounterVariable specifies the name of the variable that will be used to control the loop's execution. The initial value assigned to *CounterVariable* is specified by *Start*. *End* sets the value that when reached, will terminate the execution of the loop. Upon the first iteration of the loop, the value of *Start* is assigned to *CounterVariable*. The value of *CounterVariable* is then incremented by 1 each time the loop iterates. However, by assigning a value to the optional *Counter* parameter, you can specify the value to be used to increment the value of *CounterVariable*. The loop automatically iterates until the value assigned to *CounterVariable* equals the value assigned to *End*.

 Unlike some programming languages, in AppleScript you cannot prematurely terminate a loop's execution by setting the value of `CounterVariable` to a value that exceeds the value of End. Instead, you must use the `exit` statement to prematurely terminate the loop's execution.

To better understand how this form of the `repeat` loop works, you really need to see an example of it in action, as demonstrated here:

```
set DisplayString to ""

repeat with counter from 1 to 20 by 2

        set DisplayString to DisplayString & counter & " "
```

```
end repeat

display dialog DisplayString
```

In this example, a loop has been set up to iterate 10 times and the value assigned to `counter` is incremented by two each time the loop iterates. When executed, this example displays the output shown in Figure 4.13.

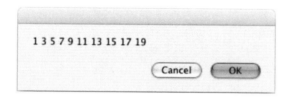

1 3 5 7 9 11 13 15 17 19

Cancel   OK

FIGURE 4.13

Counting by twos using a `repeat` loop.

Using Loops to Process Lists

The last type of loop that you can set up using the `repeat` statement is specifically designed to process all of the elements in a list. The syntax for this form of loop is shown here:

```
repeat with VariableName in List
```

The following example demonstrates how you might use this form of the `repeat` loop to process data stored in a list.

```
set UserList to {"Alexander", "William", "Molly", "Mary", "Jerry"}

repeat with x in UserList
    display dialog x buttons {"OK"}
end repeat
```

Here, a list of five names has been assigned to a variable named `UserList`. The contents of this list are then processed by a `repeat` loop. The first time the loop executes, the value of `x` is set to `"Alexander"`. The value of `x` is then displayed in a dialog window. In the same manner, each of the remaining list elements is displayed, one at a time, until the contents of the entire list have been processed. You will learn more about lists in Chapter 5, "Using Strings, Lists, and Records."

BACK TO THE APPLESCRIPT TYPING TEST GAME

Now it is time to turn your attention back to the development of the AppleScript Typing Test game. As you work on keying in this AppleScript, be sure to focus your attention on the conditional logic used to analyze player input and to determine what messages should be displayed. In addition, keep an eye on the `if` statement code block used at the end of the script to implement the conditional logic required to analyze the player's final score.

Designing the Game

The AppleScript Typing Test game will be created in 11 steps, as outlined here:

1. Create a new AppleScript and save it with a name of Typing Test.
2. Document the script and its purpose.
3. Set the player's initial score.
4. Display the first typing challenge.
5. Analyze the player's input.
6. Display and process the second typing challenge.
7. Display and process the third typing challenge.
8. Display and process the fourth typing challenge.
9. Display and process the fifth typing challenge.
10. Get the player's attention with a noise.
11. Grade the player's work.

Step 1: Creating a New AppleScript File

The first step in the creation of the AppleScript Typing Test game is to start up the Script Editor application and create a new AppleScript file named Typing Test by following the steps outlined here:

1. Start the Script Editor application.
2. Click on the File menu and select the Save As option.
3. In the sheet window that appears, enter **Typing Test** in the Save As field and specify the location where the script should be saved using the Where drop-down menu.
4. Click on the Save button.

Step 2: Providing High-Level Script Documentation

The first thing you will want to do is add a little documentation to your AppleScript file to provide a brief explanation of the game and its purpose. This documentation will go in two places, the Description tab view of the Script Editor application's data pane and as comments embedded alongside script statements.

Adding External Descriptive Text

The first documentation to be added to the script file is shown next and should be keyed in to the data area after selecting the Description tab located at the bottom of the Script Editor application.

```
The AppleScript Typing Test Game  v1.0

This game presents a series of five sentences and challenges you to type each sentence
within 20 seconds or less. You earn one point for each correctly typed sentence. Points
are not awarded unless a sentence is typed exactly as shown. No points will be awarded
if time runs out before you finish typing a sentence. To pass the typing test, you must
correctly type at least three sentences.

Developed by Jerry Lee Ford, Jr.
Copyright 2007
```

To make this information easier to read, highlight the game's name and click on the Font menu and select Bold. In response, the Script Editor application will display the text in a bold font.

Embedding Comments Inside the Script

Okay, now let's add the following comment statements at the beginning of the AppleScript to identify the name of the game and its purpose.

```
--------------------------------------------------------------------
--
-- Script Name: AppleScript Typing Test.scpt
-- Version: 1.0
-- Author: Jerry Lee Ford, Jr.
-- Date: August 2007
--
-- Description: This AppleScript tests the player's typing skills by
-- presenting a series of five sentences and challenging the player to
-- type each sentence without making any typing mistakes
-- in the time allotted.
--------------------------------------------------------------------
```

Step 3: Setting the Player's Initial Score

The next step in the development of the AppleScript Typing Test game is to define a variable that will be used to keep track of the number of correctly typed challenge sentences. To set this up, add the following statement to the end of your AppleScript file.

```
set PlayerScore to 0
```

Here, a variable named PlayerScore is assigned a starting value of zero.

Step 4: Displaying the First Typing Challenge

The next set of statements to be added to the AppleScript file, shown next, are responsible for displaying the game's first typing challenge and for collecting the player's input.

```
-- Display the first sentence
set FirstSentence to text returned of (display dialog ¬
  "Perhaps today is a good day to die." default answer "" buttons {"OK"} ¬
  giving up after 20 ¬
  with title "Type the following sentence and click on OK")
```

As you can see, the display dialog command is used to display the sentence that the player must type and also provides a text field for collecting that input. The player's input (sentence) is stored in a variable named FirstSentence. The player has 20 seconds in which to type in the sentence and click on the dialog window's OK button. This is enforced through the addition of the giving up after 20 argument as part of the display dialog command.

Step 5: Analyzing the Player's Input

Now that the code for the first typing challenge has been written, it is time to add the code responsible for analyzing the player's input to ascertain whether the player successfully typed the challenge sentence. The code statements that perform this task are shown here and should be added to the end of the script file.

```
-- Process the player's input
if FirstSentence = "Perhaps today is a good day to die." then
  set PlayerScore to PlayerScore + 1
  display dialog "Correct! Click on OK for your next typing challenge." ¬
  buttons {"OK"}
else
  display dialog "Incorrect. Click on OK for your next typing challenge." ¬
  buttons {"OK"}
end if
```

As you can see, an if statement code block has been set up to analyze the user's sentence (stored in FirstSentence) to see if it matches the challenge text. If it does, the value of PlayerScore is incremented by 1, and the display dialog command is used to notify the player of her success. However, if the player failed to precisely type the challenge sentence, the value of PlayerScore is not incremented and the display dialog command is instead used to notify the player of her error.

Step 6: Displaying and Processing the Second Typing Challenge

The statements required to display and process the second typing challenge are shown next and should be added to the end of the AppleScript file.

```
-- Display the second sentence
set SecondSentence to text returned of (display dialog ¬
  "The force is strong with you, but you are not a Jedi yet." ¬
  default answer "" buttons {"OK"} giving up after 20 ¬
  with title "Type the following sentence and click on OK")

-- Process the player's input
if SecondSentence = ¬
  "The force is strong with you, but you are not a Jedi yet." then
  set PlayerScore to PlayerScore + 1
  display dialog "Correct! Click on OK for your next typing challenge." ¬
  buttons {"OK"}
else
  display dialog "Incorrect. Click on OK for your next typing challenge." ¬
  buttons {"OK"}
end if
```

As you can see, these statements are almost identical to those that presented and processed the game's first typing challenge. The only differences are the name of the variable that is used to store the player's input and the text string that makes up the next typing challenge.

Step 7: Displaying and Processing the Third Typing Challenge

The statements that display and process the game's third typing challenge are shown next and should be added to the end of the script file.

```
-- Display the third sentence
set ThirdSentence to text returned of (display dialog ¬
  "If you lost and did not cheat, then you did not try hard enough." ¬
  default answer "" buttons {"OK"} giving up after 20 ¬
  with title "Type the following sentence and click on OK")

-- Process the player's input
if ThirdSentence = ¬
  "If you lost and did not cheat, then you did not try hard enough." then
  set PlayerScore to PlayerScore + 1
  display dialog "Correct! Click on OK for your next typing challenge." ¬
```

```
    buttons {"OK"}
else
    display dialog "Incorrect. Click on OK for your next typing challenge." ¬
    buttons {"OK"}
end if
```

Step 8: Displaying and Processing the Fourth Typing Challenge

The statements that present and process the game's fourth typing challenge are shown next and should be added to the end of your AppleScript file.

```
-- Display the fourth sentence
set FourthSentence to text returned of (display dialog ¬
    "Ask not what your country can do for you; ask what you can " & ¬
    "do for your country." default answer "" buttons {"OK"} ¬
    giving up after 20 ¬
    with title "Type the following sentence and click on OK")

-- Process the player's input
if FourthSentence = ¬
    "Ask not what your country can do for you; ask what you can " & ¬
    "do for your country." then
    set PlayerScore to PlayerScore + 1
    display dialog "Correct! Click on OK for your next typing challenge." ¬
    buttons {"OK"}
else
    display dialog "Incorrect. Click on OK for your next typing challenge." ¬
    buttons {"OK"}
end if
```

Step 9: Displaying and Processing the Fifth Typing Challenge

The code statements that display and process the game's final typing challenges are shown next and should be added to the end of the script file.

```
-- Display the fifth sentence
set FifthSentence to text returned of (display dialog ¬
    "The time may one day come when man's courage fails him, " & ¬
    "but that day is not today." default answer ¬
    "" buttons {"OK"} giving up after 20 ¬
```

```
  with title "Type the following sentence and click on OK")

-- Process the player's input
if FifthSentence = ¬
  "The time may one day come when man's courage fails him, " & ¬
  "but that day is not today." then
  set PlayerScore to PlayerScore + 1
  display dialog "Correct! Click on OK for your next typing challenge." ¬
  buttons {"OK"}
else
  display dialog "Incorrect. Click on OK for your next typing challenge." ¬
  buttons {"OK"}
end if
```

Step 10: Making a Little Noise

At this point, the game has presented all of its typing challenges and analyzed each of the player's attempts at typing each challenge sentence. It is just about time to determine whether the player has passed the typing test. However, before doing so, add the following statements to the end of the script file.

```
--Make a little noise to let the player know the test is over
beep
```

The beep command is used to play a beep sound. Its purpose is to signal the player that the test results are about to be displayed

 The beep command takes no arguments. To play a longer beep sound, simply execute the beep command several times in a row or wrap it up inside a repeat loop.

Step 11: Grading the Player's Work

The final set of statements to be added to the script file are shown next and are responsible for determining whether the player has passed the typing test.

```
-- Check the player's score and display the result
if PlayerScore ≥ 3 then -- The player has passed
  display dialog ¬
    "Congratulations. You have passed the typing test!" & ¬
    "You correctly typed " & PlayerScore & ¬
    " sentences." buttons {"OK"}
```

```
else -- The player has failed
   display dialog "Sorry. You have not passed the typing test. " & ¬
       "You mistyped " & 5 - PlayerScore & " sentences. " & ¬
       "Restart the game to try again." buttons ("OK") ¬
       with title "Test Results"
end if
```

As you can see, an if statement code block has been set up to analyze the value assigned to the PlayerScore variable. To pass the typing test, the player must successfully type at least three sentences. Therefore the value of PlayerScore must be three or more for the player to pass the test.

Testing the Execution of the AppleScript Typing Test

That's it. Assuming that you followed along carefully and did not make any typos, everything should be ready to go. If the Script Editor displays any error messages, then you most likely have a typo somewhere. Rather than going over every code statement looking for a typo, carefully study the text of the error message and use it to try and track down your error.

Once you have the game compiled, make sure you put it through its paces. By this I mean that you should experiment with the game by seeing what happens when you do not type in anything when prompted to type a sentence as well as what happens if you type slowly and run out of time when keying in a sentence. Once you are confident that your AppleScript is running correctly, share it with a few friends and see what they think.

SUMMARY

In this chapter you learned how to use different variations of the if statement to implement conditional logic with your AppleScripts. You learned how to work with different types of AppleScript operators to perform different types of comparisons and to perform more complex conditional tests. You also learned how to use the repeat statement to set up loops, allowing you to implement programming logic that can efficiently process large amounts of data or repeatedly perform the same set of code statements over and over again.

Before you move on to Chapter 5, I recommend that you set aside a little more time to work on improving the AppleScript Typing Test game by implementing the following list of challenges.

CHALLENGES

1. Expand the AppleScript Typing Test game by including additional typing challenges. For example, consider increasing the number of challenges from 5 to 10.

2. When adding new typing challenges, consider making the challenges complex enough to justify increasing the amount of time required to type them in.

3. Consider redisplaying any mistyped sentences at the end of the game to give the player the opportunity to determine what typing mistakes were made.

4. Instead of instructing the player to run the game again to retake the test, consider using a `repeat` loop to control game play and to give the player the option of retaking the test again.

Using Strings, Lists, and Records

I n prior chapters you learned different techniques for working with strings, including how to concatenate them together and how to use the continuation character to spread them over two or more lines. You were also introduced to the concept of using lists as a means for managing related collections of data. Now it is time to extend your knowledge of how to work with and manipulate strings and lists. In addition, this chapter will introduce you to records and explain how to use them to store and retrieve unordered collections of data using key-value pairs. You will also learn how to combine lists and records to create your own mini-database. On top of all this, you will learn how to create your next computer game, the Godfather Trivia Quiz.

Specifically, you will learn how to:

- Access information about strings and apply different string formatting techniques
- Compare the contents of strings, lists, and records
- Store and retrieve data using lists
- Store and retrieve data using records

PROJECT PREVIEW: THE GODFATHER TRIVIA QUIZ

This chapter's game project is the Godfather Trivia Quiz. The quiz is administered using a series of dialog windows created with the `choose from list` command. This command generates a window that contains a graphical listbox control that displays a list of items passed to the command as arguments. When started, the Godfather Trivia Quiz displays its first question, as shown in Figure 5.1.

FIGURE 5.1

All quiz questions are multiple choice.

 A *listbox* control is used to display a list of items from which the user can select one or more items. The user can use the up and down keyboard arrow buttons to move up and down the list and then press the Enter key to make a selection. If configured to support multiple selections, the user can select two or more list items by holding down the Shift or the Command key when clicking on list items.

To select an answer to a quiz question, the player must click on one of the list items. Once an answer has been selected, the dialog window's OK button is enabled, allowing the player to click on it and advance to the next question, which is shown in Figure 5.2.

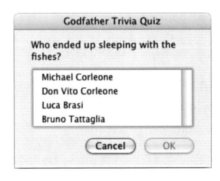

FIGURE 5.2

The second question presented by the Godfather Trivia Quiz.

Each question has just one correct answer. If the player selects the wrong answer or clicks on the dialog window's Cancel button, the game will score the question as having been incorrectly answered. Once the last quiz question has been answered, the game grades the player's answers and determines whether the player has passed or failed. To pass, the player must correctly answer at least seven out of ten questions. If the player fails the quiz, the dialog window shown in Figure 5.3 is displayed, encouraging the player to learn more about the Godfather movie and then return to take the test again.

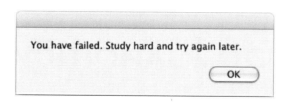

FIGURE 5.3

Players are encouraged to return and try again if they fail the quiz.

If the player passes the quiz, she is assigned a ranking that identifies her level of knowledge of the Godfather movie. This ranking assignment is based on the grading scheme outlined in Table 5.1.

TABLE 5.1		GODFATHER QUIZ RANKING ASSIGNMENTS
Rank	**No. Correct**	**Meaning**
Button Man	7	The player has demonstrated basic knowledge of the Godfather movie
Capo	8	The player has a strong understanding of the Godfather movie
Consigleri	9	The player has intimate knowledge of the Godfather movie
Godfather	10	The player has the skill and knowledge to be a Godfather character

The dialog window that is shown when the player passes the Godfather Trivia Quiz is shown in Figure 5.4.

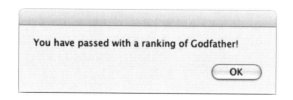

You have passed with a ranking of Godfather!

OK

FIGURE 5.4

A ranking of Godfather is assigned if the player achieves a perfect score on the quiz.

Working with Strings

The ability to work with and manipulate strings is a critical skill for any AppleScript programmer. Many scriptable applications accept string arguments and return data in the form of strings. However, the strings you need to work with may not always be in the format you need them to be. For example, an application or command may return a result as a string. However, you may only need a portion of the string. AppleScript provides you with many ways of viewing and manipulating strings and their contents.

Storing Strings in Variables

In AppleScript a string is a series of characters enclosed within matching double quotation marks, as shown here:

```
"Sam"
"freedom"
"Once upon a time there was a big bad wolf."
```

Strings can be used by inserting them directly into commands, as shown here:

```
display dialog "Once upon a time there was a big bad wolf."
```

Alternatively, strings can be assigned to variables whose values can then be referenced, as demonstrated here:

```
set OpeningLine to "Once upon a time there was a big bad wolf."
```

Beyond available memory, there is no practical limit to how large a string can be. You can also create empty strings, as demonstrated here:

```
set UserName to ""
```

Retrieving String Information

In addition to allowing you to retrieve the value of any string assigned to a variable, AppleScript also lets you retrieve information about the length of a string using the count command, which has the following syntax.

```
count String
```

String is a placeholder representing either a string or a variable that has been assigned a string. To see this command in action, take a look at the following statements.

```
set Message to "A long time ago in a galaxy far, far away…"
display dialog "There are " & (count Message) & " characters in this string."
```

Here, a variable named `Message` is defined and assigned a string that consists of 44 characters. A `display dialog` statement is then executed that uses the `count` command to retrieve the number of characters that make up the string.

In addition to using the `count` command, you can use the `String` class's `length` property to retrieve an integer value showing the number of characters in a string, as demonstrated here:

```
set Message to "A long time ago in a galaxy far, far away…"
display dialog "There are " & length of Message & " characters in this string."
```

Regardless of whether you choose to use the `count` command or the `String` class's `length` property, the result will be exactly the same for both of the preceding examples, as demonstrated in Figure 5.5.

There are 44 characters in this string.

Cancel   OK

Concatenating Strings Together

As you have already seen, you can use the & operator to merge or join strings together to create a new string, as demonstrated here:

```
set MyName to "Jerry " & "Lee " & "Ford " & "Jr."
```

In this example four small strings have been concatenated together to create a single larger string. In the following example, the contents of two string variables are concatenated together and assigned to a new variable.

```
set MyFirstName to "Jerry "
set MyLastName to "Ford"
set MyName to MyFirstName & MyLastName
display dialog MyName
```

When executed, the `display dialog` command displays the name `Jerry Ford` in a dialog window.

Formatting Strings

AppleScript provides programmers with access to a collection of escape characters that can be inserted into strings as a means of specifying formatting instructions that control the appearance of those strings when they are displayed. An *escape character* is a special sequence of characters beginning with the \ character. The \ character is followed by a letter that AppleScript recognizes and associates with a specific ASCII code. When AppleScript comes across an escape character, it knows not to display the escape character; instead, it replaces it with its ASCII equivalent. Table 5.2 lists the escape characters that AppleScript supports.

TABLE 5.2	ESCAPE CHARACTERS	
Character	**English Equivalent**	**Purpose**
\\	backslash	Inserts a backslash character inside a string
\n	new line	Adds an ASCII new line character
\r	end of line	Adds an ASCII end-of-line character
\t	tab	Inserts a tab space inside a string
\"	double quotation mark	Inserts a double quotation mark inside a string

HINT The \r and the \n escape characters are functionally equivalent. The \r escape character is traditionally used on Mac OS X and the \n escape character is traditionally used on UNIX.

To best understand how to work with these escape characters, it helps to see an example of them in action. In the following example, the display dialog command is used to display the same message using different types of formatting.

```
display dialog "Alexander looked at Molly and yelled STOP!"
display dialog "Alexander looked at Molly and yelled \t\tSTOP!"
display dialog "Alexander looked at Molly and yelled \n\nSTOP!"
display dialog "Alexander looked at Molly and yelled \r\rSTOP!"
display dialog "Alexander looked at Molly and yelled \"STOP!\""
```

TRAP If you're running this example on your computer, do not be surprised when the Script Editor removes the \t, \n, and \r escape characters and replaces them with hidden ASCII characters. This is just the way things work, and while it may look a little funny, everything will still work as expected.

When executed, these five statements generate the output shown in Figures 5.6–5.10.

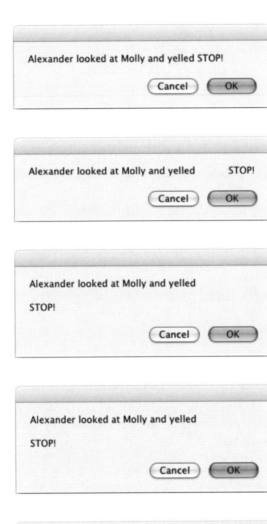

FIGURE 5.6

Displaying an unformatted string.

FIGURE 5.7

Using the \t escape character to insert tabs in a string.

FIGURE 5.8

Using the \n escape character to format a string over multiple lines.

FIGURE 5.9

Using the \r escape character to format a string over multiple lines.

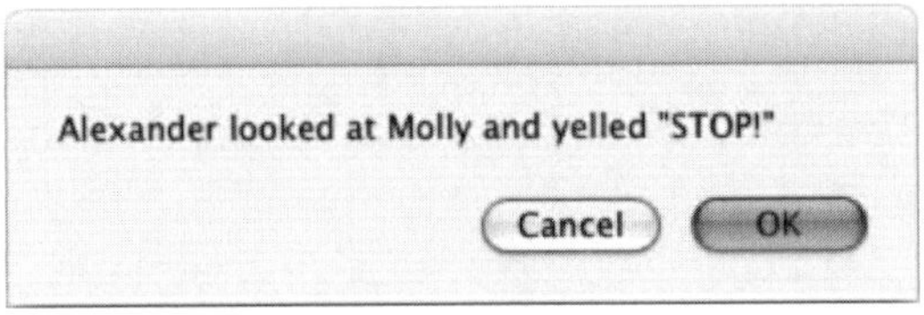

FIGURE 5.10

Using the \" escape character to display double quotes in a string.

TRICK

As was explained in Chapter 4, "Implementing Conditional Logic and Working with Loops," AppleScript provides you with access to a small collection of global properties that you can use to control string formatting. These global properties include:

- `return`
- `tab`
- `space`

These global properties are inserted into strings using the & concatenation operator, as demonstrated here:

```
display dialog "Once upon a time " & return & "there was a wicked witch."
```

When executed, this statement displays the dialog window shown in Figure 5.11.

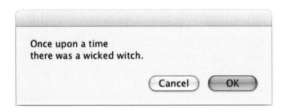

Once upon a time
there was a wicked witch.

Cancel   OK

Comparing Strings

In previous chapters you learned how to compare strings to one another to see if they were identical. In fact, the AppleScript Typing Test game, which you created in Chapter 4, worked exactly this way. AppleScript provides you with a pair of additional tools that gives you granular control over how string comparison operations are performed. These tools are provided in the form of code blocks, as outlined here:

- `considering`. Lists attributes to be considered during a comparison operation.
- `ignoring`. List attributes that are not to be considered during a comparison operation.

By embedding your string comparison operations inside these code blocks, you can tell AppleScript what to consider or ignore when comparing strings. For example, by default AppleScript performs case-insensitive comparison operations. As a result the following statement would result in a match.

```
if "apples" = "APPLES" then
     display dialog "We have a case-insensitive match"
end if
```

However, using a `considering` code block, you can instruct AppleScript to take case into consideration when comparing two strings, as demonstrated here:

```
considering case
    if "apples" = "APPLES" then
```

```
        display dialog "We have a case-insensitive match"
    else
        display dialog "We have a case-sensitive match"
    end if
end considering
```

Since case sensitivity has been taken into account this time, this example will not result in a match. In addition to case, AppleScript supports a small number of other attributes that you can include in considering and ignoring code blocks, as outlined in Table 5.3.

TABLE 5.3	ATTRIBUTES AVAILABLE IN CONSIDERING AND IGNORING CODE BLOCKS
Attribute	**Description**
case	Lowercase and uppercase characters
hyphens	Hyphen (-) character
punctuation	Punctuation characters (, . ? \ ' " ` ; :)
white space	White space (spaces, tabs, and new line and return characters)

AppleScript automatically takes into consideration all of the attributes listed in Table 5.3 except for case. By setting up an ignoring code block, you can instruct AppleScript to stop considering certain attributes, as demonstrated here:

```
set MyName to "Jerry Lee Ford, Jr."
set x to "Jerry Lee Ford Jr"
ignoring punctuation
    if MyName = x then display dialog "Hello Jerry!"
end considering
```

In this example, an ignoring code block was set up to prevent AppleScript from taking punctuation into account when comparing two strings. As a result the comparison operation resulted in a match.

Because AppleScript is such a flexible programming language, it even lets you create code blocks that include both the considering and ignoring keywords. This allows you to provide AppleScript with detailed instructions on how you want it to compare strings, as demonstrated here:

```
set MyName to "Jerry Lee Ford, Jr."
set x to "Jerry Lee Ford Jr"
considering case but ignoring punctuation and white space
    if MyName = X then display dialog "Hello Jerry!"
end considering
```

Take note of the `but` keyword that is used to tie together the `considering` and `ignoring` operations. Also note the use of the `and` keyword to allow more than one attribute to be specified.

Accessing Different Parts of a String

Another way that AppleScript lets you work with strings is through the use of the following string elements.

- `character`. An individual string character.
- `word`. A contiguous set of characters within a string, usually separated by a blank space from other characters.
- `paragraph`. A collection of characters demarcated by a return or new line character.
- `text`. A portion of text retrieved from a string using a string element specifier.

These string elements are used in conjunction with the list of *element specifiers* shown in Table 5.4 to give programmers fine-tuned access to different parts of a string.

TABLE 5.4   STRING ELEMENT SPECIFIERS

Specifier	Purpose
some	A randomly selected item inside a string.
every	Every item inside a string.
last	The last item inside a string.
end	The last item inside a string.
first, second, etc.	A specific item inside a string.
1st, 2nd, etc.	A specific item inside a string.
item 1, item 2, etc.	A specific item inside a string.
items x through z	A range of items inside a string.

The best way to learn how to work with string elements and element specifiers is to see a few examples of them in action. For starters, take a look at the following statements.

```
set MyName to "Jerry Lee Ford, Jr."
set MiddleName to second word of MyName
```

Here, a variable named MiddleName is assigned a value of "Lee" by extracting the second word found in the string assigned to MyName. As Table 5.4 shows, you can reference different parts of a string in many different ways. For example, look at the following statements.

```
set MyName to "Jerry Lee Ford, Jr."
set FirstName to first word of MyName
set Suffix to last word of MyName
```

Here, the variable FirstName is assigned a string of "Jerry" and the variable Suffix is assigned a string of "Jr".

STORING AND RETRIEVING DATA USING LISTS

Instead of working with individual pieces of data stored in variables, it is often easier to work with groups of data stored in lists. For example, if you wanted to create a script that needed to work with the names of 50 people, you could create individual variables for each name. Alternatively, you could store all the names as a single list. Lists can be used to store any type of data and can be as long as you need them to be.

 A *list* is an equivalent structure in AppleScript to what other programming languages refer to as an *array*.

Lists are an ordered collection of values. Each piece of data that is assigned to a list is referred to as an item. Lists are created by enclosing comma-separated items inside a pair of matching curly braces, as demonstrated here:

```
set MyChildren to {"Molly", "William", "Alexander"}
```

Here a list made up of three strings has been assigned to a single variable named MyChildren.

 Whether you have realized it or not, you have been working extensively with lists throughout every chapter in this book. For example, any display dialog commands for which you have specified the number of buttons to be displayed has involved the use of lists, as demonstrated here:

```
display dialog "Once upon a time…" buttons {"Yes", "No", "Cancel"}
```

Here, a list of three buttons has been passed to a display dialog command.

Lists are often returned by scriptable applications. Lists are also used to pass arguments to scriptable applications and to pass arguments to AppleScript commands like display dialog and choose from list. In addition, lists are also used by commands like choose from list to return command output.

Populating a List with Data

As you have just seen, a list can be assigned to a variable, allowing the entire list to be referenced as a unit. Lists can also be created empty, as demonstrated below, and populated with data later in a script.

```
set ListOfNames to {}
```

Lists can be used as a means of assigning a list of values to a list of variables. This simple technique is demonstrated here:

```
set {FirstName, MiddleName, LastName} to {"Jerry", "Lee", "Ford"}
```

Values are assigned to variables based on their positions in their respective lists, with the first variable in the list of variables being assigned to the first value in the list of values. If the list of values is longer than the list of variables, any extra values are ignored. However, an error will occur if the list of variables is longer than the list of values.

There is no practical limit to the size of lists. As is the case with strings, you can use the count command to retrieve an integer value representing the number of elements in a list, as demonstrated here:

```
set MyChildren to {"Molly", "William", "Alexander"}
set NoOfKids to count of MyChildren
```

When executed, a value of 3 is assigned to the NoOfKids variable. Like the String class, the List class also provides programmers with access to a small collection of properties. One such property is the length property, which can be used like so:

```
set MyList to {"Jerry", "Lee", "Ford"}
display dialog "This list has " & length of MyList & " items."
```

Here, the number of items stored in the string is displayed in a dialog window.

Concatenating Lists

Like strings, you can use the & concatenation operator when working with lists to create a new list out of other lists, as shown here:

```
set NumberList to {1, 2, 3, 4, 5}
set LetterList to {"A", "B", "C", "D", "E"}
set NewList to NumberList & LetterList
```

When executed, this example assigns a list of {1, 2, 3, 4, 5, "A", "B", "C", "D", "E"} to a variable named NewList.

Reversing the Order of Items in a List

If desired, you can reverse the order of the items stored in a list using the List class's reverse property, as shown here:

```
set SillyList to {"Me", "Myself", "I"}
set SillyList to reverse of SillyList
```

When executed, the value assigned to SillyList is reassigned as {"I", "Myself", "Me"}.

Retrieving List Elements

Because lists are ordered collections of data, they have a beginning and an end. As such, you can use the repeat loop to iterate through a list to process its contents, as demonstrated here:

```
set FruitList to {"Apples", "Oranges", "Pears", "Grapes", "Plums"}
repeat with Fruit in FruitList
     display dialog Fruit
end repeat
```

Here, a repeat loop has been set up to iterate through a list of five fruit and to display the name of each piece of fruit in the list as a separate dialog window.

In addition to processing the contents of lists using a loop, you can use any of the *item specifiers* listed in Table 5.5 to access specified items stored in a list based on their location within the list.

TABLE 5.5   ITEM SPECIFIERS APPLICABLE TO LISTS

Specifier	Purpose
some item	A randomly selected item inside a list.
every item	Every item inside a list.
beginning	The first item in a list.
middle item	The middle item in a list.
last item	The last item in a list.
end	The last item in a list.
first item, second item, etc.	A specific item in a list.
1st item, 2nd item, etc.	A specific item in a list.
item 1, item 2, etc.	A specific item in a list.
items x through z	A range of items in a list.

To demonstrate how to take advantage of the item specifiers listed in Table 5.5, consider the following example:

```
set FruitList to {"Apples", "Oranges", "Pears", "Grapes", "Plums"}
set SubList to items 2 through 4 in FruitList
```

Here, a variable named SubList is assigned {"Oranges", "Pears", "Grapes"}.

Modifying List Contents

AppleScript lets you modify the contents of lists in three ways. First, you can modify the value of any list item. Second, you can add a new item to the beginning of a list. Lastly, you can append a new item to the end of a list. For example, the first statement shown here defines a list consisting of five fruit. The next statement modifies the list by changing the value assigned to its third item.

```
set FruitList to {"Apples", "Oranges", "Pears", "Grapes", "Plums"}
set 3rd item in FruitList to "Bananas"
```

To add a new item to a list, you must use the beginning specifier, as demonstrated here:

```
set FruitList to {"Apples", "Oranges", "Pears", "Grapes", "Plums"}
set beginning of FruitList to "Bananas"
```

In a similar fashion, you can add an item to the end of a list using the end specifier, as demonstrated here:

```
set FruitList to {"Apples", "Oranges", "Pears", "Grapes", "Plums"}
set end of FruitList to "Bananas"
```

STORING DATA IN RECORDS

Another way of managing data in your AppleScript is to use records. A record is an unordered collection of data stored in *key-value* pairs, where individual pieces of data are assigned a unique key and stored as values. Records can be used to store any type of data supported by AppleScript. Many AppleScript commands and scriptable applications return data as records.

HINT   A *record* is AppleScript's equivalent to a *hash* or *dictionary* in other programming languages.

Records have a very specific format, as shown here:

```
{Key1: Value, Key2: Value …}
```

Key1 represents the key for the first value stored in the records and *Value* represents the data that is being stored. *Key2* represents the key for the next piece of data to be stored. There is no practical limit to how many key-value pairs you can store in a record.

TRAP Unlike lists, which are ordered and have a beginning and an end, records are unordered and thus their contents cannot be referenced using item specifiers like *item 1*, *beginning*, and *end*.

Creating Records

A record can be assigned as many key-value pairs as you want. For example the following record contains two key-value pairs.

```
set BuddyRecord to {name: "Mahoney", nickname: "Pizono"}
```

You can retrieve any value stored in a record using the set command, as demonstrated here:

```
set Buddy to the name of BuddyRecord
```

As you can see, to retrieve a value from a record, you must also specify the key with which it is associated as well as the name of the record that contains it. If desired, you can retrieve a list of values from a record by specifying the appropriate keys and a name for the new list, as demonstrated here:

```
set BuddyList to {name, nickname} of BuddyRecord
```

When executed, {"Mahoney", "Pizono"} is retrieved and assigned to BuddyList.

HINT You may not have realized it, but you have been working with records extensively throughout this book. Every time you have used the display dialog command to collect user input, whether it be by examining which button was clicked or by referencing the text keyed in by the user, you have been working with records. For example, the following statement generates a dialog window with two buttons and retrieves the value associated with a key named button (e.g., the button clicked by the user).

```
set answer to the button returned of (display dialog ¬
    "Click on OK to continue or Cancel to quit." ¬
    buttons {"OK", "Cancel"})
```

Likewise, the following statement generates a dialog window and retrieves the value associated with a key named text (e.g., the text keyed in by the user).

```
set answer to the text returned of (display dialog ¬
        "What is your name?" default answer "" ¬
        buttons {"OK"})
```

Like the `String` and `List` classes, the `Record` class provides programmers with access to a `length` property to ascertain the number of key-value pairs in a record, as demonstrated here:

```
set MyRecord to {Name: "Alexander", Employee_ID: 55661, Department: "IT"}
display dialog "This record contains " & length of MyRecord & ¬
    " key-value pairs. "
```

Here, a dialog window is displayed that states that the record contains 3 key-value pairs.

 Like strings and lists, you can use the & concatenation operator to join records together. When you do this, the key-value pairs in the second record are added to those in the first record, provided that there are no corresponding key-value pairs with the same key name in the first record. To see an example of how this works, take a look at the following statements.

```
set FirstRecord to {FirstName: "William", Age: 8}
set SecondRecord to {FavoriteColor: "Orange", Age: 9}
set NewRecord to FirstRecord & SecondRecord
```

When executed, the statements result in the creation of a new record that consists of the following.

```
{FirstName: "William", Age: 8, FavoriteColor: "Orange"}
```

Note that the second key-value pair was not added to the new record because a key of the same name was already in the first record. However, the second key-value pair was added.

Changing Record Value Assignments

You can change the value assigned to any key by specifying the name of the key and a new value using the `set` command, as demonstrated here:

```
set MyRecord to {Name: "Alexander", Employee_ID: 55661, Department: "IT"}
set Department of MyRecord to "Accounting"
```

Here, the string associated with the department key has been changed from "IT" to "Accounting".

Creating a Small Database Using Lists and Records

To realize the power of records, you need to group them together into lists. In doing so, you can generate your own small database. For example, take a look at the following statements.

```
set VendorDB to {¬
    {name: "XYZ, Inc.", account: 12345, product: "Lawn Supplies"}, ¬
    {name: "ABC Co.", account: 67890, product: "Roofing Materials"}, ¬
    {name: "AAA Lumber Yard", account: 44444, product: "Lumber"}, ¬
    {name: "BIG Tools", account: 55555, product: "Power Tools"}, ¬
    {name: "Office Mart", account: 98765, product: "Office Supplies"}}

set ProductCategories to {}

repeat with i in VendorDB
    set end of ProductCategories to product of i
end repeat
```

Here a list named VendorDB is created and assigned five records. Each record stores information about a different fictional company. Together this list and its records form a small database. Since lists are ordered collections of data, you can set up a loop to process their contents. In this example, a loop is set up to iterate through every record in the list and extract the value associated with the product key. Each time the loop iterates, the value of i is assigned the value associated with one of the products stored in the database. When the loop first runs, the value of i will be set to Lawn Supplies. The value of i is set to Roofing Materials on the loop's second iteration. This process continues until every record in the database has been processed. Upon the final iteration of the loop, the value of i will be set to Office Supplies.

By expanding the data stored in records and the number of records stored in the VendorDB list, you can create a small database that stores all kinds of information, which can easily be searched and processed using loops.

SEARCHING STRING, LISTS, AND RECORDS

AppleScript provides you with access to a collection of containment operators that you can use to search the contents of strings, lists, and records. These containment operators are listed in Table 5.6.

TABLE 5.6	APPLESCRIPT CONTAINMENT OPERATORS	
Operator	**Applies to**	**Description**
contains	strings, lists, records	Searches the first operand to see if it contains the second operand.
is in	strings, lists, records	Searches for the second operand in the first operand.
does not contain	strings, lists, records	Searches the first operand to verify that it does not contain the second operand.
is not it	strings, lists, records	Searches for the second operand in the first operand to ensure that it is not present.
begins with	strings, lists	Searches the first operand to see if it begins with the second operand.
ends with	strings, lists	Searches the first operand to see if it ends with the second operand.

 The reason that the begins with and ends with containment operators are not applicable to records is because records are unordered lists and, as such, do not have a beginning or ending.

To get a feel for how these containment operators work, let's look at a few examples that work with the contains operator. In the first example, shown next, an if statement code block has been set up to look for the occurrence of "Lee" inside a larger string. Since the first string does include the second string, a dialog window will be displayed declaring that a match has been found.

```
if "William Lee Ford" contains "Lee" then
    display dialog "Match!"
end if
```

In a similar fashion, the contains operator can be used to search lists, as demonstrated here:

```
if {"Alexander", "William", "Molly"} contains {"Molly"} then
    display dialog "Match!"
end if
```

Here, a list made of three strings is searched to see if it contains {"Molly"}, which in this example it does. Because lists are ordered, you must specify your search string with this fact in mind, as demonstrated here:

```
if {"Alexander", "William", "Molly"} contains {"William", "Molly"} then
    display dialog "Match!"
end if
```

Since {"William", "Molly"} can be found in this exact order in the first list, a match will occur. On the other hand, the following example will not result in a match because the order in which list items have been specified does not match the order in which they are stored in the first list.

```
if {"Alexander", "William", "Molly"} contains {"Molly", "William"} then
    display dialog "Match!"
end if
```

As a final example of how to work with containment operators, take a look at the next set of statements.

```
set MyRecord to {FirstName: "Jerry", LastName: "Ford", Age: 42}

if MyRecord contains {LastName: "Ford"} then display dialog "Match!"
if MyRecord contains {Age:40} then display dialog "Match!"
```

Here, a record named MyRecord has been assigned three key-value pairs. Next a pair of if statements are executed. The first if statement searches MyRecord to see if it contains a key-value pair of LastName: "Ford", which it does. The second if statement searches MyRecord for a key-value pair of Age: 40, which it does not find.

BACK TO THE GODFATHER TRIVIA QUIZ

Okay, now it is time to turn your attention back to the development of the Godfather Trivia Quiz. The development of this game relies on the use of lists when displaying quiz questions in dialog windows using the choose from list command. The player's answer to each quiz question is also returned as a list.

Designing the Game

The Godfather Trivia Quiz, like every other game project presented in this book, will be created in a series of steps. Specifically, the development of this game will be completed in seven steps, as outlined here:

1. Create a new AppleScript and save it with a name of Godfather Trivia Quiz.
2. Document the script and its purpose.
3. Define and initialize global variables.
4. Develop the programming logic for the first quiz question.

5. Develop the remaining quiz questions.
6. Add the programming logic required to grade the quiz.
7. Display quiz results.

Step 1: Creating a New AppleScript File

The first step in the creation of the Godfather Trivia Quiz is to open the Script Editor application and create a new AppleScript file named Godfather Trivia Quiz by performing the following steps.

1. Start the Script Editor application.
2. Click on the File menu and select the Save As option.
3. In the sheet window that appears, enter **Godfather Trivia Quiz** in the Save As field and specify the location where the script should be saved using the Where drop-down menu.
4. Click on the Save button.

Step 2: Providing High-Level Script Documentation

Since good script development also includes the provision of good documentation, let's begin the development of this script by providing a little basic documentation. This documentation will be embedded inside the script file as comment statements as well as written to the Script Editor application's Description tab.

Adding External Descriptive Text

Let's begin this AppleScript by documenting the script's name, version, rules, author, and copyright information on the data view field after selecting the Script Editor's Description tab view, as shown here:

```
The Godfather Trivia Quiz  v1.0


This game tests the player's knowledge of the Godfather movie by challenging him to
correctly answer at least 7 out of 10 questions related to the movie. If the player
passes the game, a rank will be assigned to him based on the following criteria.


7 correct   = Button Man
8 correct   = Capo
9 correct   = Consigleri
10 correct = Godfather


Developed by Jerry Lee Ford, Jr.
Copyright 2007
```

To help make this information easy to read, highlight the name of the game and select the Bold option located on the Font menu. The Script Editor will display this text in bold, making it stand out.

Embedding Comments Inside the Script

By now you should be used to embedding comment statements at the beginning of every script file. This is a very important programming practice, and I strongly encourage to you continue this practice in all your AppleScript projects. Although there is plenty of room for improvement, through the addition of other information, for now just add the following comment statements to the beginning of your new AppleScript.

```
-------------------------------------------------------------------------
--
-- Script Name: Godfather Trivia Quiz.scpt
-- Version: 1.0
-- Author: Jerry Lee Ford, Jr.
-- Date: August 2007
--
-- Description: This AppleScript tests the player's knowledge of the
-- Godfather movie by presenting a list of multiple-choice questions
-- and challenges the player to select the correct answers.
-------------------------------------------------------------------------
```

Step 3: Declaring and Initializing Global Variables

The Godfather Trivia Quiz will make frequent use of two variables throughout the script file. The first is responsible for storing the number of correctly answered questions. The second variable is used to store a string containing the name of the game. Many display dialog statements will reference this string when the script is running to display a consistent title bar message in the game's dialog windows. To define these variables, add the following statements to the end of the AppleScript file.

```
-- Define and initialize variable values
set NoCorrect to 0 -- Keeps a count of correctly answered questions
set GameTitle to "Godfather Trivia Quiz" -- Stores the game's name
```

As you can see, the value of the NoCorrect variable has been assigned an initial value of 0 and the value of the variable GameTitle has been assigned a string of "Godfather Trivia Quiz".

Step 4: Formulating the First Quiz Question

The next step in the development of the Godfather Trivia Quiz is to present the game's first quiz question. This is accomplished by adding the following statements to the end of the AppleScript.

```
-- Present the first question
set Q1 to choose from list {"Santino Corleone", "Fredo Corleone", ¬
    "Connie Corleone", "Tom Hagen"} ¬
    with prompt "What was the name of the Godfather's oldest child?" ¬
    with title GameTitle
```

As you can see, a variable named Q1 is assigned the value, in the form of a list, that is returned from the choose from list command. The choose from list command is passed a list of four strings, which it then displays as list items in a listbox control on a dialog window. The actual quiz question is presented by assigning a text string containing the question and passing it to the choose from list command as an argument using the with prompt parameter. Finally, the name of the game is displayed in the dialog window's title bar by passing it to the choose from list command as an argument using the with title parameter.

Step 5: Developing the Rest of the Quiz Questions

The code statements required to present and collect the results of the remaining quiz questions are provided below and should be added to the end of the AppleScript. As you can see, each of the following set statements is basically just a minor variation of the first set statement that was used to present the game's first question (with a different variable name, a new set of possible answers, and a new question).

```
-- Present the second question
set Q2 to choose from list {"Michael Corleone", "Don Vito Corleone", ¬
    "Luca Brasi", "Bruno Tattaglia"} ¬
    with prompt "Who ended up sleeping with the fishes?" ¬
    with title GameTitle

-- Present the third question
set Q3 to choose from list {"Johnny Fontane", "Moe Greene", ¬
    "Amerigo Bonasera", "Pete Clemenza"} ¬
    with prompt "Upon whose services did the Godfather call when " & ¬
    "his son was killed?" with title GameTitle

-- Present the fourth question
set Q4 to choose from list {"Causeway Tollboth", "Vegetable Market", ¬
```

```
          "Connie's apartment", "Tessio's Territory"} ¬
          with prompt "Where was Solenzio killed?" with title GameTitle

   -- Present the fifth question
   set Q5 to choose from list {"Italy", "Sardinia", "Sicily", "England"} ¬
          with prompt "To what country was Michael sent after killing the " & ¬
          "Turk?" with title GameTitle

   -- Present the sixth question
   set Q6 to choose from list {"Tom Hagen", "Luca Brasi", ¬
          "Salvatore Terrio", "Pete Clemenza"} ¬
          with prompt "Who was Don Corleone's consigleri" with title GameTitle
   -- Present the seventh question
   set Q7 to choose from list {"Grocery", "Flea market", ¬
          "Olive Oil", "Music store"} ¬
          with prompt "What kind of business did the Godfather operate?" ¬
          with title GameTitle

   -- Present the eighth question
   set Q8 to choose from list {"A Request", "A loan", ¬
          "A dance", "A hug"} ¬
          with prompt "What can't a Sicilian refuse on his daughter's " & ¬
          "wedding day?" with title GameTitle

   -- Present the ninth question
   set Q9 to choose from list {"Luca Brasi", "Kay Adams", ¬
          "Don Vito Corleone", "Pete Clemensa"} ¬
          with prompt "Who taught Michael how to cook?" with title GameTitle

   -- Present the tenth question
   set Q10 to choose from list {"Cat", "Dog", "Bird", "Fish"} ¬
          with prompt "What type of pet did the Godfather have?" ¬
          with title GameTitle
```

Step 6: Grading the Quiz

Now that all of the quiz questions have been presented and the player's answers collected, it is time to grade each question. This is accomplished by adding the following statements to the end of your AppleScript.

```
-- Analyze the player's answers and tally the number of correct answers
if Q1 = {"Fredo Corleone"} then set NoCorrect to NoCorrect + 1
if Q2 = {"Luca Brasi"} then set NoCorrect to NoCorrect + 1
if Q3 = {"Amerigo Bonasera"} then set NoCorrect to NoCorrect + 1
if Q4 = {"Causeway Tollboth"} then set NoCorrect to NoCorrect + 1
if Q5 = {"Sicily"} then set NoCorrect to NoCorrect + 1
if Q6 = {"Tom Hagen"} then set NoCorrect to NoCorrect + 1
if Q7 = {"Olive Oil"} then set NoCorrect to NoCorrect + 1
if Q8 = {"A Request"} then set NoCorrect to NoCorrect + 1
if Q9 = {"Pete Clemensa"} then set NoCorrect to NoCorrect + 1
if Q10 = {"Cat"} then set NoCorrect to NoCorrect + 1
```

As you can see, a series of 10 if statements have been defined. Each if statement is designed to analyze the list that was returned when the player responded to each of the game's 10 choose from list commands. In the case of the first if statement, the player's answer is correct if the choose from list command returns a list made up of a single item indicating that the player selected an answer of Fredo Corleone (e.g., {"Fredo Corleone"}). For each correctly answered quiz question, the value assigned to the NoCorrect variable is incremented by one. By the time the last question has been analyzed, the value assigned to NoCorrect will reflect the player's score on the quiz.

Step 7: Posting the Player's Score

With the player's score now available, it is time to determine if the player did well enough to pass the quiz. If this is the case, a ranking is assigned that describes the player's perceived knowledge of the Godfather movie.

```
-- Determine whether or not the player passed and what ranking,
-- if applicable, should be assigned
if NoCorrect < 7 then
    display dialog ¬
        "You have failed. Study hard and try again later." buttons {"OK"}
else if NoCorrect = 7 then
    display dialog ¬
        "You have passed with a ranking of Button man!" buttons {"OK"}
else if NoCorrect = 8 then
    display dialog ¬
        "You have passed with a ranking of Capo!" buttons {"OK"}
else if NoCorrect = 9 then
    display dialog ¬
```

```
            "You have passed with a ranking of Consigleri!" buttons {"OK"}
else if NoCorrect = 10 then
     display dialog ¬
            "You have passed with a ranking of Godfather!" buttons {"OK"}
end if
```

If the value of NoCorrect is less than seven, then the player has failed the quiz and a dialog window is displayed that suggests the player return and take the quiz again after learning more about the movie. If, on the other hand, the player has passed the quiz, a ranking is assigned based on the number of correctly answered questions.

Testing the Execution of the Godfather Trivia Quiz

All right! That's everything you need to get your own copy of the Godfather Trivia Quiz up and running. As long as you followed along carefully and did not make any typos when keying in the script's statements, you should be ready to test things out. To make sure that the quiz is operating as expected, test it in a number of different ways. For starters, test it by making sure that you correctly answer every question. Take it again answering nine questions correctly. Next answer eight questions correctly. Keep this testing up until you are one hundred percent confident that the quiz is ready for distribution to your friends and colleagues.

If you run into any errors along the way, read the error message that is generated very carefully and use it to track down and fix the error.

SUMMARY

In this chapter you learned the ins and outs of working with strings, lists, and records. This included learning how to retrieve information about strings, concatenate them together, and exercise control over string formatting. You learned how to perform advanced comparison operations allowing you to ignore or consider case, punctuation, and white space. You also learned how to access string contents using string elements, including characters, words, and paragraphs. This chapter also provided you with more information on how to work with lists. You learned how to create lists, extract list elements, and to add new list elements. Finally, you learned how to store and retrieve data using key-value pairs stored in records.

Before you move on to Chapter 6, "Improving Script Organization with Handlers," I suggest you set aside a little extra time to improve the Godfather Trivia Quiz game by tackling the following list of challenges.

CHALLENGES

1. Currently, every question in the Godfather Trivia Quiz includes four mutually exclusive answers. Consider expanding the length of the test and when doing so include a question or two in which the player must select two or more answers to successfully answer the question. Hint: Add `with multiple selections` to the end of each set statement that presents the player with quiz questions and instruct the user to make multiple selections by holding down the Shift or Command key. Hint: Player answers will be returned as a list so you might want to use a loop to process the player's answer.

2. To make the player think a little harder, consider adding a question or two to the Godfather Trivia Quiz for which none of the listed answers apply. Hint: Expand the `with multiple selections` argument to `with multiple selections and empty selection allowed`.

3. As it is currently written, the Godfather Trivia Quiz does not tell the player how many questions were missed when the player fails the quiz. Consider modifying the game to provide this information.

4. To help the player keep track of his progress when taking the quiz, consider adding a number to the beginning of each question (e.g., 1. or even Question 1 of 10).

IMPROVING SCRIPT ORGANIZATION WITH HANDLERS

N ow that you have learned how to work with variables, lists, records, conditional logic, loops, and other key AppleScript programming constructs, it is time to look at how to improve the overall organization and manageability of your AppleScripts through the implementation of handlers. A *handler* is a group of program statements enclosed inside a named code block that can be called upon to execute as necessary from different parts of your AppleScripts. Handlers facilitate modular program design and code reuse. They can be used to make your AppleScript easier to read and understand. This chapter will also cover the use of event handlers. An *event handler* is a special type of handler that is automatically called in response to certain program events, like script startup and termination. In addition to learning the ins and outs of working with handlers, this chapter will also guide you through the creation of your next AppleScript game, the AppleScript Shell game.

Specifically, you will learn to:

- Improve script organization through the implementation of handlers
- Control variable scope using handlers
- Develop handlers that process arguments

- Develop handlers that return a result
- Integrate support for event handlers into your AppleScripts

PROJECT PREVIEW: THE APPLESCRIPT SHELL GAME

This chapter's game project is the AppleScript Shell game. This game is based on the traditional shell guessing game in which the player is challenged to guess under which of three shells a ball is being hidden. In this game, the player is given a $10 bank account with which to start the game. The game begins by displaying the dialog window shown in Figure 6.1.

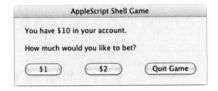

FIGURE 6.1

The player can specify how much money she wishes to gamble.

The first step in playing the game is to determine how much to bet. This is done by clicking on one of the dialog window's buttons. Once a bet has been made, the player is presented with the dialog window shown in Figure 6.2.

FIGURE 6.2

Each shell is represented by a button control.

The game randomly assigns a virtual ball to one of the three shells. The player must click on one of these shells in order to play. If the player guesses wrong, a dialog window like the one in Figure 6.3 is displayed, letting the player know that her guess was wrong.

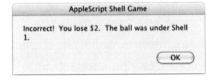

FIGURE 6.3

Money is automatically deducted from the player's account for each wrong guess.

The player is prompted to make another bet, as demonstrated in Figure 6.4.

FIGURE 6.4

The player is reminded of how much money is in her account at the beginning of each round of play.

If the player correctly guesses the location of the ball, a dialog window like the one shown in Figure 6.5 is displayed.

FIGURE 6.5

The amount of money added to the player's account for a winning guess depends on the size of the bet that was placed.

Game play is automatically terminated if the player goes broke. If this happens, the dialog window shown in Figure 6.6 is displayed.

FIGURE 6.6

The game ends if the player runs out of money.

Alternatively, the player can elect to stop playing at any time by clicking on the Quit Game button when prompted to place a new bet. When this happens, the game displays the dialog window shown in Figure 6.7, inviting the player to return and play again.

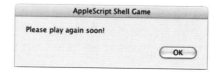

FIGURE 6.7

The game ends only after encouraging the player to play again.

LEVERAGING THE POWER AND CONVENIENCE OF HANDLERS

So far, all of the AppleScript games that you have worked on have consisted of various program statements that work together as a group to perform a particular task. For small scripts, like the AppleScript games you have worked on so far, this approach has worked well. As your AppleScripts grow in size and complexity, they will become more difficult to develop and maintain. To make them more manageable, you need to learn how to develop and organize your AppleScripts in a modular fashion using handlers. As I mentioned at the beginning of this chapter, a handler is a named group of statements, sometimes referred to as a subroutine or function, that can be called upon to execute from different locations within a script. Handlers allow for the development of small scripts by allowing collections of program statements to be called on whenever necessary from different locations within your script file, thus eliminating the need to duplicate programming logic in different parts of your scripts.

AppleScript supports two types of handlers: custom handlers and event handlers. Using *custom handlers*, you can build your AppleScript in a building block approach, adding and testing program code a module (handler) at a time. Custom handlers provide you with a means for separating program statements into related groups. For example, instead of grouping together all the programming statements that make up an AppleScript, you can use custom handlers to separate related statements into different logical groups. For example, you might develop a handler to collect user input and then another handler to verify that the input is valid. You could then set up a handler to process the input and perhaps one more handler to display any result generated by the script. Once you have developed each of these handlers, you could then write controlling program logic that calls upon each handler when it is needed, using the handlers as building blocks upon which your script is built.

Unlike custom handlers, which you create and control, *event handlers* are predefined handlers that AppleScript manages and makes available to you. Using event handlers, you can develop AppleScripts that are capable of reacting to predefined events, like script startup and termination.

Developing Your Own Custom Handlers

Custom handlers provide you with the building blocks you need to properly organize and produce modular AppleScripts that are easier to maintain. Handlers are created as code blocks within which you can embed any number of code statements. Handlers begin with the on keyword, followed by the name assigned to the handler and a pair of parentheses using the syntax outlined here:

```
on HandlerName()
     Statements
end HandlerName
```

As you can see, the end of the handler is identified by the end keyword followed by the name of the handler, this time without the parentheses. The reason for the parentheses at the beginning of the handler code block is to provide handlers with the ability to accept and process arguments, which AppleScript maps to parameters specified inside the parentheses. You'll learn how to create custom handlers that accept and process arguments a little later in this chapter.

Creating and Calling Upon Custom Handlers

To give you a better understanding of how to create and work with custom handlers, let's look at an example of how to create one and then look at how to call on it to execute. Using the syntax outlined in the preceding section, let's develop a custom handler named DisplayHelp() that displays a small amount of help information in a dialog window whenever it is called. The code that makes up this handler is shown here:

```
on DisplayHelp()
    display dialog "Help files are available in this application's " & ¬
        "installation directory."
end DisplayHelp
```

In this example, the handler does not accept any arguments. It does not return a result back to the statement that calls on it to execute. When called, it uses the display dialog command to display a message. Once executed, process control returns back to the location in the script where the call to the handler was made and resumes with the statement that follows the calling statement.

 Handlers cannot be defined within other handlers. Except for this rule, AppleScript does not enforce any restrictions on the locations in your scripts where you can define handlers. However, I strongly recommend that you group all of your handlers together in one location. For example, going forward in this book, I will group all handlers together and place them at the end of all scripts. This will make locating them easy and will help separate any controlling programming logic from the handlers that it calls upon to execute.

In order to execute, you must explicitly call upon your custom handlers. Otherwise, AppleScript will ignore them. One way of calling upon a handler is to type its name, along with any required arguments. In the case of the DisplayHelp() handler, no arguments are accepted, so to call on it to execute, all you have to do is add the following statement at the appropriate location within the AppleScript that contains the handler.

```
DisplayHelp()
```

As you will see a little later in this chapter, handlers can be set up to return a result back to the statements that call upon them to execute. In order to capture its information, you will need to use the set command to formulate your handler call using the syntax outlined here:

```
set VariableName to HandlerName()
```

VariableName represents the name of the variable in which the result returned by the handler will be stored and *HandlerName()* identifies the handler to be called.

Developing Custom Handlers that Process Arguments

As has already been stated, handlers can be set up to process any number of arguments passed to them by calling statements. In AppleScript, there are two ways to set up handlers to process arguments. The first option is to set up the handler to make parameter assignments based on the order in which they are defined. The second option is to define named parameters, allowing arguments to be passed in different order as long as their name is included.

TRAP   AppleScript has no restrictions on the types of data that you can pass to a handler. Therefore, it is up to you to ensure that the arguments that are passed are of the type expected and supported by your handlers. For example, suppose you write a script that added three numbers supplied by the user via dialog windows. The best way to handle things in this scenario would most likely be to validate the user's input as soon as it is collected and to reject it if it is not correct. One way of doing this is to use the class command to validate that the appropriate type of data has been supplied. The class command was covered in Chapter 3, "Working with Values, Variables, and Classes."

Working with Ordered Arguments and Parameters

To set up a handler that requires arguments to be passed to it in a predetermined order, you must specify one or more comma-separated variables inside the parentheses that follow the handler's name. These variables will be assigned the values of arguments passed to the handler when it is called upon to execute. These variables, referred to in this context as parameters, will automatically be assigned data that is passed to them based upon the order in which the arguments are passed. For example, look at the following custom handler.

```
on AddSomeNumbers(x, y, z)
    set TotalValue to x + y + z
    display dialog x & " + " & y & " + " & z & " = "  & TotalValue as string
end AddSomeNumbers
```

Here, a custom handler named AddSomeNumbers() has been defined. The handler has been set up to process three arguments. The first argument passed to the handler will be assigned to

x. The second argument passed will be assigned to y. The third argument passed will be assigned to z. Once the script maps out the arguments passed to the handler to the parameters defined in the handler, the statements located inside the handler are executed. The first statement inside the handler takes the value assigned to these three arguments and adds them together, assigning the resulting value to a variable named TotalValue, which is then displayed in a dialog window. Once written, you can call on the AddSomeNumbers() handler from anywhere in your script. When you do, you will need to remember to pass the appropriate arguments, as demonstrated here:

```
AddSomeNumbers(1, 2, 3)
```

In addition to passing literal values, you could just as easily pass variables as arguments, as demonstrated here:

```
set {a, b, c} to {1, 2, 3}
AddSomeNumbers(a, b, c)
```

Here, the values assigned to variables named a, b, and c are passed as arguments to AddSomeNumbers().

 TRAP Be very careful to pass the right number of arguments to your custom handlers. If you pass too many or too few, an error will occur.

Passing Arguments by Name

Instead of setting up your custom handlers to process arguments passed to them based in a predefined order, AppleScript also lets you assign a name or label to individual handler parameters. When written this way, you can call upon a handler and pass it arguments in any order you want, as long as you remember to reference parameter names. To see how this works, let's modify the AddSomeNumbers() handler to work with named parameters, as shown here:

```
on AddSomeNumbers given FirstNum:x, SecondNum:y, ThirdNum:z
     set TotalValue to x + y + z
     display dialog x & " + " & y & " + " & z & " = " & TotalValue as string
end AddSomeNumbers
```

Once rewritten, you can call upon this handler to pass it argument data, as demonstrated here:

```
set TotalSum to AddSomeNumbers given FirstNum:1, SecondNum:2, ThirdNum:3
```

As previously stated, as long as you pass the names associated with each parameter as part of the call to the handler, you can pass the arguments in any order you want, as demonstrated here:

```
AddSomeNumbers given SecondNum:2, FirstNum:1, ThirdNum:3
```

From a functional standpoint, this statement is no different from the previous statement. Both statements call the AddSomeNumbers() handler and pass it the same three arguments. Ultimately, it is more a matter of personal preference than anything else regarding whether you choose to set up your handlers to accept arguments based on order or name. Chances are if you are familiar with programming using another programming language, you will feel more comfortable passing arguments based on order. If you are new to programming, you may find it more intuitive to pass arguments by name.

Passing Arguments by Value and by Reference

By default, any variable passed to a handler as an argument is passed *by value*. This means that a copy of the variable being passed as an argument is passed to the handler. As such, changes made to the copy of the data within the handler have no effect on the value of the variable outside of the handler. However, any data passed to a handler as a list or record is passed *by reference*. What this means is that any changes made to a list or record passed as argument data to a handler are reflected in the value of the list or record outside of the handler.

Since lists and records are handled differently from variables, you must take additional care when passing them to your custom handlers. One easy way of handling this situation is to modify your handlers to make a copy of any argument data passed to them and then to work only with the copy of the data, thus leaving the original data that was passed intact and unaltered, as demonstrated here:

```
on AddSomeNumbers(ArgList)
     set TempList to ArgList
     statements
end AddSomeNumbers
```

Here, a handler named AddSomeNumbers() has been set up to process a list of data passed to it as an argument that is mapped to an internal variable named ArgList. Any changes made to the data stored in the ArgList would be reflected as changes outside of the handler. To prevent this from happening, the first statement in the handler assigns a copy of the contents of ArgList to a variable named TempList. This way, any changes made to the contents stored in TempList are not reflected in ArgList or anywhere else in the AppleScript.

Creating Handlers That Return a Result

In addition to accepting incoming arguments for processing, you can create custom handlers that can return a result to any statements that call on them. AppleScript provides two ways of returning a result from a handler: explicitly and implicitly. Both of these options are discussed in the sections that follow.

Explicitly Return a Result

Using the `return` command, you can explicitly return a result from a handler back to the statement that called upon the handler to execute. The syntax of the `return` command is outlined here:

```
return result
```

The value assigned to *result* can be a variable, list, or record. By using the `return` command to return a result back to the calling statement, you make your program code easier to read and understand. To see how the `return` command works, look at the following example.

```
on AddSomeNumbers(x, y, z)
    set TotalValue to x + y + z
    return TotalValue
end AddSomeNumbers
```

Here the `AddSomeNumbers()` handler that was presented earlier in the chapter has been modified so that it no longer displays the value assigned to `TotalValue` in a dialog window when the handler is called. Instead, the value assigned to `TotalValue` is now passed back to the calling statement.

To call upon this new version of the handler, you must use the `set` command, as demonstrated here:

```
set InterimValue to AddSomeNumbers(1, 2, 3)
```

Here, the `AddSomeNumbers()` handler is called and passed three numbers. The result returned by the handler (e.g., 6) is then assigned to a variable named `InterimValue`.

Implicitly Returning a Result

As an alternative to explicitly returning a result from a handler, you can implicitly return a result. By default, AppleScript will return the value of the last expression executed in a handler as its result. Therefore, if you wanted, you could rewrite the preceding example as shown here:

```
on AddSomeNumbers(x, y, z)
    set TotalValue x + y + z
end AddSomeNumbers
```

When executed, AppleScript will automatically return the value assigned to `TotalValue` to the statement that calls on the handler to execute. I recommend against implicitly returning a handler's value because it makes your source code a little more difficult to read.

USING EVENT HANDLERS TO INITIATE ACTION

Using event handlers, you can develop AppleScripts that are capable of reacting to predefined events, like script startup and termination. AppleScript supports a number of different event handlers, including those listed here:

- `run`. Automatically executes whenever the AppleScript is run.
- `open`. Automatically runs whenever a file, folder, or disk is dragged and dropped onto an AppleScript file.
- `idle`. Automatically runs on a periodic basis whenever an AppleScript enters an idle state.
- `quit`. Automatically runs when an AppleScript receives a Quit command.
- `reopen`. Automatically runs when a docked AppleScript application is reactivated.

 Note that when you work with event handlers, you do not include a pair of parentheses at the end of the handler's name, as demonstrated here:

```
on run
        statements
end run
```

Working with the run Event

The `run` event is triggered whenever an AppleScript is started. The `run` handler does not support any parameters. If you have added a `run` event handler to an AppleScript, it is automatically executed when the script is run. However, use of this handler is somewhat superfluous. If you execute a script that does not have a `run` handler, the script's top-level statements are executed. To demonstrate what I mean, look at the following one-line AppleScript.

```
display dialog "Hello World!"
```

When executed, this script displays a message in a dialog window. Now, let's rewrite this script using the `run` event handler.

```
on run
    display dialog "Hello World!"
end run
```

This script behaves and runs the same as the preceding script; therefore, you may be asking yourself what is the point? Well, one reason for using the run event handler is to distinguish AppleScript applications (applets) from AppleScript droplets, which are created based on the open event. You will learn about droplets in the next section of this chapter. Unless you have a lot of applets and droplets and want to use the run handler as a way of visually distinguishing your droplets from your applets, you shouldn't have much need for working with this event handler.

Working with the open Event

The open event is triggered whenever a file, folder, or disk is dragged and dropped onto an AppleScript file. Any AppleScript that has an open event handler is referred to as a droplet. The open handler supports a single parameter, which is a list of the items dragged and dropped onto it. If the AppleScript file contains an open event handler, the code statements inside that handler are executed. If, however, the AppleScript is run from inside the Script Editor or by double clicking on it when saved as an application, the code statements inside the open event handler are not executed. Using this event handler, you can create AppleScripts that process lists of files and folders that are dropped on them.

 The run and the open event handlers are mutually exclusive, meaning that AppleScript can run one or the other but never both. So if you start an AppleScript saved as an application by double clicking on it, its run handler, if present, is executed. On the other hand, if the AppleScript contains an open event handler and you drag and drop a file or folder on it, the open event will execute instead of the run handler.

To get a better idea of how to work with the open event handler, look at the following example.

```
on open ArgumentList

    repeat with ListItem in ArgumentList
        display dialog ListItem as string
    end repeat

end open
```

Here, an open event handler is added to an AppleScript. The open handler is passed a list made up of all the files and folders dropped on it. Inside the handler, the repeat command has been used to create a code block that will loop through each item in the argument list and display its file or folder name in a dialog window. Using this example as a template, you could create a host of AppleScripts. For example, you might create a droplet that renames any files dropped on it by adding a date or time stamp.

Working with the idle Event

The idle event is triggered whenever an AppleScript enters an idle state. To enter an idle state, an AppleScript must be saved using the Stay Open option. When saved with this option, an AppleScript remains active after it finishes executing or when the code in its run or open event handler is finished executing. In this scenario, an icon is added to the dock representing the AppleScript, allowing the script to be accessed again later and to remain running until the user clicks on the Quit menu item located on AppleScript's Application menu. Any statements placed inside the AppleScript idle event handler, if present, will be executed on a periodic basis.

Using the idle event handler, you can create a script that, when executed, attempts to perform a particular task and, if it is unable to perform that task, can keep running, attempting to perform its task until it accomplishes its job. By default, the idle event handler is set to execute every 30 seconds. However, you can specify a different time interval by passing an integer value representing the number of seconds the idle event should wait before re-executing when returning a result from the idle event handler.

Working with the quit Event

The quit event is triggered whenever an AppleScript finishes executing. By including a quit event handler in an AppleScript, you can execute code statements that perform any required clean-up actions. For example, you might use the quit event handler to display a dialog window for all your AppleScripts that provides the user with information about you, your website, and so on.

For an application that has been saved with the Stay Open option, the application can only be terminated if you add the following statement to the AppleScript's quit event handler.

```
continue quit
```

Working with the reopen Event

The reopen event is triggered whenever an AppleScript application is reactivated. This occurs when the user clicks on a docked AppleScript or when the user double clicks on an AppleScript application's icon when an instance of that application is docked.

A Quick Event Handler Example

Okay, now let's take what you have learned about AppleScript event handlers and use this information to create a fun little AppleScript that demonstrates how to work with the run, idle, reopen, and quit event handlers. Begin by creating a new AppleScript called Event Demo. Save this script as an application using the Stay Open option. Next, add the following statements to your new AppleScript.

```
on run
    say "I'll get you and your little dog too!" using "Vicki"
end run

on idle
    say "There is no escape. Now hand over those ruby slippers." ¬
    using "Vicki"
    return 10
end idle

on reopen
    say "Pay no attention to the man behind the curtain." using "Vicki"
end reopen

on quit
    say "Oh no, I'm melting." using "Vicki"
    continue quit
end quit
```

Compile and save your new script. Now locate and double click on it. As soon as you do, you should hear a female voice saying the message written out in the script's run event handler. Immediately after this, you should hear the message written out in the idle event handler. Remember, the idle event occurs immediately after the run event and then on a recurring basis. Wait 10 seconds and you should hear the message written out in the idle event handler again. Next, look for the icon representing your AppleScript application in the dock and click on it. You should now hear a male voice saying the message outlined in the reopen event handler. Repeat any of the above actions as many times as you want. When ready, click on the Quit Event Demo menu item located on the AppleScript application's Event Demo menu. When you do this, you will hear the message outlined in the script's quit event handler, after which the AppleScript will be removed from the dock and will stop executing.

UNDERSTANDING A HANDLER'S EFFECT ON VARIABLE SCOPE

As has already been mentioned, a variable's scope defines the location from within a script where a variable and its value can be accessed. You already know that variables defined within `if` and `repeat` statement code blocks are local to those code blocks, meaning that they cannot be accessed and do not exist outside of those code blocks.

By default, any variable declared inside an event handler is local in scope, meaning that it cannot be accessed outside of the handler. However, using the `global` command, you can explicitly declare variables as being accessible anywhere within an AppleScript, regardless of where they are declared.

Working with Local Variables

Any variables declared within a handler are local to that handler and as such can only be accessed within that handler. AppleScript lets you explicitly declare variables as being local using the `local` command, which has the following syntax.

```
local VariableName
```

VariableName is the name of the variable being declared as local in scope. For example, the following statements make up a handler named `GuessMyAge()`.

```
on GuessMyAge()
    local Age
    set Age to text returned of ¬
        (display dialog "How old are you?" default answer "")
    return Age
end GuessMyAge
```

When called, this handler declares a local variable named `Age`, which is assigned a value collected from the user using a dialog window. The handler then explicitly returns this value to the calling statement. Had the `return` statement not explicitly returned the value of `Age`, there would not be any other way that its value could be accessed from elsewhere within the AppleScript.

Creating Global Variables

Since variables declared within code blocks (like `if` and `repeat` code blocks, as well as event handlers) are local in scope, you must take an extra step in order to make these variables accessible outside of the handlers that contain them. This is accomplished using the `global` command, which has the following syntax.

```
global VariableName
```

VariableName is the name of the variable being declared as global in scope. A variable declared as being global can be accessed from any location within an AppleScript.

 HINT Any variable that is declared outside of a code block is by default global in scope. However, for a handler to access a variable that is declared outside of itself, that variable must be explicitly declared as being global in scope.

Too see how the global command works, consider the following example.

```
on DemoHandler()
    global MyName
    set MyName to "Jerry Ford"
end DemoHandler
```

```
DemoHandler()
display dialog "Welcome " & MyName
```

Here, a handler named DemoHandler has been set up. Within the handler, a variable named MyName has been declared as global and assigned a value. Next, the handler is called on to execute, thus establishing the value of MyName, which is then referenced and displayed in a dialog window. As this example demonstrates, using the global command, a variable and its value can be accessed from outside of the handler where it was initially declared.

Now, let's take a look at another example.

```
global GameTitle
set GameTitle to "Demo Game"
```

```
on DisplayMsg()
    display dialog "Welcome!" with title GameTitle
end DisplayMsg
```

```
DisplayMsg()
```

Here, a variable named GameTitle has been declared as being global. The variable is then accessed from within a handler named DisplayMsg(), where its value is used to populate the title bar of a dialog window. If you were to remove the global statement from this example, an error would occur when the Script Editor attempts to compile the AppleScript, stating that a variable named GameTitle is not defined. This example demonstrates that variables declared outside of handlers are accessible inside handlers only if they were previously declared as being global in scope.

AppleScript does not require you to declare a variable as being global when that variable is first used. Instead, it lets you wait, as demonstrated here:

```
set GameTitle to "Demo Game"

on DisplayMsg()
     global GameTitle
     display dialog "Welcome!" with title GameTitle
end DisplayMsg

DisplayMsg()
```

In this example, the GameTitle variable is not declared as being global until just before it is accessed in the DisplayMsg() handler.

 HINT I suggest you get into the habit of declaring variables global at the beginning of your AppleScript as opposed to embedding global commands somewhere deeper in your AppleScript. This will make your scripts easier to read and understand.

Now, let's take a look at one more example of the use of the global command, as shown here:

```
on FirstHandler()
     global Total
     set Total to 100
end FirstHandler

on SecondHandler()
     set Score to Total
end SecondHandler

FirstHandler()
SecondHandler()
```

This time two handlers have been set up. The first handler declares a variable named Total as being global. It then assigns a value of 100 to Total. The second handler attempts to reference the value assigned to Total in order to assign it to a variable named Score. Both handlers are then called on to execute. While, intuitively, everything may seem in order, it's not. When executed, the first handler runs correctly. However, when the second handler runs, an error is generated because even though Total has been declared as being global, the second handler cannot access it. This is because a variable declared as being global in one handler cannot be accessed from another handler unless the other handler also declares that variable as being global. Therefore, to fix the preceding example, you would have to add the `global` command to the second handler, as demonstrated here:

```
on FirstHandler()
    global Total
    set Total to 100
end FirstHandler

on SecondHandler()
    global Total
    set Score to Total
end SecondHandler

FirstHandler()
SecondHandler()
```

With both handlers now declaring Total as a global variable, everything works and the second handler is able to assign the value of Total to Score.

BACK TO THE APPLESCRIPT SHELL GAME

All right, it is time to turn your attention back to the development of this chapter's game project, the AppleScript Shell game. The design of this game relies extensively on the use of custom handlers. In developing this AppleScript, you will gain additional experience in developing handlers that accept and process arguments and which also return a result back to the statements that call on them.

Designing the Game

The AppleScript Shell game is created by following 10 steps, as outlined here:

1. Create a new AppleScript and save it with a name of Shell Game.
2. Document the script and its purpose.
3. Declare the game's global variable.
4. Initialize variable starting values.
5. Develop the high-level programming logic for the game.
6. Display the game's closing messages.
7. Create the GetRandomNumber() handler.
8. Create the GetBet() handler.
9. Create the GetGuess() handler.
10. Create the ProcessGuess() handler.

Step 1: Creating a New AppleScript File

The first step in creating the AppleScript Shell game is to start up the Script Editor application and create a new AppleScript file named Shell Game, by performing the following steps.

1. Start the Script Editor application.
2. Click on the File menu and select the Save As option.
3. In the sheet window that appears, enter **Shell Game** in the Save As field and specify the location where you want to save the script file using the Where drop-down menu.
4. Click on the Save button.

Step 2: Providing High-Level Script Documentation

By now, the importance of properly documenting your AppleScript should be well understood. As such, the next step in the development of the AppleScript Shell game is to begin documenting the script file. This documentation will consist of embedded comment statements as well as descriptive text written to the Script Editor application's Description tab.

Adding External Descriptive Text

The text to be added to the AppleScript file using the Script Editor's Description tab view is provided here:

```
The AppleScript Shell Game  v1.0


This game challenges the player to compete against the computer in a traditional shell
game. The objective of this game is for the player to guess under which of three shells
the game's virtual ball is hidden.


Developed by Jerry Lee Ford, Jr.
Copyright 2007
```

To spruce things up just a bit, highlight the game's name and select the Bold option located on the Font menu, instructing the Script Editor to display this text in a bold font.

Embedding Comments Inside the Script

Next, add the following comment statements to the beginning of the AppleScript to provide some starting documentation that identifies the name of the script and a high-level description of its purpose.

```
----------------------------------------------------------------------
--
-- Script Name: AppleScript Shell Game.scpt
-- Version: 1.0
```

```
-- Author: Jerry Lee Ford, Jr.
-- Date: August 2007
--
-- Description: This AppleScript game challenges the player to guess under
-- which of three shells the game's virtual ball is hiding.
--
-------------------------------------------------------------------------
```

Step 3: Declaring the Game's Global Variable

The AppleScript Shell game will reference a variable named `GameTitle` globally throughout the script. To ensure that this variable is globally available, you will need to use the `global` command as shown here:

```
-- Declare the following variable as having a global scope
global GameTitle
```

By declaring the variable as global, you ensure that it can be accessed from any location within the script file.

Step 4: Assigning Initial Variable Values

The next step in the development of the AppleScript Shell game is to assign initial values to two variables. The code that accomplishes this is outlined next and should be added to the end of the script file.

```
-- Define and initialize variable values
set AcctBalance to 10 -- The amount of money in the player's account
set GameTitle to "AppleScript Shell Game" -- Stores the game's name
```

The `AcctBalance` variable is set to 10. This value represents the amount of money added to the player's virtual bank account at the beginning of the game. The value of `GameTitle` will be used throughout the script file by all its `display dialog` commands in order to ensure the consistent display of each dialog window's title bar.

Step 5: Developing the Game's High-Level Programming Logic

The overall controlling logic for this script is outlined next in a `repeat` statement code block. These code statements are responsible for managing game play, calling on various handlers as required to perform specific tasks, and then terminating the script's execution when the player goes broke or decides to stop playing.

```
-- Loop until the player goes broke or decides to quit
repeat until AcctBalance is less than or equal to 0
```

```
-- Call the handler that collects the player's bet
set Bet to GetBet(AcctBalance)

--Analyze the player's input
if Bet = "Quit Game" then --The player clicked on the Quit Game button
    exit repeat
else -- The player has made a bet
    if Bet = "$1" then set Bet to 1
    if Bet = "$2" then set Bet to 2
end if

-- Call the handler that generates random numbers
set randomNumber to GetRandomNumber()

-- Call the handler that collects the player's guess
set Guess to GetGuess()

-- Call the handler that processes the player's guess
set AcctBalance to ProcessGuess(Guess, randomNumber, AcctBalance, Bet)

end repeat
```

As you can see, the repeat statement code block has been set up to execute until the value assigned to AcctBalance is less than or equal to zero (e.g., the player goes broke). The first statement inside the code block calls upon the GetBet() handler, passing it an argument of AcctBalance. This handler is responsible for prompting the player to specify the size of her bet, which is returned by the handler and assigned to the Bet variable.

Next an if statement code block is set up. It begins by checking to see if the value of Bet is "Quit Game", indicating that instead of making a bet, the player decided to quit playing the game. If this is the case, the exit repeat command is executed, terminating the repeat statement code block and effectively ending the game. On the other hand, if the player did place a bet, the else portion of the code block executes, in which case the value of Bet is reset to an integer value based on the size of the bet made by the player.

Next, the GetRandomNumber() handler is called on to execute. This handler is responsible for generating a random number between 1 and 3, representing the shell under which the game's virtual ball is hidden. The handler returns this value, which is then assigned to the randomNumber variable.

The GetGuess() handler is executed next. This handler's job is to prompt the player to guess under which shell the ball is hidden. This handler returns an integer value between 1 and 3, representing the player's guess, which is then assigned to the Guess variable.

The last handler to be called before the repeat loop runs again is the ProcessGuess() handler. This handler is passed the values of Guess, randomNumber, AcctBalance, and Bet as arguments. This handler is responsible for analyzing the player's guess to see if it is correct. The handler returns an integer representing the amount of money in the player's bank account. This value is then assigned to the AcctBalance variable.

Step 6: Displaying Closing Dialog Windows

Game play continues either until the player goes broke or decides to stop playing, at which time the repeat statement code block is exited. The last set of statements to be executed before the AppleScript stops running are shown next and should be added to the end of the script file.

```
-- To get here, the player has either quit the game or gone broke
if AcctBalance is less than or equal to 0 then
    display dialog "Game over. You have gone broke."
else
    display dialog "Please play again soon!" buttons {"OK"} ¬
        with title GameTitle
end if
```

As you can see, an if statement code block has been set up to determine whether the player has gone broke. This is accomplished by checking to see if the value assigned to AcctBalance is less than or equal to zero. If it is, the display dialog command is used to display a message that informs the player that she has busted. If the player did not go broke, then she must have clicked on the Quit Game button when prompted to place a bet. In this case, the else portion of the code block is executed and the display dialog command is used to display a message that encourages the player to return and play the game again.

Step 7: Creating the GetRandomNumber() Handler

The code statements that make up the GetRandomNumber() handler are listed next and should be added to the end of the script file.

```
-- This handler generates a random number between 1 and 3 representing
-- the shell under which the ball is hidden
on GetRandomNumber()

    -- Generate a random number between 1 and 3
```

```
set randomNo to random number from 1 to 3

return randomNo -- Return the random number to the calling statement
```

end GetRandomNumber

This handler uses the `random number` command to generate a number between 1 and 3, which is then assigned to a local variable named `randomNo`. The value of `randomNo` is then returned back to the program statement that called upon the handler to execute.

Step 8: Creating the GetBet() Handler

The code statements that make up the `GetBet()` handler are listed next and should be added to the end of the script file. This handler takes as an argument a value representing the amount of money in the player's bank account, which it stores in a local variable named `AcctBalance`.

 HINT   Note that although the `GetBet()` handler uses a variable named `AcctBalance`, this variable is local to the handler. It is not the same variable used elsewhere in the script. Any variable used outside of a handler and not declared as global is not accessible inside any of the script's handlers. Conversely, any variables declared inside a handler are local to that handler and cannot be accessed from anywhere else.

```
-- This handler prompts the player to make a bet or to quit
on GetBet(AcctBalance)

    -- Prompt the player for the size of her bet or to Quit
    set Amount to button returned of (display dialog "You have $" & ¬
        AcctBalance & " in your account. " & return & return & ¬
        "How much would you like to bet?" ¬
        buttons {"$1", "$2", "Quit Game"} with title GameTitle)

    return Amount -- Return the player's selection
```

end GetBet

This handler uses the `display dialog` command to display a dialog window in order to prompt the player to make a bet of $1 or $2. Alternatively, the player can click on the Quit Game button to terminate game play. The button that the player clicks on is assigned to a variable named `Amount`, which is then returned back to the statement that called upon the handler.

Step 9: Creating the GetGuess() Handler

The code statements that make up the GetGuess() handler are listed next and should be added to the end of the script file. This handler is responsible for displaying a dialog window that prompts the player to click on one of three buttons representing each of the game's three shells.

```
-- This handler prompts the player to guess which shell the ball is under
on GetGuess()

    -- Prompt the player to guess which shell the ball is under
    set reply to button returned of (display dialog "OK, now that you " & ¬
        "have made your bet, it is " & ¬
        "time to make a guess.  Which shell do you think the " & ¬
        "ball is under?" buttons {"Shell 1", "Shell 2", "Shell 3"} ¬
        with title GameTitle)

    -- Translate the player's selection into a number
    if reply = "Shell 1" then
        set reply to 1
    else if reply = "Shell 2" then
        set reply to 2
    else if reply = "Shell 3" then
        set reply to 3
    end if

    return reply -- Return a number representing the player's guess

end GetGuess
```

The button clicked on by the user is assigned to a variable named reply (as "Shell 1", "Shell 2", or "Shell 3"). The value assigned to reply is then processed by an if statement code block, which reassigns a value of 1, 2, or 3 to reply based on the button that the player clicked on. Finally, the value of reply is returned back to the statement that called upon the handler to execute.

Step 10: Creating the ProcessGuess() Handler

The code statements that make up the ProcessGuess() handler are listed next and should be added to the end of the script file. This handler is responsible for determining whether the player's guess was correct and for recalculating the balance of the player's account.

```
-- This handler processes the player's guess and determines whether the
-- player has won or lost
on ProcessGuess(Guess, randomNumber, AcctBalance, Bet)

    -- Determine if the player's guess was right or wrong
    if Guess = randomNumber then -- The player's guess was correct
        set AcctBalance to AcctBalance + Bet --Adjust the player's account
        display dialog "Correct!  You win $" & Bet ¬
            buttons {"OK"} with title GameTitle
    else -- The player's guess was not correct
        set AcctBalance to AcctBalance - Bet --Adjust the player's account
        display dialog "Incorrect!  You lose $" & Bet & ¬
            ".  The ball was under Shell " & ¬
            randomNumber & "." buttons {"OK"} with title GameTitle
    end if

    return AcctBalance -- Return the player's new account balance

end ProcessGuess
```

This handler accepts four arguments, representing the player's guess, a number representing the shell under which the ball is hidden, the amount of money stored in the account, and the size of the player's bet. The handler compares the value assigned to the Guess argument to see if it is equal to the randomNumber argument. If it is, the player's guess was correct and the value of the AcctBalance argument is incremented based on the size of the player's bet. If, on the other hand, the player's guess was incorrect, the value assigned to the AcctBalance argument is decremented. The value of AcctBalance is then returned back to the statement that called upon the handler to execute.

Testing the Execution of the AppleScript Shell Game

At this point, your copy of the AppleScript Shell game should be ready for testing. Assuming that you did not make any typos when keying in the code statements for this AppleScript, the game should operate as described at the beginning of this chapter. When you first test it, make sure that you use different size bets and that your bank account is adjusted correctly after each round of play. Also, make sure that the game properly terminates if you run out of money. If you run across any errors when testing your script, use the information provided by the error message to locate and fix the error.

SUMMARY

In this chapter, you learned how to develop custom handlers and to use them to improve the overall organization of your AppleScripts. In doing so, you learned how to create handlers that can accept and process input and also return a result to calling statements. Learning how to use custom handlers to organize your program code will result in modular code that is easier to read and maintain. Your script code will also be more efficient because of its support for code reuse. This chapter also explained how handlers impact variable scope. In addition to all this, you learned about AppleScript's built-in support for event programming, and you learned the basic steps involved in working with different types of events.

Now, before you move on to Chapter 7, "Accessing Files and Folders," why don't you set aside a little extra time to improve the AppleScript Shell game by tackling the following list of challenges.

CHALLENGES

1. As currently written, the AppleScript Shell game does not provide the player with any instruction regarding the rules of the game. Why don't you save the game as an AppleScript application and enable its Startup screen in order to provide this information?

2. Consider modifying the game so that after a given number of turns, say 20 plays, the size of bets doubles from $1 and $2 to $2 and $4 dollars. Hint: you'll need to add a variable that keeps track of the number of plays and add programming logic to increment it at the end of each round of play. In addition, you will need to modify the display of the dialog window that collects the player's bet as well as include additional conditional logic to appropriately modify the player's account balances after the size of the bets have doubled.

3. Using your new understanding of event programming, consider making the game dockable, allowing the player to start the game and play a while and then send the application to the dock. This way the player can come back and play some more later without having to start over.

Part

III

ACCESSING FILES AND FOLDERS

I n Chapters 3 through 6, you were introduced to the basics of AppleScript programming. This chapter is the first of four chapters dedicated to covering advanced programming topics. The primary focus of this chapter is on teaching you how to develop AppleScripts that can interact with and control files and folders. You will learn how to interact with the Mac file system and establish file references. You will also learn how to read from and write to text files. In addition, you will learn how to create your next AppleScript game, the AppleScript Lottery Picker game.

Specifically, you will learn how to:

- Identify the location of files and folders
- Open and close text files
- Read data from text files
- Write data to text files

PROJECT PREVIEW: THE APPLESCRIPT LOTTERY PICKER GAME

This chapter's game project is the AppleScript Lottery Picker game. When executed, this game assists the player in generating a list of randomly selected lottery numbers. To play, the player must provide three pieces of information. First, the player must identify the range of numbers from which the game must choose. Second, the player must specify how many numbers must be selected to complete a ticket, and finally, the player must tell the game how many tickets she plans on purchasing. With this information in hand, the game will generate a list of lottery numbers. The game will even offer to save them in a text file and print them out if the player wants.

When first started, the AppleScript Lottery Picker game begins by prompting the player for required information, as demonstrated in Figure 7.1.

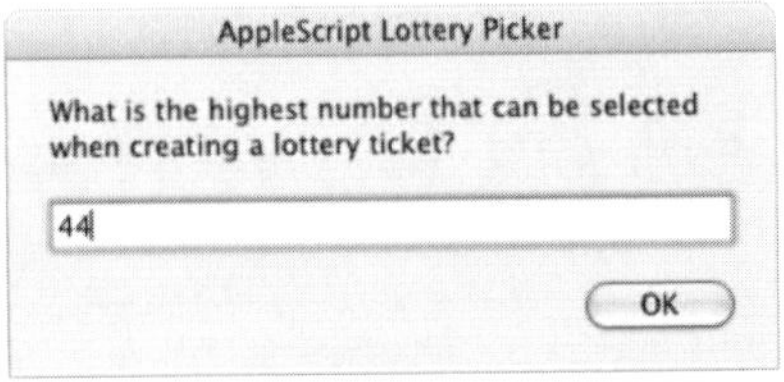

FIGURE 7.1

The game asks the player for a range of numbers from which to choose.

Because different lottery games have different rules, the game needs to know the range of numbers from which it should draw upon when generating lottery ticket numbers. Next, the game prompts the player to specify how many numbers it takes to complete a lottery ticket, as demonstrated in Figure 7.2.

FIGURE 7.2

The game needs to know how many numbers to select for each ticket.

Next, the game prompts the player to enter how many lottery tickets she wants to purchase, as demonstrated in Figure 7.3.

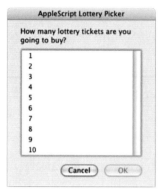

FIGURE 7.3

The game will generate a list of up to 10 lottery number selections.

Once the game has collected answers to all its questions, it will generate a list of randomly selected lottery number selections for the player, as demonstrated in Figure 7.4.

FIGURE 7.4

An example of five lottery tickets generated by the game.

If the player wants, she can print a listing of the game's lottery number selections by clicking on the Print button. With a printed copy of the lottery numbers in hand, the player is now ready to visit her local convenience store to purchase her lottery tickets.

WORKING WITH THE MAC OS X FILE SYSTEM

Originally, Mac computers ran a proprietary operating system created by Apple programmers. However, since the introduction of Mac OS X, UNIX has served as the underlying operating system. As a UNIX operating system, Mac OS X uses POSIX path names to identify the names and locations of files and folders. POSIX was developed back in the 1980s as a standard designed to unify differences that abounded in the many different flavors of UNIX available at the time.

However, Apple has continued to provide Mac users with support for pre-Mac OS X Mac-styled path names. Therefore, Mac users have two options for specifying path names. It is important that you understand and know how to work with both of these options, because as you interact with AppleScripts developed by other programmers, you are going to see both used.

Using Mac-Styled Paths

Mac-styled path names use the : character to separate drives, folders, and file names, as demonstrated here.

```
Macintosh HD:Users:Jerry:Documents:DemoFile.txt
```

As this example demonstrates, AppleScript requires that you supply file extensions as part of any file's name. Omitting a file's file extension will result in a script error.

 Because Mac OS X can be configured to hide file extensions, it is not always obvious what type of file extension a particular file has. However, you can view any file's extension by selecting it using Finder and then selecting the Get Info menu item located on the File menu.

Using POSIX-Styled Paths

POSIX path names use the / character to separate drives, folders, and filenames, as demonstrated here.

```
/Users/Jerry/Documents/DemoFile.txt
```

Note the use of the opening / character. The initial / character is used to represent the root of the computer's file system.

Specifying a Folder's Path

In the two preceding sections, you learned how to specify the path for a file using Mac-styled and POSIX-styled paths. To specify a folder instead of a file using a Mac-styled path, you need to append a trailing : character to the end of the path, as demonstrated here:

```
Macintosh HD:Users:Jerry:Documents:
```

Similarly, to specify a folder instead of a file using a POSIX path, you must specify an extra / character at the end of the path, as demonstrated here:

```
/Users/Jerry/Documents/
```

WORKING WITH FULL AND RELATIVE PATHS

AppleScript lets you work with both absolute and relative paths. All of the examples of paths that you have seen so far have been absolute paths. An *absolute path* is one that specifies the disk drive, folder, and subfolders in which a file or folder is stored, as demonstrated here.

```
Macintosh HD:Users:Jerry:Documents:DemoFile.txt
```

When you work with relative paths, you specify the location of a file or folder relative to the current working directory. By default, the current working directory is the folder in which an AppleScript is stored. For example, suppose an AppleScript was stored in a folder located in the following folder:

```
Macintosh HD:Users:Jerry:Documents:
```

If the AppleScript needed to reference a file named `DemoFile.txt` stored inside the same folder, you could reference it using its absolute path, as shown here:

```
Macintosh HD:Users:Jerry:Documents:DemoFile.txt
```

Alternatively, you could reference the file using its absolute path, as shown here:

```
DemoFile.txt
```

Since the AppleScript and the text file reside in the same folder, you can omit any path specification. Mac OS X provides a number of shortcuts that you can use when working with relative paths, as outlined in Table 7.1.

TABLE 7.1	POSIX PATH REFERENCE CHARACTERS
Characters	**Value**
.	The current folder or directory
..	The parent folder or directory
~	The current user's home directory

To get a better feel for how to use these shortcuts, take a look at the following example.

```
./Homework/TermPaper.txt
```

Here, a relative path has been used to specify the location of a file named `TermPaper.txt` related to the current working directory. The reference starts at the current working directory, as specified by the `.` special character, and denotes the text file resides in a subfolder named `Homework`.

Retrieving File and Folder Information

AppleScript gives you access to information about files and folders through the `info for` command, which has the following syntax.

```
info for file FileName
```

FileName represents the complete path and filename of the file or folder for which information is to be retrieved. To see this command in action, take a look at the following statement.

```
set FileData to ¬
    (info for file "Macintosh HD:Users:jerryford:Documents:PartsDB.txt")
```

Here, the `info for` command is being used to retrieve file information for a file named `PartsDB` located in `Macintosh HD:Users:jerryford:Documents:`. The `info for` command retrieves a great deal of information about the target file or folder. For example, the previous statement will return a record containing information like the following when executed.

```
{name:"PartsDB.txt", creation date:date "Sunday, August 20, 2006 2:59:19 PM",
modification date:date "Sunday, August 20, 2006 2:59:19 PM", icon position:{0,
0}, size:376.0, folder:false, alias:false, package folder:false, visible:true,
extension hidden:false, name extension:missing value, displayed name:"PartsDB.txt",
default application:alias "Macintosh HD:Applications:TextEdit.app:", kind:"Text
document", file type:"TEXT", file creator:"ttxt", type
identifier:"com.apple.traditional-mac-plain-text", locked:false, busy
status:false, short version:"", long version:""}
```

Since the `info for` command returns its result as a record, you can easily retrieve data by specifying the appropriate key name, as demonstrated in the following example.

```
set FileData to ¬
    (info for file "Macintosh HD:Users:jerryford:Documents:PartsDB.txt")

display dialog "File size: " & size of FileData & return & ¬
    "Created : " & creation date of FileData & return & ¬
    "File type: " & kind of FileData buttons {"OK"} ¬
    with title "File Name: " & name of FileData
```

Here, information about the file's size, creation date, and file type is retrieved and displayed, as demonstrated in Figure 7.5.

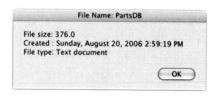

FIGURE 7.5

Using the info for command to retrieve information about a file.

WORKING WITH THE FILE CLASS

In order to work with a file, you need to tell AppleScript the name and location of the stored file. This is typically done by assigning the name and path of the file as a string to a variable, setting up a file reference that can then be used repeatedly throughout an AppleScript without having to respecify the file and path each time you need to refer to it. In order to set up the file reference, you need to know how to work with the file class.

Using the file class you can establish a file object reference. The syntax that you must follow when using the file class to set up a file reference is outlined here:

```
set FileReference to "FileNameAndPath"
```

FileReference is a variable that will be used to reference the file specification (*"FileNameAndPath"*) that follows the file class keyword. For example, the following statement will set up a file reference to a file named GroceryList.txt, which is located in "Macintosh HD:Users:Jerry:Documents:".

```
set MyFile to "Macintosh HD:Users:Jerry:Documents:GroceryList.txt"
```

Once established, the file can be referenced by referring to the MyFile variable. Of course, if you prefer, you could just as easily use the UNIX POSIX path when setting up the file reference, as shown here:

```
set MyFile to POSIX "/Users/Jerry/Documents/GroceryList.txt"
```

Referencing Commonly Accessed Folders

Mac OS X automatically creates many different types of folders. You probably work with many of the folders all the time and take their presence for granted. For example, every user of any Mac OS X computer is automatically assigned her own Documents folder. Other folders you probably interact with include the Applications folder, where most applications are installed, and the Desktop folder, which contains all of the items displayed on your desktop.

Recognizing that these and many other folders are commonly accessed, AppleScript provides you with access to a collection of predefined path arguments that you can use as shortcuts when you need to access commonly used folders. Referencing the predefined path arguments saves you the trouble of having to type out commonly used folder's full path names. In addition, since all you have to do to reference one of these folders is refer to its path argument, you do not have to even know the folder's complete path, just its path argument. Table 7.2 provides a list of commonly used path arguments that you will want to take advantage of when you are writing your AppleScripts.

TABLE 7.2	PREDEFINED PATH ARGUMENTS
Argument	**Description**
applications folder	"Macintosh HD:Applications:"
desktop	"Macintosh HD:Users:*username*:Desktop:"
trash	"Macintosh HD:Users:*username*:Trash:"
startup disk	"Macintosh HD:"
system folder	"Macintosh HD:System:"
users folder	"Macintosh HD:Users:"
utilities folder	"Macintosh HD:Applications:Utilities:"
documents folder	"Macintosh HD:Users:*username*:Documents:"
home folder	"Macintosh HD:Users:*username*:"
library folder	"Macintosh HD:Library:"
pictures folder	"Macintosh HD:Users:*username*:Pictures:"
movies folder	"Macintosh HD:Users:*username*:Movies:"
music folder	"Macintosh HD:Users:*username*:Music:"
shared documents	"Macintosh HD:Shared:"
public folder	"Macintosh HD:Users:*username*:Public:"
scripts folder	"Macintosh HD:Users:*username*:Library:Scripts:"
temporary items folder	"Macintosh HD:private:tmp:501:TemporaryItems:"
current application	Path to current execution script

HINT

Macintosh HD is the default name for the startup disk on Mac OS X. Depending on how your computer was set up, a different name may have been assigned to this drive. *username* represents the name (user account) of the user who actually runs the AppleScript.

Setting Up File References Using Path Arguments

By taking advantage of path arguments, you can reduce the number of keystrokes required to identify the location of commonly accessed folders, thus reducing the likelihood of making typos. To take advantage of path arguments, you need to set up your file referencing using the syntax outlined here:

```
set FileReference to (path to PathArgument folder)
```

Here, *FileReference* is a variable that will be used to reference the target folder. This folder is specified as *PathArgument*. Note the use of parentheses around the folder specification and the use of the path to command and the placement of the folder keyword.

Using path arguments, you could rewrite the following statement

```
set MyFile to "Macintosh HD:Users:Jerry:Documents:GroceryList.txt"
```

as

```
set MyFile to (path to documents folder as string) & "Grocerylist.txt"
```

and AppleScript will know exactly where to go to find the GroceryList.txt file. Here the documents path argument is specified. Note that to allow for the specification of a filename at the end of the statements, it was necessary to add the as string keywords as part of the path specification. By default, the value returned by the path to command is an alias. An *alias* is a reference to an object and not a string, so to append a string representing a file to the end of the path, you must first convert the alias to a string. Note the use of the & concatenation operator in the previous statement, which allows for the formulation of a statement that includes both the path and filename. Using the documents path argument, as shown above, is preferable to hard coding the full path to the user's documents folder because it creates more portable code.

Instead of having to create a different version of your AppleScript, each with a hardcode path representing the path to a different user's documents folder, you can just refer to the document path argument and the script will automatically know how to find the documents folder for any user that runs the script. Therefore, I recommend you keep Table 7.2 in mind whenever you are working on a script that requires folder access, and that you use path arguments whenever the opportunity to do so arises.

WRITING APPLESCRIPTS THAT INTERACT WITH TEXT FILES

At this point you have learned how to work with traditional MAC and POSIX paths and are now familiar with how to use the file class to establish references to files and folders. With this information now in hand, you are ready to learn how to read from and write to text files. In the sections that follow, you will learn how to open and close files and to extract and modify their contents while you have them open.

Programmatically Opening a Text File

Once you have established a reference to a particular text file, you can open it and begin reading from it or writing text to it. This is accomplished using the open for access command, using the following syntax.

```
set TargetFile to open for access file FileReference
```

TargetFile is a variable that will be used by successive commands when reading from or writing to the file being opened. *FileReference* is the variable name previously assigned as the file reference. For example, the following statements set up a file reference and then open the file.

```
set MyFile to "Macintosh HD:Users:Jerry:Documents:GroceryList.txt"
set WorkingFile to open for access file MyFile
```

In this example, a variable named WorkingFile is assigned a reference that points to MyFile (e.g., "Macintosh HD:Users:Jerry:Documents:GroceryList.txt"). The equivalent POSIX example of this example is shown here:

```
set MyFile to POSIX "/Users/Jerry/Documents/GroceryList.txt"
set WorkingFile to open for access POSIX file MyFile
```

Note the requirement to include the POSIX keyword after the open for access command. Once a file is opened, you can read from it or write to it.

 TRAP Whenever you open a file, you must also remember to close it. If you forget, the file may get corrupted and you may not be able to access it the next time you try to open it. To close a file that has been opened, you will need to execute the close access command, as explained a little later in this chapter.

Choosing a File Using the choose file Command

Instead of programmatically opening a text file using the open for access command, AppleScript provides you with access to the choose file command, which displays a standard Choose a File dialog window from which the user can navigate the Mac OS X file system and select a file. The choose file command supports a number of optional parameters, including:

- with prompt. Displays a message prompt.
- of type. Specifies the types of files that are displayed.
- default location. Sets the default location.

- invisibles. A Boolean value indicating whether invisible files and folders are displayed.
- multiple selections allowed. A Boolean value indicating whether the user can select more than one file.

When used without any parameters, a generic Choose a File dialog window, like the one shown in Figure 7.6, is displayed.

FIGURE 7.6

Using the choose file command to display a dialog from which the user can specify a file selection.

Using any combination of the optional parameters, you can customize the Choose a File dialog window to meet your particular needs. For example, the following statement will display the Choose a File dialog window, displaying a custom prompt and setting the default location to the user's Documents folder.

```
set TargetFile to choose file ¬
    with prompt "Select a document file with which you want to work" ¬
    default location (path to documents folder)
```

Once you have made a file selection, the name of the selected file is returned as an alias, which you can then use to open the file and read from or write to it.

HINT

You can select a folder using the choose folder command. An alias is returned for the selected folder.

Closing a Text File

When your AppleScript is done working with a file, it should close it. Closing a file ensures that any data not yet written to the file gets written and prevents the file from becoming corrupted, which can happen if your script terminates without closing any open files. To close an open text file, use the close access command, which has the following syntax.

```
close access FileReference
```

FileReference is a variable that has been assigned the full path and filename of the file being closed. *FileReference* is established earlier in the script by the open for access command. For example, the following statements define the path and filename of a file, open the file, and then immediately close it.

```
set MyFile to "Macintosh HD:Users:Jerry:Documents:GroceryList.txt"
set WorkingFile to open for access file MyFile
close access WorkingFile
```

Reading from and Writing to Text Files

Okay, now you know the steps involved in setting up a file reference and then using that reference to open and then close the file. Let's look at what it takes to read from and write to a text file. To read from a file, you will need to use the read command. Similarly, to write to a file, you will need to use the write command.

Reading Text from a File

In the sections that follow, you will learn how to use the read command to retrieve the contents of a text file. In order to simplify things, let's assume up front that all examples of how to read from a file will be made using the text file shown here:

Assuming that you are keying in and trying out each of the examples covered in this chapter, there is no need for you to re-key the text file shown below. You will find a copy of this text file named ThreePigs.txt located on this book's companion website at www.courseptr.com/downloads.

```
Once upon a time there were three little pigs who lived happily near the edge of a
great forest. One day a wolf appeared and told the pigs that he had just eaten
a large goat but that tomorrow he would be back to eat one of the three pigs.
In a panic the three little pigs scurried off to build houses in which they
would hide from the wolf. The first pig quickly built his house out of
straw and slept the afternoon away dreaming of Disneyland. A short time later
the second pig finished building a house made of sticks and ran off to play
tennis. But the third little pig worked hard all day and night building his
house out of brick. When his work was done, he went inside to sleep the
afternoon away. When the wolf returned that evening he quickly began to eat his
way through the first little pig's house, but the taste of straw made him feel
sick so he moved on to the second little pig's house, which he began to quickly
```

eat his way through. However, the wolf soon got a splinter in his lip and angrily left. Finally, the wolf arrived at the third little pig's house and broke down the door to find that the third pig, having built his house in the middle of an open field with no shade, had been baked alive by the heat of the hot afternoon sun, once again proving that when it comes to building a house, nothing is more important than finding a good location.

In order to read from a file, you must first open it, as demonstrated here:

```
set StoryFile to (path to documents folder as string) & ¬
    "ThreePigs.txt"
set InputFile to open for access file StoryFile
```

Here, the variable `InputFile` has been set up to reference `ThreePigs.txt`, which has been stored in the `users` folder. By default, all files opened as demonstrated above are made ready for reading. So, you can now use the `read` command, as demonstrated here:

```
set EntireStory to read InputFile as string
```

This statement reads the entire contents of the `ThreePigs.txt` file and stores it in a variable named `EntireStory`. The `read` command, by default, reads the entire file in a single operation. As previously mentioned, once your AppleScript has finished working with a file that has been opened, it is critical that you remember to close it. This is accomplished using the `close access` command, which has the following syntax.

```
close access FileReference
```

`FileReference` is a variable that has been assigned the full path and filename of the file being closed. In the case of the preceding example, you would close the `ThreePigs.txt` file as shown here:

```
close access InputFile
```

To prove that the entire `ThreePigs.txt` file has been read and stored in the `EntireStory` variable, let's use the `display dialog` command to display the contents of the variable, as demonstrated here:

```
display dialog EntireStory
```

When fully assembled, the previous statements come together to produce the following AppleScript.

```
set StoryFile to (path to users folder as string) & "ThreePigs.txt"
set InputFile to open for access file StoryFile
```

```
set EntireStory to read InputFile as string
close access InputFile

display dialog EntireStory
```

When executed, the dialog window shown in Figure 7.7 is displayed.

Once upon a time there were three little pigs who lived happily near the edge of a great forest. One day a wolf appeared and told the pigs that he had just eaten a large goat but that tomorrow he would be back to eat one of the three pigs. In a panic the three little pigs scurried off to build houses in which they would hide from the wolf. The first pig quickly built his house out of straw and slept the afternoon away dreaming of Disneyland. A short time later the second pig finished building a house made of sticks and ran off to play tennis. But the third little pig worked hard all day and night building his house out of brick. When his work was done, he went inside to sleep the afternoon away. When the wolf returned that evening he quickly began to eat his way through the first little pig's house, but the taste of straw made him feel sick so he moved on to the second little pig's house, which he began to quickly eat his way through. However, the wolf soon got a splinter in his lip and angrily left. Finally, the wolf arrived at the third little pig's house and broke down the door to find that the third pig, having built his house in the middle of a open field with no shade, had been baked alive by the heat of the hot afternoon sun, once again proving that when it comes to building a house, nothing is more important than finding a good location.

Cancel | OK

FIGURE 7.7

Proof that the AppleScript has read the entire contents of ThreePigs.txt.

Reading Portions of a Text File

In addition to allowing you to read an entire text file, the read command also accepts a number of arguments that allow limited read operations to just portions of the text file. These arguments are outlined in Table 7.3.

To best understand how to work with the arguments listed in Table 7.3, it helps to see a few examples, as provided here:

```
set StoryFile to (path to users folder as string) & "ThreePigs.txt"
set InputFile to open for access file StoryFile
set Exert to (read InputFile for 16)  -- Once upon a time
set Exert to (read InputFile for 24)  -- there were three little pigs
set Exert to (read InputFile until return as string)  -- Remainder of story
close access InputFile
```

TABLE 7.3	READ ARGUMENTS
Argument	**Description**
`as` *type*	Coerces a value to the specified data type
`to` *offset*	Reads the file up to the specified character position
`for` *length*	Reads the specified number of characters
`from` *offset*	Reads the file beginning at the specified character position
`using delimiter` *character*	Sets a delimiter character
`using delimiters` *list*	Sets a list of delimiter characters
`before` *character*	Reads the file up to but not including the first instance of the specified character
`until` *character*	Reads the file up to and including the first instance of the specified character

The string read by each `read` operation is noted to the right of each set statement as a comment.

You can also mix and match different `read` arguments, using them in combination, as demonstrated here:

```
set StoryFile to (path to users folder as string) & "ThreePigs.txt"
set InputFile to open for access file StoryFile
set Exert to (read InputFile from 18 to 91)
```

When this example is run, the `read` command skips the first 17 characters and then reads the 18th through the 91st characters in the text file.

Writing Text to a File

Writing to a text file is not too different from reading from it. You still have to set up a reference and open the file. Once this is done, you can use the `write` command, using the syntax outlined next, to write to the specified text file.

```
write TextOutput to FileReference
```

TextOutput represents the text output to be written to the text file as specified by *FileReference*. For example, the following statements demonstrate how to write output to a text file named `GroceryList.txt`.

```
set GroceryFile to (path to desktop folder as string) & "GroceryList.txt"
set OutputFile to open for access file GroceryFile with write permission
```

```
write "Bread\rButter\rCheese\rMilk\rOrange Juice" to OutputFile
close access OutputFile
```

Here, a text string is written to `GroceryFile.txt`, which is saved to the user's desktop. Since the `open for access` command automatically opens the file for reading, it is necessary to add `with write permission` to the end of the second statement to open the file in write mode. If the `GroceryFile.txt` file already exists on the user's desktop, it will be overwritten. If it does not already exist, it will be created and then written to. Also, take note of the addition of the `\r` escape characters embedded inside the text string. These escape characters were added to control the format of the text string, spreading it out over five lines. Figure 7.8 shows how this file will look when opened using the TextEdit application.

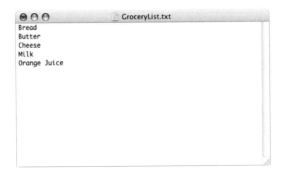

FIGURE 7.8

Examining the contents of `GroceryFile.txt`.

The `write` command accepts a number of arguments that affect its operations. These arguments are outlined in Table 7.4.

TABLE 7.4	WRITE COMMAND ARGUMENTS
Argument	**Description**
as *type*	Coerces a value to a the specified data type
for *length*	Writes a specific number of characters
starting at *offset*	Sets the character position where writing begins

Overwriting Existing File Contents

When performing a write operation, AppleScript will create a new text file if it does not already exist in the target folder. If the specified file already exists, AppleScript will automatically overwrite its contents. However, if the amount of text written to an existing file is less than the amount of text already stored in it, then some of the file's original data will remain in the file, which typically results in an ugly mess. Fortunately AppleScript provides you with a way of avoiding this situation using the set eof command. This command can be used to remove any preexisting data from the file.

The syntax of the set eof command is outlined here:

```
set eof of FileReference to IntegerValue
```

IntegerValue is a value in bytes that tells AppleScript how to set the length of the file. By setting *IntegerValue* to 0, you effectively remove any text previously written to it, as demonstrated here:

```
set eof of OutputFile to 0
```

Appending to the End of Text Files

If you want to add text to the end of a text file instead of overwriting its contents, then you will need to set things up so that the write command will begin writing its output starting at the end of the text file. To set this up, you will need to work with the get eof command, using the following syntax.

```
get eof FileReference
```

When executed, the get eof command retrieves a value representing the end of file location within the specified file. For example, the following example sets up a file reference, opens a file for writing, and then appends a text string to the end of the file. When done, the text file is closed.

```
set GroceryFile to (path to desktop folder as string) & "GroceryList.txt"
set OutputFile to open for access file GroceryFile with write permission
write "\rJelly\rHotdogs\rRice\rEggs\rBacon" to OutputFile ¬
    starting at (get eof OutputFile)
close access OutputFile
```

PRINTING TEXT FILES

Although you will not learn how to interact with and automate Mac OS X applications until Chapter 8, "Automating Mac OS X Applications," I thought I'd go ahead and show you how to use the TextEdit application to print text files that you generate with your AppleScripts. TextEdit is a free text editing Mac OS X application supplied as part of the operating system.

To interact with and control the TextEdit application, you will need to use the `tell` command to set up a code block in which you will embed commands that you want AppleScript to pass along to TextEdit for processing, as demonstrated here:

```
tell application "TextEdit"
    print (path to desktop folder as string) & "GroceryList.txt"
end tell
```

Here, TextEdit's `print` command is executed and passed the path and filename of the text file to be printed.

BACK TO THE APPLESCRIPT SHELL GAME

Okay, let's turn our attention back to the development of this chapter's project, the AppleScript Lottery Picker game. This game generates a random list of lottery numbers based on input provided by the player. This game leverages your newfound knowledge of how to interact with the Mac OS X file systems by providing the player with the option of printing (after saving) a listing of the lottery numbers generated by the game.

Designing the Game

The AppleScript Lottery Picker game will be created in 11 steps, as outlined here:

1. Create a new AppleScript and save it with a name of Lottery Picker.
2. Document the script and its purpose.
3. Declare the game's global variables.
4. Develop the overall controlling logic.
5. Document the location of the script's handlers.
6. Create the `GetPlayerInput()` handler.
7. Create the `GetTicketSize()` handler.
8. Create the `GetNoOfTickets()` handler.
9. Create the `CreateTicket()` handler.
10. Create the `GetRandomNumber()` handler.
11. Create the `PrintLotteryTickets()` handler.

Step 1: Creating a New AppleScript File

The first step in creating the AppleScript Lottery Picker game is to open the Script Editor application and create a new AppleScript file named Lottery Picker by following the steps outlined here:

1. Start the Script Editor application.
2. Click on the File menu and select the Save As option.

3. In the sheet window that appears, enter Lottery Picker in the Save As field and specify the location where you want to save the script file using the Where drop-down menu.
4. Click on the Save button.

Step 2: Providing High-Level Script Documentation

As with all the scripts that you have worked on in this book, the development of the AppleScript Lottery Picker game starts off by adding documentation to the script file that identifies the script and its purpose. This documentation will consist of embedded comment statements as well as descriptive text written to the Script Editor application's Description tab.

Adding External Descriptive Text

The text that is to be added to the Script Editor's Description tab view is provided here:

```
The AppleScript Lottery Picker Game  v1.0


This game generates a list of randomly generated lottery ticket numbers. The game will
generate up to 10 lottery ticket selections at a time, each of which can consist of up
to 10 numbers.

Developed by Jerry Lee Ford, Jr.
Copyright 2007
```

To make the name of the game stand out, highlight it and select the Bold option located on the Font menu, instructing the Script Editor to display this text in a bold font.

Embedding Comments Inside the Script

Next, add the following comment statements to the beginning of the AppleScript. These statements document the name of the script, its version, author, and creation date. In addition, a brief description of the script is also provided.

```
-------------------------------------------------------------------------
--
-- Script Name: AppleScript Lottery Picker Game.scpt
-- Version: 1.0
-- Author: Jerry Lee Ford, Jr.
-- Date: August 2007
--
-- Description: This AppleScript game generates a list of lottery ticket
-- numbers and will print the list if instructed by
```

```
-- the player to do so.
```

Step 3: Declaring High-Level Variables

Now it is time to define and initialize variables that are used throughout the AppleScript. This is accomplished by adding the following statements to the end of the script file.

```
-- Declare the following variable as having a global scope global GameTitle

-- Stores the list of lottery ticket numbers generated by the game set TicketList to ""

-- Tracks the number of tickets that have been generated set TicketCount to 0

-- Stores the game's name
set GameTitle to "AppleScript Lottery Picker"
```

For starters, a variable named GameTitle is declared as being global. This variable will be referenced throughout the script file, including from inside the script's handlers to provide a consistent title bar message in each of the game dialog windows. The next variable defined is TicketList. This variable will be used to build a string that contains the list of lottery numbers generated by the game. The next variable defined is TicketCount. It will be used to keep track of the number of lottery ticket numbers generated by the game. Lastly, the GameTitle variable is assigned a value of "AppleScript Lottery Picker".

Step 4: Developing the Script's Controlling Logic

With the script's high-level variables now defined and initialized, it is time to develop the programming statements that will be responsible for the overall execution of the AppleScript. The code statements that perform this part of the script are listed next and should be added to the end of the script file.

```
-- Call handler that prompts the player to specify the range
-- of lottery numbers from which lottery tickets numbers should be
--randomly selected
set Range to GetPlayerInput()

-- Call handler that prompts the player to specify how many numbers
-- it takes to make up one lottery ticket
set TicketSize to GetTicketSize()

-- Call handler that prompts the player to specify how many lottery
```

```
-- tickets are to be generated
set NoOfTickets to GetNoOfTickets()

-- This loop is responsible for managing the creation of the
-- appropriate number of lottery tickets, iterating once for each
-- ticket that is to be created
repeat NoOfTickets times

    -- Increment each time a new ticket is being generated
    set TicketCount to TicketCount + 1

    -- Call the handler responsible for generating individual
    -- lottery tickets
    set ticket to CreateTicket(Range, TicketSize)

    -- Format the display of individual lottery tickets
    if TicketCount < 10 then
        set ticket to TicketCount & ")   " & ticket
    else
        set ticket to TicketCount & ")   " & ticket
    end if

    -- Add the new number to the list of numbers generated by the game
    set TicketList to TicketList & ticket & return & return

end repeat

-- Display the list of lottery ticket numbers that have been generated
set reply to button returned of (display dialog ¬
    "Here are your Lottery Ticket numbers:" & return & return ¬
    & TicketList buttons {"OK", "Print"} with title GameTitle)

-- Check to see if the player has elected to print a list of the
-- lottery ticket numbers
if reply = "Print" then
    PrintLotteryTickets(TicketList)
end if
```

As you can see, the script's controlling logic incorporates a number of calls to various handlers that will be added to the script in subsequent steps. The first handler to be called is the `GetPlayerInput()` handler, which is responsible for prompting the player to specify the range of numbers that the game should use when generating lottery numbers. The value returned by `GetPlayerInput()` is stored in a variable named `Range`.

The `GetTicketSize()` handler is executed next. This handler is responsible for prompting the player to specify how many numbers are in each lottery ticket. The value returned by this handler is stored in the `TicketSize` variable. The `GetNoOfTickets()` handler is then called. This handler prompts the player to specify the number of lottery tickets to be purchased. The value returned by this handler is assigned to the `NoOfTickets` variable.

Next, a `repeat` statement code block is set up to repeat once for each lottery ticket that is to be created. Each time the loop iterates, the value assigned to `TicketCount` is incremented by one. Then the `CreateTicket()` handler is executed and passes the `Range` and `TicketSize` variables as arguments. This handler is responsible for generating a complete lottery ticket number set, which is returned and assigned to the `Ticket` variable. An `if` statement code block is then used to analyze the value of `TicketCount`. If its value is less than the value of `Ticket`, it is modified to be equal to the value of `TicketCount`, followed by a string made up of the right parenthesis character and three blank spaces followed by the original value assigned to `Ticket`. If the value of `TicketCount` is equal to 10, the value assigned to `Ticket` is still updated but this time the string containing the right parenthesis only has two blank spaces. The end result is a reformatted ticket that includes a number representing the number of the lottery ticket (e.g., 1, 2, 3...10), followed by the) character, a little blank space, and then the ticket's actual lottery numbers. Each time a new ticket number set is generated and reformatted, it is then appended to a string variable named `TicketList`. As a result, `TicketList` is ultimately assigned a formatted list of lottery ticket numbers.

The `repeat` loop code block ends once the last lottery ticket number set has been generated. This list of lottery numbers is then displayed in a dialog window. This window displays two buttons, OK and Print. An `if` statement code block is then set up to execute the `PrintLotteryTickets()` handler if the player elected to print the list of lottery ticket numbers created by the game.

Step 5: Documenting the Location of Handlers

The rest of this AppleScript consists of a collection of custom handlers. To help visually organize the contents of the scripts, add the following statement to the end of the script file.

```
--------------------------- HANDLER SECTION ---------------------------
```

These comment statements help to clearly separate the script's controlling logic from its handlers.

Step 6: Creating the GetPlayerInput() Handler

The first handler to be added to the AppleScript is the `GetPlayerInput()` handler. The code statements that make up this handler, shown next, should be added to the end of the script file. This handler prompts the player to specify the range of lottery ticket numbers the game should use when generating lottery numbers. This handler consists of a `repeat` statement code block that executes until the value assigned to `ValidInput` is set equal to `true`.

```
-- This handler prompts the player to tell the game the range of
-- numbers from which lottery ticket numbers should be selected
on GetPlayerInput()

        -- This variable is used to control loop execution
        set ValidInput to false

        repeat until ValidInput = true -- Loop until valid input is collected

            -- Prompt the player to specify the range of numbers to be used
            set NoRange to text returned of (display dialog ¬
                "What is the highest number that can be selected when " & ¬
                "creating a lottery ticket?" default answer "44" ¬
                buttons {"OK"} with title GameTitle)
            -- The range must be at least 3 and no larger than 59
            if (NoRange > 2) and (NoRange < 60) then
                set NoRange to NoRange as integer --Convert the player input
                return NoRange -- Return the player's input
            else -- Display an error message if the input is not valid
                display dialog "Error: You must enter an integer value " & ¬
                    "between 3 and 59" with title GameTitle
            end if

        end repeat

end GetPlayerInput
```

As you can see, the player's input is collected using a dialog window. A default value of 44 is provided. The player can click on the window's OK button to accept the suggested default value or overtype it with another value. An if statement code block is then set up to validate the player's input. If the player enters a value that is greater than 2 or less than 60, the value is returned back to the handler's calling statement as an integer value. Otherwise, an error message is displayed after which the loop iterates, prompting the player once again to specify the range of numbers to be used by the game when generating lottery numbers.

Step 7: Creating the GetTicketSize() Handler

The GetTicketSize() handler, shown next, should be added to the end of the script file. This handler is responsible for displaying a list of numbers that make up a complete lottery ticket and prompting the player to make a selection.

```
-- This handler prompts the player to specify how many numbers it takes
-- to make up a lottery ticket
on GetTicketSize()

    -- Use a list to populate the listbox control from which the
    -- player will specify how many numbers make up a lottery ticket
    set TicketSize to choose from list ¬
        {1, 2, 3, 4, 5, 6, 7, 8, 9, 10} ¬

        with prompt "How many numbers do you need to select for each" & ¬
" lottery ticket?" with title GameTitle

    -- If the player clicked on the Cancel button instead of selecting a
    -- number, then set 6 as the default
    if TicketSize = false then set TicketSize to 6

    -- Coerce the player's input into an integer
    set TicketSize to TicketSize as integer

    return TicketSize -- Return the player's input

end GetTicketSize
```

This handler begins by prompting the player to select from a list of 1 to 10 numbers using the choose from list command. If the player clicks on the Cancel button without making a selection, a default value of 6 is specified. Since the choose from list command returns a list representing the selected value, it must be converted to an integer before it is returned to the statement that called upon the handler to execute.

Step 8: Creating the GetNoOfTickets() Handler

The code statements that make up the GetNoOfTickets() handler, shown next, should be added to the end of the script file. This handler is responsible for prompting the player to specify the number of tickets that are to be purchased.

```
-- This handler prompts the player to tell the game how many lottery
-- tickets the player plans on purchasing
on GetNoOfTickets()

    -- Use a list to populate the listbox from which the player will
    -- specify how many lottery tickets are to be purchased
    set NoTickets to choose from list ¬
        {1, 2, 3, 4, 5, 6, 7, 8, 9, 10} ¬
        with prompt "How many lottery tickets are you going " & ¬
        "to buy?" with title GameTitle

    -- If the player clicked on the Cancel button instead of selecting a
    -- number, then set 1 as the default
    if NoTickets = false then set NoTickets to 1

    -- Coerce the player's input into an integer
    set NoTickets to NoTickets as integer

    return NoTickets -- Return the player's input

end GetNoOfTickets
```

The handler uses the choose from list command to display a list of numbers from 1 to 10. As with the previous handler, a default value is assigned in the event the player clicks on the dialog window's Cancel button instead of making a selection. Since the choose from list command returns a list representing the selected value, it must be converted to an integer before it is returned to the statement that called upon the handler to execute.

Step 9: Creating the CreateTicket() Handler

The code statements that make up the CreateTicket() handler, shown next, should be added to the end of the script file. This handler is responsible for creating one complete lottery ticket number set, which is then returned back to the statement that called upon the handler to execute.

```
-- This handler is responsible for generating one complete lottery ticket
-- number set
on CreateTicket(Range, TicketSize)

    -- Define and initialize variables used within the handler
    set ValidTicket to false
    set NumberCount to 0
    set TempList to {}

    -- Loop until a valid ticket number set has been generated
    repeat until ValidTicket = true

        -- Retrieve a randomly generated number within the range
        -- specified by the player
        set randomNumber to GetRandomNumber(Range)

        -- Ensure that the number has not already been selected
        if randomNumber is not in TempList then

            -- Pad single digit numbers with an extra blank space
            if randomNumber < 10 then
                set randomNumber to " " & randomNumber
            end if

            -- Add the random number to the list of numbers
            -- generated for the lottery ticket
            set TempList to TempList & randomNumber & "   "

            -- Keep track of the number of valid lottery ticket numbers
            -- generated so far
            set NumberCount to NumberCount + 1

        end if

        -- Determine when a complete ticket's worth of numbers has
        -- been generated
        if NumberCount = TicketSize then
            set ValidTicket to true
```

```
        end if

    end repeat

    return TempList -- Return the completed list of lottery ticket numbers

end CreateTicket
```

The handler begins by defining several variables. `ValidTicket` is assigned a value of `false` and will be used to control the execution of the handler loop. `NumberCount` is set to zero and will be used to keep track of the number of lottery ticket number sets as they are created. `TempList` is a list that is set up as an empty string. `TempList` will be used to store all of the numbers that make up the lottery ticket number set being created.

Next a `repeat` loop code block is set up to execute until a complete lottery ticket number set has been created. Within the loop, the `GetRandomNumber()` handler is called. This handler generates a random number between 1 and the value of the upper level range previously collected from the player and passed to the handler as `Range`. The value returned by `GetRandomNumber()` is assigned to `randomNumber`. This value is then analyzed by a number of `if` statement code blocks. First, the value of `randomNumber` is checked to see if it is stored within `TempList`. If it is found in `TempList`, then the number has previously been added to the lottery ticket number set and should be discarded since an individual lottery ticket cannot contain the same number more than once. If the number is not already in `TempList`, then it is examined to see if it is less than 10 and if it is, it is pre-appended with a 0 to yield a two-digit value (e.g., 01, 02, 03, 04, 05, 06, 07, 08, and 09). Once the game has ensured that the random number consists of two digits, it is appended to the end of `TempList` and the value assigned to `NumberCount` is incremented by 1. At the end of each execution of the loop, the value of `NumberCount` and `TicketSize` are compared to see if they are equal, and if they are, then the lottery ticket number set is complete. If this is the case, the value of `ValidTicket` is set to true, and as a result, the loop will stop executing, and the `TempList` will be returned back to the statement that called upon the handler to execute.

Step 10: Creating the GetRandomNumber() Handler

The code statements that comprise the `GetRandomNumber()` handler are shown next and should be added to the end of the AppleScript file. This handler is responsible for generating a random number between 1 and the value of the upper-level range previously collected from the player and passed to the handler as `Range`.

```
-- This handler generates a random number representing a lottery
-- ticket number
```

```
on GetRandomNumber(Range)

    -- Generate a random number representing a lottery ticket
    set randomNo to random number from 1 to Range

    return randomNo -- Return the random number to the calling statement

end GetRandomNumber
```

The `random number` command is used to generate the game's random numbers, which are then returned back to the calling statement.

Step 11: Creating the PrintLotteryTickets() Handler

The last handler to be added to the game is the `PrintLotteryTickets()` handler, which is shown next. This handler processes one argument, `TicketList`, which is a string variable containing a formatting string representing all of the lottery ticket number sets generated by the game. The handler then saves a temporary text file containing these numbers and uses the TextEdit application to print it out.

```
-- This handler uses the TextEdit application to print a list of the
-- lottery ticket numbers generated by the game
on PrintLotteryTickets(TicketList)

    -- Save the lottery ticket as a temporary text file
    set LotteryFile to (path to temporary items folder as string) & ¬
        "Lottery.txt"

    -- Open the file for writing
    set OutputFile to open for access file LotteryFile ¬
        with write permission

    -- Overwrite any text already written to the file
    set eof of OutputFile to 0

    -- Finish formatting text output
    set TicketList to ¬
        "Lottery Ticket Numbers" & return & return & TicketList

    -- Write the lottery ticket to the file
```

```
    write TicketList to OutputFile

    -- Close the text file
    close access OutputFile

    -- Use TextEdit to print the lottery ticket
    tell application "TextEdit"
        print LotteryFile
    end tell

    -- Notify the player that the list of lottery ticket numbers has been
    -- sent to the printer
    display dialog "Your lottery ticket numbers have been submitted " & ¬
        "to the printer." buttons {"OK"} with title GameTitle

end PrintLotteryTickets
```

The handler starts out by establishing a reference to the operating system's temporary items folder to which a string of "Lottery.txt" is appended, creating a complete path name. Next, the file is opened for writing and the set eof command is used to ensure that the Lottery.txt file is overridden if it already exists. A string representing a header is then written to the file followed by the list of lottery tickets stored in TicketList.

Once the lottery ticket information has been written to the text file, the file is closed. Next, the tell command is used to send the print command to the TextEdit application. Finally, the display dialog command is used to display a dialog window that informs the player that the list of lottery ticket number sets has been sent to the printer.

Testing the Execution of AppleScript Lottery Picker Game

All right, you now have everything you need to develop the AppleScript Lottery Picker game. Assuming that you didn't make any typos, the game should run as described at the beginning of this chapter.

SUMMARY

In this chapter you learned how to open and close files and to read from and write to files. You also learned how to interact with the Mac OS X file systems and to work with relative and absolute file references. Using the information presented in this chapter, you now possess the knowledge required to generate reports as well as text and log files.

Now, before you move on to Chapter 8, why don't you set aside a little extra time to improve the AppleScript Lottery Picker game by tackling the following list of challenges.

CHALLENGES

1. As currently written, the game does not provide the player with any instruction on how the game is played. Consider adding specific instructions to the text stored in the Description tab and then saving the game as an AppleScript application with the `Startup screen` option enabled to provide this information.

2. Rather than just allowing the player to print the lottery ticket number sets, consider adding a Save File button and allowing the player to save the lottery numbers as a text file at the destination folder of her choice.

3. As currently written, the game assumes the player understands that when specifying the highest number that can be selected on a lottery ticket, the number specified must be at least 3 but no larger than 59. Consider modifying the game to make this requirement explicitly clear.

AUTOMATING MAC OS X
APPLICATIONS

I n this chapter, you will learn the basic steps involved in taking control of and automating Mac OS X applications. This includes learning more about how to use application dictionaries to locate the classes and commands that you will need to work with to automate these applications. By learning how to incorporate the functionality of other applications into your AppleScripts, you can significantly extend the reach of your AppleScripts to build automated workflows that can save you time and help you to work more efficiently. In short, by developing AppleScripts that leverage the capabilities of different Mac OS X applications, you can develop your own scripts and applications that are greater than the sum of their individual parts. On top of all this, you will learn how to create your next AppleScript game, the AppleScript Number Guessing game.

Specifically, you will learn how to:

- Target and send commands to Mac OS applications
- Locate and take advantage of AppleScripts already on your computer or available on the Internet
- Search application dictionaries to find application classes, elements, properties, and commands
- Automate Finder, TextEdit, Mail, DVD Player, Safari, iTunes, Help View, and other Mac OS X applications

Project Preview: The AppleScript Number Guessing Game

This chapter's game project is the AppleScript Number Guessing game. This game challenges the player to guess a randomly generated number in the range of 1 to 100 in as few guesses as possible. The game begins by generating a secret random number and prompting the player to guess it, as demonstrated in Figure 8.1.

FIGURE 8.1

To play the player must type in a number from 1 through 100.

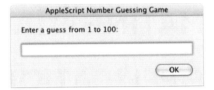

If the player guesses the game's secret number, she wins. Otherwise, the game displays a message that helps guide the player's next guess. For example, Figure 8.2 shows the message displayed in the event the player's guess is too high.

FIGURE 8.2

The player's guess was too high.

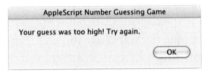

Similarly, Figure 8.3 shows the message displayed in the event that the player's guess is too low.

FIGURE 8.3

The player's guess was too low.

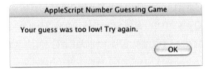

The game continues to prompt the player for guesses until the player finally guesses the game's secret number. When this happens, a dialog window similar to the one shown in Figure 8.4 displays.

FIGURE 8.4

Game statistics display at the end of each game.

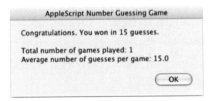

The window lets the player know she has won and how many guesses it took to win the game. In addition, the window also displays the number of games that the player has played so far and the average number of guesses that the player has made per game.

Once the player dismisses the dialog window by clicking on its OK button, the game prompts the player to start another round of play, as demonstrated in Figure 8.5.

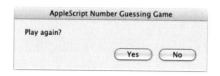

FIGURE 8.5

The game allows the player to play as many times as she wants.

The player must click on the Yes button to start a new round of play. Clicking on the No button initiates game termination. If the player elects to play a new round, the game will generate a new random number and then begin prompting the player to start making guesses. If the player elects to stop play, the dialog window shown in Figure 8.6 displays.

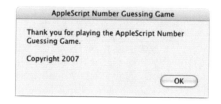

FIGURE 8.6

The closing window of the AppleScript Number Guessing game.

Game play ends when the player clicks on the window's OK button.

BOSSING AROUND YOUR MAC OS X APPLICATIONS

The primary focus of this chapter is to show you how to develop AppleScripts that take control of and automate the actions of Mac OS X applications. Automating the operation of applications is the primary reason that AppleScript exists. As such, I would be remiss if I did not provide you with a number of different and varied examples of AppleScripts that automate different Mac OS X applications. To cover as much ground as possible, I am going to avoid going into too much depth with any one particular application.

After reading this chapter and re-creating and experimenting with each of the examples that will be presented, you should have a strong understanding of the basic steps involved in automating any Mac OS X application. As a result, you will be well on your way to learning how to unlock the true power of AppleScript programming: the development of automated workflows that combine the capabilities of one or more Mac OS X applications to automate a task that no one application alone is capable of doing.

TAKING ADVANTAGE OF APPLESCRIPTS TO WHICH YOU ALREADY HAVE ACCESS

As you already know, any new Mac OS X installation automatically includes AppleScript. In addition, it also includes many dozen AppleScripts. You can access and immediately start running these AppleScripts. In addition, you can edit and review them to see what makes them tick. You will find most of these AppleScripts located in /Library/Scripts. You will also find most of them in the Script menu, assuming that you have turned it on as described in Chapter 1, "AppleScript Basics."

Scripts on the Scripts menu are organized into categories, like Finder Scripts, Mail Scripts, Navigation Scripts, Printing Scripts, and Script Editor Scripts. As an example of the types of AppleScripts you will find here, look inside the Navigation Scripts collection. Here you will find scripts that when executed open an assortment of new windows. In addition, you will find a script named Open Special Folder. When executed, the Open Special Folder Script displays a listing of Mac OS X special folders in a dialog window, as demonstrated in Figure 8.7.

FIGURE 8.7

Running the Open Special Folders AppleScript.

You can instruct the AppleScript to open any special folder that is listed by selecting it and then clicking on the OK button.

The ultimate source of free AppleScripts is the Internet. In particular, I would point you to http://www.apple.com/applescript/apps/. This Apple web page, shown in Figure 8.8, displays a list of scriptable Mac OS X applications. You can click on the icons representing each application to learn more about the application. In addition, when you click on many of the application's icons, collections of free AppleScripts await you.

FIGURE 8.8

There is no shortage of scriptable applications on Mac OS X.

FIGURING OUT HOW TO COMMUNICATE WITH MAC OS X APPLICATIONS

You can create AppleScripts to automate any scriptable Mac OS X applications. This includes both Mac OS X applications supplied by Apple as well as any scriptable third-party applications that are installed on your computer. You will find that in many instances you can automate a particular application feature using just a handful of lines of program code. This chapter will provide you with a number of working examples that demonstrate how to interact with and automate applications, including:

- TextEdit
- iTunes
- Finder
- Terminal
- DVD Player
- Mail
- QuickTime

- Safari
- System Events
- Help Viewer

Digging into Application Dictionaries

Scriptable Mac OS X applications publish script terminology in application dictionaries, which you can access using the Script Editor's Dictionary Browser window. Without the Dictionary Browser, or a similar application, determining what classes, commands, and properties are supported by a given application would be extremely challenging. While many applications support similar commands such as open or make, these commands may vary in regards to the actions they perform. In addition, the same command may exist in different applications under different names, making it difficult to identify. Since different applications support different terminologies, you must become comfortable working with the Dictionary Browser application if you are going to be successful in developing AppleScripts that automate the actions of other Mac OS X applications. For example, Figure 8.9 shows the contents of the TextEdit application's dictionary.

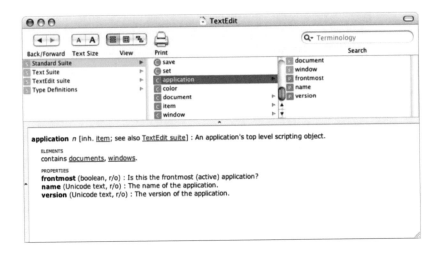

FIGURE 8.9

Examining terminology stored in the TextEdit dictionary.

Dictionary terminology is organized into suites, each of which contains different collections of related classes and commands. Many application classes also provide access to various properties. Typically, when you start looking through an application's dictionary for the first time, you will want to begin by examining the application class entry. This class represents the application itself. Within the class entry, you will find elements belonging to that class. For example, the TextEdit application's application class contains an element named document. This element is used to create new text documents, and it is required to perform most any TextEdit task.

Each dictionary element has a definition that you can read to learn about the element and its purpose. Properties associated with different elements identify application attributes, which you can examine and modify. Take for example Figure 8.10, which shows properties belonging to the document element. These properties include modified, name, and path.

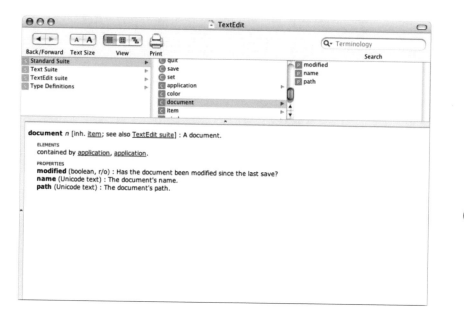

FIGURE 8.10

Examining properties belonging to the TextEdit document element.

Application dictionaries also identify commands to which the application will respond and execute. For example, TextEdit supports the make command, which can be used to create a new document. The make command has a required argument named new.

Using the class, command, and property terminology outlined in an application's dictionary, you have access to all the information required to create AppleScripts that can interact with and automate the operation of an application. For example, the following AppleScript uses the TextEdit terminology explained above to take control of the TextEdit application and create a new document upon which some text is written.

```
tell application "TextEdit"
   activate
   make new document at the front
   set text of front document to "Once upon a time in a far away land..."
end tell
```

Here, the `tell` command code block targets the TextEdit application and then activates it. Next, the `make` command is executed, generating a new TextEdit document. Take note of the inclusion of the `new` keyword. You should also note that `at the front` has been added to the end of the `make` statement, instructing TextEdit to display the new document on top of any other text windows that might already be open. The last statement inside the code block writes a test string to the TextEdit document using the `set` command to assign a string to the document's `text` property.

When executed, this AppleScript activates the TextEdit application and writes text to a new document, as demonstrated in Figure 8.11.

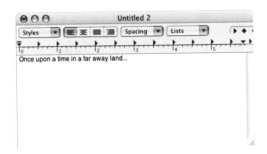

FIGURE 8.11

An example of an AppleScript that automates the TextEdit application.

Using Universal Application Commands

AppleScript supports several universal commands that you can use when interacting with any Mac OS X application. Table 8.1 lists each of these commands and provides a high-level description of their purpose.

TABLE 8.1	UNIVERSAL APPLICATION COMMANDS
Command	**Description**
activate	Starts the application if it is not already running and brings it to the forefront of any other applications
quit	Closes the application
launch	Starts the application but does not bring it to the forefront

Since these commands are universal, you will not find them defined in any individual application's dictionary. Fortunately, there are only three of them so it should not be too hard to remember what they are and what their purpose is.

Sending Commands to Mac OS X Applications

In order for AppleScript to interact with and control a Mac OS X application, it must have a way of communicating with it. This is accomplished through the `tell` command, which has the following syntax.

```
tell application ApplicationName
    statements
end tell
```

ApplicationName is the name of the application to be targeted and *statements* represents embedded code statements that are executed against the targeted application when the `tell` statement code block is executed. For example, earlier in this chapter you saw an example of how to use the `tell` command to interact with and control the execution of the TextEdit application.

Each statement embedded inside the `tell` statement code block is directed to the specified application in the form of inter-application messages. The target application will then attempt to process these messages. However, any messages not recognized by the application (unsupported terminology) will not be processed by the application. If this happens, the commands will be ignored, leaving it to AppleScript to process them. If AppleScript cannot process the command, an error will be generated.

AUTOMATING MAC OS X APPLICATIONS

When learning how to use AppleScript to develop scripts that automate different types of Mac OS X applications, it helps to have a large number of working examples from which to learn. In the sections that follow, I will provide you with a number of different sample AppleScripts, spanning an assortment of Mac OS X applications. This approach will provide you with a broad view of AppleScript's capabilities and hopefully spur your interest in different ways that you can leverage AppleScript to develop more efficient automated processes.

Using iTunes to Play Music

iTunes is a media player created by Apple and supplied as a free application on Mac OS X. iTunes is a music management application that organizes and plays digital music and audio and video files. iTunes is very scriptable, allowing you to develop AppleScripts that can, for example, manage tracks, playlists, and control the operation of iTunes. For example, using the iTunes `play` command, you can write a small AppleScript that plays the most recently listened to song, as demonstrated here:

```
tell application "iTunes"
     play
end tell
```

With very little effort, you can modify this example to play a specific track in any playlist, as demonstrated here:

```
tell application "iTunes"
     play track 5 of playlist "MyFavorites"
end tell
```

Here, an AppleScript has been set up to play the fifth track in a playlist named MyFavorites. Using iTunes commands like play, pause, and stop, you can exercise precise control over music playback.

Automating Finder Tasks

As you learned back in Chapter 7, "Accessing Files and Folders," AppleScript has built-in capabilities for opening, closing, and reading from and writing to files. However, AppleScript cannot, for example, rename, delete, or move files. Instead, most AppleScript programmers rely on the Finder application to perform file and folder administration tasks.

As this section will demonstrate, Finder is a very scriptable application. Because Finder is so useful and flexible, there is not enough room in this section to cover all its capabilities. Instead, I have chosen to provide you with a number of specific examples that together will provide you with a good understanding of Finder's scriptable capabilities.

In this first example, an AppleScript has been set up to activate Finder and then open a Finder window displaying the contents of the user's desktop.

```
tell application "Finder"

     activate
     open desktop

end tell
```

As you can see, the real work performed by this AppleScript is done using the Finder's open command, which takes as an argument the resource to be opened. Figure 8.12 demonstrates how the window that Finder opens looked when run on my computer.

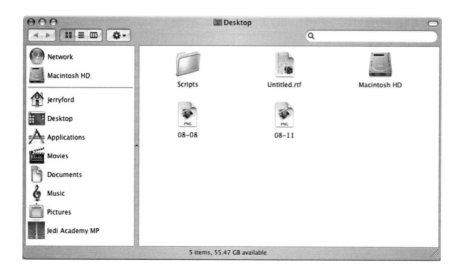

FIGURE 8.12

Telling Finder to display the contents of the desktop folder.

This next example uses Finder's count command to return a value representing the number of files located on the user's desktop and then displays this number in a dialog window.

```
tell application "Finder"

    set FileTotal to count of every file in the desktop
    display dialog "There are " & FileTotal & ¬
        " files on your desktop" buttons {"OK"}

end tell
```

HINT The count command retrieves a numeric count of the number of elements for a particular class. In the case of the previous example, the file class is referenced.

In the following example, an AppleScript has been set up to open a specific file.

```
tell application "Finder"

    activate
    open (path to pictures folder as string) & "Kids.jpg"

end tell
```

In this example, the open command is used to open and display the contents of a file. Because Mac OS X natively supports JPEG files, the image file is opened and displayed, as demonstrated in Figure 8.13.

FIGURE 8.13

Telling Finder to open and display a JPEG file.

Finder also provides you with access to commands for creating new files and folders. For example, the following AppleScript uses the make command to create a new folder (based on the folder class) on the user's desktop.

```
tell application "Finder"

    make new folder at desktop with properties {name:"MyFiles"}

end tell
```

As this example demonstrates, a name can be assigned to a new folder by referencing a record and assigning a new folder name as a string assigned to the name key.

You can also use Finder's `copy` and `move` commands to copy and move files and folders from one place to another. For example, the following AppleScript checks to see if a folder named `MyFiles` exists on the user's desktop, and creates the folder if it does not already exist. Then Finder's `move` command is then used to move every file located on the user's desktop into the `MyFiles` folder.

```
tell application "Finder"

    if not (the folder "MyFiles" of desktop exists) then
        make new folder at desktop with properties {name:"MyFiles"}
    end if
    move every file of desktop to folder "MyFiles" of desktop

end tell
```

In addition to the `copy` and `move` commands, you will find a number of other useful file and folder administration commands listed in Finder's dictionary. These commands include `sort`, `delete`, `make`, and `print`.

This final example demonstrates how to use Finder to empty Mac OS X trash.

```
tell application "Finder"

    empty trash

end tell
```

As you can see, the `tell` statement code block contains a single statement that executes the `empty trash` command.

Because Finder is such an enormously helpful application, capable of handling many different types of tasks, I felt it necessary to provide you with a number of different examples. Hopefully, this section has impressed upon you the importance of learning how to work with this application. As such, I strongly recommend you set aside a little time to peruse Finder's application dictionary to get a better understanding of its scriptable capabilities.

Executing Command-Line Commands

If you are used to working with the UNIX command prompt, then you will be pleased to learn that the Terminal application, which provides a command-line interface to the UNIX command shell, is also scriptable. Specifically the Terminal application provides access to a command named `do script`, which you can use to execute any UNIX command or shell script.

For example, the following AppleScript demonstrates how to activate a Terminal session and then execute the do script command.

```
tell application "Terminal"
     activate
     do script "ls > DirList.txt"
end tell
```

 HINT ls is a UNIX command that lists the contents of the current working directory. In UNIX, the > character is a redirection operator that takes the output of one command and passes it to another resource, typically another command or a file.

Here, the do script command is used to execute the UNIX ls command. The output generated by the ls command is then saved to a text file named DirList.txt in the current working directory.

Playing DVDs

DVD Player is an application that is supplied as part of Mac OS X and used to play DVDs. This application supplies a number of commands that you can use to control DVD playback, including play dvd, pause dvd, stop dvd, and eject dvd. The following AppleScript provides an example of how to automate the DVD Player application.

```
tell application "DVD Player"
     activate
     set viewer size to max
     set controller visibility to false
     play dvd
end tell
```

Here, the DVD Player application is activated. Next, the DVD Player application class's viewer size property is set to max to maximize the display of the DVD Player application. Next, the controller visibility property is set equal to false, which tells the DVD Player application not to display its controller window. Finally, the play dvd command is executed to play the currently loaded DVD.

Sending Mail

Another scriptable application that you may want to automate using AppleScript is the Mail application, which you can use to create and send automated e-mail messages, as demonstrated here:

```
tell application "Mail"
    set MessageText to make new outgoing message
    tell MessageText to make new to recipient
    set sender of MessageText to "jlf04@yahoo.com"
    set subject of MessageText to "Reader Comment"
    set content of MessageText to "I really like your new book."
    set address of recipient of MessageText to "jerry@tech-publishing.com"
    send MessageText
end tell
```

Here, the `tell` command is used to target the mail application. The first statement inside the `tell` statement code block uses the `make` command to create a new e-mail message using the `outgoing message` class. Then the `make` command is used to create a `recipient` object. Next, the following properties, all belonging to the `outgoing message` class, are set. The first property is `sender`, which is assigned a text string representing the e-mail account being used to send the e-mail. The second property is `subject`, which assigns a text string that will be used to add a subject header to the e-mail. The third property is `content`, which is assigned a text string representing the text of the e-mail message. Next, the `recipient` class's `address` property is assigned a text string representing the e-mail address to which the e-mail will be sent. Finally, the `send` command is used to submit the e-mail to the Mail application, which will then send out the e-mail.

Playing QuickTime Movies

Apple's QuickTime Player is a multimedia Mac OS X application. QuickTime can be used to play digital video and music and display text and image files. As the following example demonstrates, QuickTime is highly scriptable.

```
set SelectedFile to ¬
    choose file with prompt ¬
        "Select a movie" default location (path to movies folder)

set SelectedFile to SelectedFile as string

tell application "QuickTime Player"

    activate
    open file SelectedFile
    play movie

end tell
```

Here, an AppleScript has been developed that displays the Choose a File dialog window, prompting the user to specify the name of a movie file. Once the user has located and selected a movie file and then clicks on the window's Choose button, the AppleScript will start Quick-Time and load the selected movie into the movie player, as demonstrated in Figure 8.14.

FIGURE 8.14

Using AppleScript to Start QuickTime and load a movie specified by the user.

The keys to making this AppleScript work are QuickTime's open command, which opens a file, and QuickTime's play command, which plays the movie selected by the user.

Telling Safari to Load Web Pages

Safari is a web browser developed by Apple for its Mac OS X operating system, but has since been made available to Windows users as well. It is enormously popular with Mac OS X users. As the following example demonstrates, Safari is also scriptable.

```
tell application "Safari"
    activate
    open location "http://www.courseptr.com"
end tell
```

Here, the open command is used to load the http://www.courseptr.com URL. Using the example outlined above, it would very easy to create an AppleScript that provides the user with access to online help, which might be accessed by clicking on a dialog window button.

Automating System Events

Mac OS X runs a special behind-the-scenes application known as System Events. System Events is active at all times and is responsible for starting the operating system at boot time and for managing the execution of other Mac OS X applications. System Events is highly scriptable.

For example, the following AppleScript demonstrates how to tell the System Events application to put the computer into a sleep state.

```
tell application "System Events"
    sleep
end tell
```

You can just as easily substitute the sleep command with the log out command to log out the current user, the restart command to restart the computer, and the shut down command to perform a system shutdown. These commands make up the System Events application dictionary's power suite.

The following example demonstrates how to use the name property belonging to the System Events application's process class (part of the processes suite) to retrieve a list of active processes running on the computer, as demonstrated in Figure 8.15.

Please make your selection:

```
loginwindow
Dock
SystemUIServer
Finder
iTunesHelper
UniversalAccess
System Events
HPEventHandler
HP IO Classic Proxy 2
HP IO Classic Proxy
DashboardClient
DashboardClient
DashboardClient
DashboardClient
DashboardClient
Script Editor
TextEdit
```

Cancel   OK

FIGURE 8.15

Using an AppleScript to display a list of active processes.

```
tell application "System Events"
    set AppList to name every process
end tell

set reply to choose from list AppList
set reply to reply as string
```

```
tell application reply
    activate
end tell
```

The list of active processes is displayed as a dialog window generated by the `choose from list` command. The window lets the user activate any active process by selecting it and clicking on the dialog window's OK button.

Automating the Help Viewer Application

Another Mac OS X application that is scriptable is Help Viewer. This application provides access to Mac OS X help files. For example, the following AppleScript can be used to provide the user with a simple interface for searching Mac OS X help files using the Help Viewer.

```
set UserQuery to text returned of ¬
    (display dialog "What do you want to search for?" ¬
    Default answer "" buttons {" OK"})


tell application "Help Viewer"
    activate
    search looking for UserQuery
end tell
```

When executed, this AppleScript displays a dialog window that prompts the player to enter a topic for which she requires help, as demonstrated in Figure 8.16.

FIGURE 8.16

Using an AppleScript as a simple front end to the Help Viewer application.

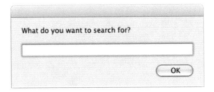

The search topic entered by the user is assigned to a variable named `UserQuery`, which is then used by the Help Viewer application's `search` command. For example, Figure 8.17 shows the results returned by the Help Viewer when the user enters `Display` as a search topic.

By building off this example, you can create an AppleScript that provides your users with access to Mac OS X help information.

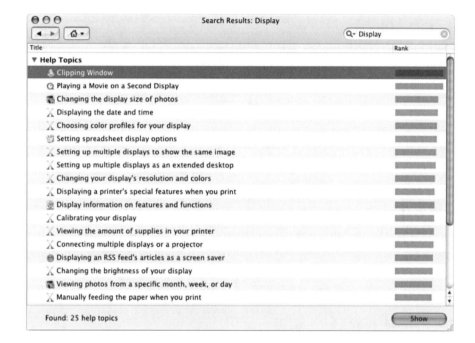

FIGURE 8.17

Viewing the results of a Help Viewer search.

BACK TO THE APPLESCRIPT NUMBER GUESSING GAME

All right, it is time to turn your attention back to this chapter's game project, the AppleScript Number Guessing game. This game challenges the player to guess a randomly generated number in the range of 1 to 100 in as few guesses as possible. To assist the player, the game provides her with a hint at the end of each turn, which lets her know if the answer is too high or too low.

Designing the Game

The AppleScript Number Guessing game will be created in 10 steps, as outlined here:

1. Create a new AppleScript and save it with a name of Number Guess.
2. Document the script and its purpose.
3. Declare the game's global variables.
4. Generate the game's first random number.
5. Develop the game's controlling programming logic.
6. Display the game's closing window.
7. Separate controlling code from script handlers.
8. Create the `GetRandomNumber()` handler.
9. Create the `PlayAgain()` handler.
10. Create the `DisplaySplashScreen()` handler.

Step 1: Creating a New AppleScript File

Begin the creation of the AppleScript Number Guessing game by opening the Script Editor application and creating a new AppleScript file named Number Guess by following the steps outlined here:

1. Open the Script Editor application.
2. Click on the File menu and select the Save As option.
3. In the sheet window that appears, enter **Number Guess** in the Save As field and specify the location where you want to save the script file using the Where drop-down menu.
4. Click on the Save button.

Step 2: Providing High-Level Script Documentation

Let's begin the development of the AppleScript Number Guessing game by adding a little documentation to the script file identifying the script's name and its purpose. This documentation will consist of embedded comment statements as well as descriptive text written to the Script Editor application's Description tab.

Adding External Descriptive Text

The text to be added to the Script Editor's Description tab view is shown here:

```
The AppleScript Number Guessing Game   v1.0


This AppleScript game challenges the player to guess a number between 1
and 100 in as few guesses as possible. Hints are provided at the end of each
guess to help guide the player in making her next guess. Game statistics
are provided at the end of each round of play.



Developed by Jerry Lee Ford, Jr.
Copyright 2007
```

Following the pattern established in previous game development efforts, let's make the name of the game stand out by highlighting it and then selecting the Bold option located on the Font menu. This instructs the Script Editor to display the game's name in a bold font.

Embedding Comments Inside the Script

Now let's add the following comment statements to the beginning of the AppleScript.

```
-----------------------------------------------------------------------
--
-- Script Name: AppleScript Number Guessing Game (Number Guess.scpt)
```

```
-- Version: 1.0
-- Author: Jerry Lee Ford, Jr.
-- Date: August 2007
--
-- Description: This AppleScript game challenges the player to try to
-- guess a number between 1 and 100 in as few guesses as possible.
--
-------------------------------------------------------------------------
```

These statements document the AppleScript's name, its version, author name, and creation date. In addition, a brief description of the script has also been provided.

Step 3: Declaring Global Variables

The next step in the development of the AppleScript Number Guessing game is to define variables that will be used globally throughout the script, as well as those variables used to drive the game's main programming logic. This is accomplished by adding the following statements to the end of the script file.

```
-- Declare the following variable as having a global scope
global GameTitle

-- Define variables used by the statements that control the AppleScript's
-- overall controlling logic

set NumberGuessed to false -- Used to control loop execution

set NoGamesPlayed to 1 -- Keeps track of the number of games played

-- Keeps track of the number of guesses made in the current round of play
set NumberOfGuesses to 0

-- Keeps track of the number of guesses made since the game was started
set TotalGuesses to 0

-- Keeps track of the average number of guesses made per game
set AvgGuesses to 0 --

-- Stores the game's name
set GameTitle to "AppleScript Number Guessing Game"
```

These statements begin by declaring a variable named `GameTitle` as being global in scope. Next, a variable named `NumberGuessed` is assigned a value of `false`. This variable will be used to control a `repeat` loop used later in the script to control the game's main programming logic. A variable named `NoGamesPlayed` is then assigned an initial value of 1. This variable will be used to keep track of the total number of games played. Next, a variable named `NumberOfGuesses` is assigned a value of 0. This variable will be used to keep count of the number of guesses made by the player during the current round of play. Next, two variables, `TotalGuesses` and `AvgGuesses`, are assigned an initial value of 1. These variables will be used to keep count of the total number of guesses made by the player for every game played and the average number of turns taken per game. Lastly, the `GameTitle` variable is assigned a string value of `"AppleScript Number Guessing Game"`. This variable will be referenced by `display dialog` commands used throughout the AppleScript, including its handlers, to display a consistent message in each dialog window's title bar.

Step 4: Generating the Game's Initial Random Number

As soon as the game is started, it prompts the player to begin making guesses. However, before the first dialog window is displayed, the game needs to generate a random "correct" number for the player to guess. This is accomplished by adding the following statements to the end of the program file.

```
-- Generate the game's initial random number
set randomNumber to GetRandomNumber()
```

As you can see, a handler named `GetRandomNumber()` is called. The handler executes, generating a random number between 1 and 100; then the number is returned and assigned to the `randomNumber` variable.

Step 5: Developing the Game's Controlling Logic

Now it is time to set up the `repeat` statement code block that is responsible for controlling the overall execution of the game. This is accomplished by adding the following statements to the end of the script file.

```
-- This loop controls overall game play, calling on handlers as necessary
-- to perform specific functions
repeat until NumberGuessed = true

    beep -- Make some noise to get the player's attention

    -- Prompt the player to make a guess between 1 and 100
    set PlayerGuess to text returned of (display dialog ¬
```

```
            "Enter a guess from 1 to 100:" default answer ¬
            "" buttons {"OK"} with title GameTitle)

-- Keep track of the number of guesses made in this round of play
set NumberOfGuesses to NumberOfGuesses + 1


-- Coerce the player guess from a string to an integer
set PlayerGuess to PlayerGuess as integer


-- Validate the player's guess, which must be greater than 1 or equal
-- to 1 and less than or equal to 100
if PlayerGuess < 1 or PlayerGuess > 100 then
    beep -- Make some noise to get the player's attention
    -- Display an error message informing the player of the error
    display dialog "Error: Guesses must be between 1 and " & ¬
        "100." buttons {"OK"} with title GameTitle
else
    if PlayerGuess < randomNumber then -- Player's guess was too low
        beep -- Make some noise to get the player's attention
        -- Provide the player with a hint
        display dialog "Your guess was too low! Try again." ¬
            buttons {"OK"} with title GameTitle
    end if

    if PlayerGuess > randomNumber then -- Player's guess was too high
        beep -- Make some noise to get the player's attention
        -- Provide the player with a hint
        display dialog "Your guess was too high! Try again." ¬
            buttons {"OK"} with title GameTitle
    end if

    -- The player's guess was correct and the game has been won
    if PlayerGuess = randomNumber then

        -- Update the total number of guesses made so far
        set TotalGuesses to TotalGuesses + NumberOfGuesses

        -- Calculate the average number of guesses made per game
```

```
            set AvgGuesses to TotalGuesses / NoGamesPlayed

            beep -- Make some noise to get the player's attention

            -- tell the player the good news and display game statistics
            display dialog "Congratulations. You won in " & ¬
                NumberOfGuesses & " guesses." & return & return & ¬
                "Total number of games played: " & NoGamesPlayed & ¬
                return & "Average number of guesses per game: " & ¬
                AvgGuesses buttons {"OK"} with title GameTitle

            -- Call the handler that prompts the player to play
            -- another round
            set KeepPlaying to PlayAgain()

            -- Analyze the player's input
            if KeepPlaying = "No" then
                -- Set variable value to true to terminate the loop
                set NumberGuessed to true
            else --Reset key variables to prepare for a new round
                set NoGamesPlayed to NoGamesPlayed + 1
                set NumberOfGuesses to 0
                set randomNumber to GetRandomNumber()
            end if

        end if

    end if

end repeat
```

The handler is set up to execute until the value assigned to NumberGuessed is equal to true. The handler begins by executing the beep command to get the player's attention and to bring attention to the dialog window that is then displayed. This window prompts the player to make a guess, which is assigned to the PlayerGuess variable. Once the player submits a guess, the value of NumberOfGuesses in incremented by 1.

Because the display dialog command only returns input as a string, the next statement converts it to an integer, allowing it to be evaluated in the statements that follow. Next, an if statement code block is set up that analyzes the value of `PlayerGuess` to see if it is less than 1 or greater than 100. If either of these tests evaluates as being `true`, an error message is displayed, reminding the player that guesses must be in the range of 1 to 100.

If, on the other hand, the value of `PlayerGuess` is valid, the `else` portion of the code block is executed. The first set of statements that are executed are a pair of embedded `if` statement code blocks. The first code block checks to see if the player's guess was too low and displays a hint to help guide her as she makes her next guess. The second code block checks to see if the player's guess was too high and once again displays a hint to help guide her next guess.

The rest of the statements in the `repeat` statement code block are embedded inside an `if` statement code block that checks the value assigned to `PlayerGuess` to see if it is equal to `randomNumber`, in which case the player has guessed the game's secret number. If this is the case, the value of `NumberOfGuesses` is added to `TotalGuesses`. Next, the value of `AvgGuesses` is recalculated by assigning it the value of `TotalGuesses` divided by `NoGamesPlayed`. Next, the `display dialog` command is used to display a dialog window that lets the player know she has won the game. In addition, the values of `NumberOfGuesses`, `NoGamesPlayed`, and `AvgGuesses` are also displayed. To see if the player wants to play another game, the `PlayAgain()` handler is called. If the player elects to quit, the value of `NumberGuessed` is set equal to `true`. If, however, the player elects to keep playing, the values assigned to `NoGamesPlayed` and `NumberOfGuesses` are reset to their starting values and the `GetRandomNumber()` handler is executed to generate a new random number for the player to guess.

Step 6: Displaying a Closing Window

Once the player has played long enough and decides to stop, the `repeat` statement code block terminates and a closing dialog window is displayed, thanking the player for playing the game. This is accomplished by adding the following statements to the end of the game file.

```
-- Before the games ends, call on the following handler to
-- thank the player for playing.
DisplaySplashScreen()
```

Step 7: Visually Separating Control Logic from Handlers

The remainder of the AppleScript will be made up of a collection of custom handlers. To help visually organize the contents of the script, add the following statement to the end of the script file.

```
--------------------------- HANDLER SECTION ---------------------------
```

This comment statement helps to separate visually the script's controlling logic from its custom handlers.

Step 8: Creating the GetRandomNumber() Handler

The code statements for the GetRandomNumber() handler are shown next and should be added to the end of the script file.

```
-- This handler generates random numbers representing the game's
-- secret number
on GetRandomNumber()

    -- Generate a random number between 1 and 100
    set randomNo to random number from 1 to 100

    return randomNo -- Return the random number to the calling statement

end GetRandomNumber
```

This handler is responsible for generating a random number for the player to guess. This is accomplished by using the random number command to generate a number between 1 and 100. This value is then returned to the statement that called upon the handler to execute.

Step 9: Creating the PlayAgain() Handler

The code statements for the PlayAgain() handler are shown next and should be added to the end of the script file.

```
-- This handler displays a dialog window that prompts the player
-- for permission to start a new round of play
on PlayAgain()

    beep -- Make some noise to get the player's attention

    -- Prompt the player to play again
    set reply to button returned of (display dialog ¬
        "Play again?" buttons {"Yes", "No"} with title GameTitle)

    return reply -- Return the player's response

end PlayAgain
```

This handler is responsible for prompting the player to play another round once the game's secret number has been guessed. This is accomplished by displaying a dialog window that displays two buttons labeled Yes and No. A string representing the button clicked by the player is then returned by the handler.

Step 10: Creating the DisplaySplashScreen() Handler

The code statements for the `DisplaySplashScreen()` handler are shown next and should be added to the end of the script file.

```
-- This handler displays a dialog window that thanks the player
-- for playing the game.
on DisplaySplashScreen()

    beep -- Make some noise to get the player's attention

    -- Display the game's final window
    display dialog "Thank you for playing the AppleScript Number " & ¬
        "Guessing Game. " & return & return & ¬
        "Copyright 2007" buttons {"OK"} with title GameTitle

end DisplaySplashScreen
```

This handler is responsible for displaying the game's closing dialog window at the end of the game—a text message thanking the player for playing .

Testing the Execution of the AppleScript Number Guessing Game

Okay, at this point you should have everything you need to develop the AppleScript Number Guessing game. As long as you have not made any typing mistakes, the game should run as advertised. As you test out your new AppleScript, try supplying it both valid and invalid guesses and make sure that the game responds correctly. For example, in addition to guessing numbers in the range of 1 to 100, try entering negative numbers and numbers greater than 100. Try entering letters and special characters as well.

 Note that if you try to enter a real number that includes a decimal point, the game has been set up to automatically convert the number to an integer.

SUMMARY

In this chapter, you learned how to take control of and automate all kinds of Mac OS X applications, including Finder, TextEdit, QuickTime, Safari, and Help Viewer, just to name a few. By building upon the information and examples provided in this chapter, you can start developing processes that automate repetitive and complex application tasks. If you take things further and start developing AppleScripts that coordinate the automation of two or more Mac OS X applications, you can develop workflows capable of performing an assortment of complex tasks that no one application is capable of performing by itself.

Before you move on to Chapter 9, "Debugging Your AppleScripts," I suggest you set aside a little additional time to further enhance the AppleScript Number Guessing game by addressing the following challenges.

CHALLENGES

1. As it is currently written, the AppleScript Number Guessing game is hard-coded to generate secret numbers within the range of 1 to 100. Consider prompting the player at the beginning of the game to pick from a list of different ranges, including 1 to 10, 1 to 100, 1 to 1,000, and 1 to 10,000.

2. As currently written, the player can take as many guesses as is required to guess the game's secret number. As such, the player can never really lose, because eventually the secret number will be guessed. Consider enforcing an arbitrary limit on the number of guesses that the player can make before losing a game. You might also want to warn the player when she is down to her final guess.

3. If you elect to declare games to be lost after a predefined number of incorrect guesses, also consider tracking the number of games lost as another game statistic.

DEBUGGING YOUR
APPLESCRIPTS

Until this point in the book, you have been encouraged to review any error
messages encountered with the AppleScript games to glean what information you could from them. This chapter's primary focus is to explain
how and why programming errors occur and to provide you with instruction on
how to prevent errors from occurring. In addition, this chapter will also provide
instruction on how to develop error handling logic that can trap and respond to
errors when they occur. On top of all this, you will learn how to create your next
AppleScript, the Rock, Paper, Scissors game.

Specifically, you will learn:

- About different types of script errors
- How to develop error handlers using the try statement
- Different ways of tracking the logical flow of script execution
- Different ways of reporting errors and keeping track of variable values
- How to interpret error messages

PROJECT PREVIEW: THE ROCK, PAPER, SCISSORS GAME
This chapter's game project is the Rock, Paper, Scissors game. In this game, the
player is challenged to compete against the computer in a head-to-head game

based on the classic children's game, Rock, Paper, Scissors. In this game, there are three valid moves, Rock, Paper, and Scissors. The player makes her move by selecting one of these items from a dialog window containing a listbox control. The computer's move is generated by the game as a random number that is then associated with a move. The following list outlines the rules used to analyze the player's and the computer's move to determine the results of a round of play.

- Rock will crush scissors, resulting in a win
- Paper will cover rock, resulting in a win
- Scissors will cut paper, resulting in a win
- Matching moves result in a tie

Game play begins as soon as the player starts the game, as demonstrated in Figure 9.1.

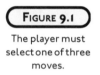

FIGURE 9.1

The player must select one of three moves.

To play the player must select Rock, Paper, or Scissors and then click on the OK button. If instead, the player clicks on the Cancel button, the game responds by redisplaying the dialog window once again prompting the player to select a move. Once a valid move has been selected, the game generates a random number representing the computer's move and then analyzes the player's move and the computer's move to determine the results. Once the analysis is complete, the results of the current round of play are displayed in a dialog window like the one shown in Figure 9.2.

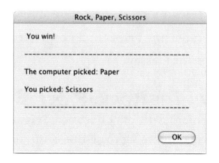

FIGURE 9.2

In this example, the player has won the game because scissors cut paper.

Once the player has finished viewing the results and clicks on the OK button, the game prompts the player to play another round, as demonstrated in Figure 9.3.

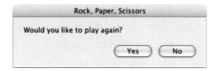

Once the player has had enough and decides to stop playing, the dialog window shown in Figure 9.4 is displayed, thanking the player for playing the game.

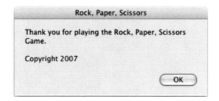

EXAMINING THE THREE BASIC TYPES OF ERRORS

All modern programming languages, including AppleScript, are subject to three basic types of errors. These errors are listed next and are explained in the sections that follow.

- Syntax errors
- Logical errors
- Runtime errors

Fixing Syntax Errors

No doubt you have made at least a few typos as you have worked on re-creating the different AppleScripts and game scripts presented in this book. The Script Editor discovers typos and makes them known whenever you compile or try to run your AppleScripts. As you have observed, your AppleScripts will not execute as long as a single syntax error, such as a typo, exists within your scripts.

A syntax error occurs whenever you fail to follow AppleScript's syntax rules as you write your AppleScript statements. Syntax errors occur whenever you make a typing error when keying in an AppleScript command or keyword. Syntax errors also occur if you fail to properly format your code statements, which would be the case if, for example, you omitted a required keyword.

The easiest way of dealing with syntax errors is to avoid making them in the first place. This means taking your time when keying in code statements and double-checking the syntax of any commands and keywords that you are not accustomed to working with. Still, even the most careful programmer cannot avoid making a few syntax errors every now and again. Fortunately, AppleScript makes finding and fixing syntax errors a relatively painless process because it generates an error message every time it discovers one. For example, suppose you wrote an AppleScript that contained the following statement.

```
display dialog "Now is the winter of our discontent
```

If you executed this AppleScript, instead of running and displaying the expected dialog window, the error message shown in Figure 9.5 would be displayed.

FIGURE 9.5

An example of a typical AppleScript syntax error message.

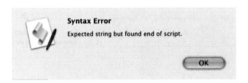

Syntax Error
Expected string but found end of script.

OK

By reviewing the information provided in this message, you can often determine what the cause of the error is. For example, this error message clearly states that the syntax error was generated because AppleScript failed to find an expected ". After clicking on the OK button associated with the error message, the Script Editor will dismiss the error message and then reposition the cursor to the approximate location of the syntax error within the script file, making it easier to track down and fix the error. This, combined with the information provided in the error message, is usually all you need to track down and fix the vast majority of syntax errors.

AppleScript's error messages are not always easy to understand, and you may find yourself scratching your head from time to time trying to figure out what a particular error message means. While the Script Editor does a pretty good job of placing the cursor in the vicinity of where an error occurred, it does not always pinpoint the correct statement. Therefore, you may have to look backward or forward a statement or two to find the line where the error being reported resides. Still, on the whole, you'll find that compared to the other types of errors that you will run into, locating and fixing syntax errors is fairly straightforward.

Coping with Runtime Errors

A second category of error that plagues all programmers is runtime errors. A *runtime* error is an error that occurs when a fully compiled AppleScript begins executing and then comes across an illegal action. For example, the following statements provide an example that is syntactically correct and therefore will compile without issue.

```
set Result to text returned of (display dialog "Enter a number:" ¬
    default answer "" buttons {"OK"})


set Total to 5 + Result
```

Here, the user is prompted to enter a number that is then added to 5 and assigned to a variable named Total. As long as the user enters a numeric value as instructed, these statements will execute without incident. However, should the user enter text or special characters in place of a numeric value, the runtime error shown in Figure 9.6 will be displayed, terminating the script's execution.

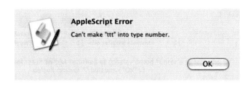

FIGURE 9.6

An example of an AppleScript runtime error message.

In this example, a runtime error was generated because the user failed to provide the proper input and the script did not perform any data validation. Runtime errors can occur for a variety of reasons. For example, runtime errors can occur if an AppleScript tries to access a disk drive that does not exist or tries to call upon an application that is not installed on the computer where the AppleScript is running.

Many times, runtime errors can be managed by adding an error handler to your AppleScript. An *error handler* is a special type of handler that is specifically designed to detect and deal with runtime errors.

Runtime errors do not affect compilation because they are not detectible by AppleScript's compiler. Runtime errors do not make themselves known until later when the AppleScript that contains them is executed. In most cases, runtime errors result in an error message and the immediate termination of the script.

The last thing any programmer wants is to allow users to experience runtime errors. The resulting loss of confidence in you and your AppleScripts can be quite damaging. One way of dealing with runtime errors is to carefully plan out and design your AppleScript. Another important step is to develop your AppleScripts in a modular fashion using custom handlers and extensively test each handler as you add it to your script file.

When your AppleScript is complete, it is important that you test its operation and validate that everything works as expected. It is equally important that you test your AppleScripts by doing everything you can think of to make your scripts fail. By this I mean attempting to do things like deliberately providing invalid input to make sure that your script appropriately deals with it. Another way of dealing with runtime errors is to develop error handlers that trap errors when they occur and then deal with them, as discussed later in this chapter.

Dealing with Logical Errors

The third category of error to which all computer programs are susceptible is logical errors. A *logical error* is one that occurs when you make a mistake in the way you formulate your programming logic. For example, a logical error would occur if you wrote an AppleScript that was supposed to add up the number of files located on the user's desktop and the user's home directory, but instead of adding the number of files found in both folders you subtracted one from another, yielding an invalid result.

A poorly formulated loop that never provides a means for terminating itself is an example of another type of logical error. This type of loop is referred to as an *endless loop*. Endless loops prevent your AppleScript from terminating, and they result in an AppleScript that needlessly consumes computer resources. For example, the following statement sets up an endless loop that was intended to count from 1 to 100. However, in formulating the loop, an error was made and instead of counting to 100 by 1, the loop instead counts by negative 1. As a result, the value assigned to Counter gets smaller with each iteration. Since the value of Counter will never reach 100, the loop will run forever, consuming processor and memory resources and preventing the rest of the script from accomplishing its task.

```
set Counter to 1
repeat until Counter > 100
    set Counter to Counter - 1
end repeat
```

 One possible sign of an AppleScript with an endless loop is that the script does not terminate when it is supposed to and instead keeps on running. If this is the case, you can force the termination of your AppleScript by clicking on the Apple menu and selecting the Force Quit option. In response, Mac OS X displays a list of all currently active applications. Select the AppleScript from within this list and then click on the Force Quit button. You will be asked to confirm this instruction by clicking on the Force Quit button again, after which your AppleScript will be terminated.

Because there is technically nothing wrong with the code statements involved in logical errors, the compiler cannot detect them. They only make themselves known when your AppleScript runs and behaves in an unexpected manner or produces unexpected results. Like runtime errors, careful planning and testing should prevent, or at the very least detect, endless loops early in the development process.

DEALING WITH ERRORS

As with other programming languages, the basic process involved in debugging an AppleScript is to write a few lines of code, compile and run the script file, and then fix any errors that are reported. This process is repeated until the program is fully written and all errors have been identified and eliminated. In addition to following this basic set of steps, there are a number of other good programming practices that you should follow. These programming practices, listed next, become increasingly important as your AppleScripts grow in terms of size and complexity.

- Always begin script development with a plan, taking time to lay out the overall design of your AppleScript before you write the first line of code.
- Avoid using overly complex programming logic when a simpler solution is available.
- Apply consistent naming schemes for all your variables and handlers and make them descriptive of their purpose.
- Build your AppleScripts in a modular fashion and be sure to test out every handler.
- Whenever possible, simplify the design of your dialog windows to make them easier to understand, thus reducing the possibility of confusing the user.
- Incorporate clear language and provide instruction or access to help information whenever possible.
- Validate user input as thoroughly as possible and always make sure files and folders exist before attempting to access them.
- Attempt to anticipate the locations within your AppleScript where errors are most likely to occur and add programming logic to try to prevent these errors from occurring.
- Always set aside extra time to test your AppleScripts, and, whenever possible, get someone else to test them as well.

BUILDING ERROR HANDLERS

Try as you may, it is not possible to anticipate and prevent every possible error. Hard drives crash. Network and Internet connections fail. Files and folders get moved around or accidentally deleted. And users often behave in extremely unexpected ways. The best that you can sometimes do is to anticipate where errors are most likely to occur and then add a little program code to try to prevent them. For example, you can often add input validation handlers to process and ensure good user input, or use default data in the event the user fails to provide input. You can check for the existence of files and folders before attempting to access them. Still, some problems like a crashed disk drive or a failed Internet connection cannot be prevented. In these situations, you can at least provide the user with a clear explanation of the problem and apologize. That's certainly better than just allowing your AppleScript to crash and display one of AppleScript's cryptic error messages.

Catching Errors with the try Statement

One of the most helpful tools provided by AppleScript for dealing with errors is the try command. Using the try command, you can set up a code block within which any errors that occur are trapped and prevented from terminating your AppleScript. To be able to effectively use the try command, you must be able to anticipate the location within your AppleScript where an error may occur and then enclose that portion of your script inside a try statement code block.

To better understand the try command, take a look at the following set of statements.

```
tell application "Finder"
    open desktop
end tell
```

Here a small AppleScript has been set to open a Finder window that displays the contents of the user's desktop. Now, take at look at the following AppleScript.

```
tell application "Finder"

    set reply to button returned of ¬
        (display dialog "Close Desktop window?" buttons {"Yes", "No"})

    if reply = "Yes" then
        close Finder window "Desktop"
    end if

end tell
```

When this AppleScript runs, it closes the window opened by the previous AppleScript. However, if in between the execution of the first and second script the user manually closes the

Desktop window, a runtime error occurs when the second AppleScript executes, as demonstrated in Figure 9.7.

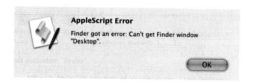

FIGURE 9.7

A runtime error caused when an AppleScript is unable to find an open folder.

In this scenario, it is perfectly okay for the user to manually close the Desktop window if she wants and there is no reason why doing so should result in an error when the second AppleScript is executed. By embedding the statements where an error may occur inside a try statement code block, as demonstrated next, you can modify the second AppleScript so that it is tolerant of any errors that may occur when the close command is executed.

```
tell application "Finder"

set reply to button returned of ¬
    (display dialog "Close Desktop window?" buttons {"Yes", "No"})

    try

        if reply = "Yes" then
            close Finder window "Desktop"
        end if

    end try

end tell
```

When executed, this AppleScript closes the Desktop window if it is open. If it is not open, the try statement code block prevents the script from terminating with an error.

TRICK

You may enclose as many programming statements as necessary within your try statement code block. The first statement within the code block that generates an error will be trapped. Any statements that follow in the code block are skipped.

Specifying Recovery Actions Using an on error Handler

The previous set of scenarios demonstrated how to use the `try` statement to set up code blocks that ignore errors if they occur. However, this approach to error handling is not always practical. Sometimes you may want to take an action other than simply ignoring the error. This is accomplished by adding the `on error` handler inside the `try` statement code block. When added, any statement inside the `on error` code block will be executed, allowing you to either try to fix the error or, at the very least, terminate your AppleScript gracefully, by closing any open files and perhaps displaying a user-friendly error message. For example, consider the following AppleScript.

```
tell application "Finder"

set reply to button returned of ¬
        (display dialog "Close Desktop window?" buttons {"Yes", "No"})

    try

        if reply = "Yes" then
            close Finder window "Desktop"
        end if

    on error

        display dialog "You must have closed the window already."

    end try

end tell
```

This time an `on error` handler has been included inside the `try` statement code block. As a result, any error that occurs in the code block will trigger the execution of any statements that follow the `on error` handler, allowing you to attempt whatever corrective actions make sense for the situation.

Catching Specific Errors

Every AppleScript runtime error has an associated error message and number. If you want, you can modify the `on error` handler to capture this information when it executes. To make this happen, all you have to do is add arguments to the end of the `on error` statement, as demonstrated in the following example.

```
set UserAge to text returned of (display dialog ¬
    "How old are you?" default answer "" buttons {"OK"})

try

    set UserAge to UserAge as integer

    if UserAge < 19 then
        display dialog ¬
            "Go away. You are too young to play this game." ¬
            buttons {"OK"}
        return
    end if

on error ErrorMsg number ErrorNo

    display dialog "Error: " & ErrorMsg & return & "Number: " & ¬
        ErrorNo & return & return & ¬
        "You must enter a number!" buttons {"OK"}
    return
end try

display dialog "OK, let's play!" buttons {"OK"}
```

Here, the player is prompted to enter her age in a dialog window. This value is then validated to determine whether the player is old enough to play the game. While it is expected that the player will enter an integer value, there is no guarantee. Since invalid input may result in a runtime error, some validation checking needs to be performed. This is accomplished by setting up a try statement code block that handles any errors that may occur when analyzing the data supplied by the player, and some good old-fashioned conditional logic. The first statement inside the try statement code block explicitly coerces the value supplied by the player into an integer. An error will occur if the user has provided non-numeric input. If this is the case, the on error event handler is executed. If the player has supplied a number, an error will not occur.

The on error handler has been set up to capture the error message and error number for any error that occurs within the try statement code block. This information is then used to display an error message that explicitly informs the player of the error, as demonstrated in Figure 9.8.

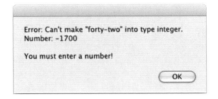

FIGURE 9.8 figure**FIGURE 9.8**

Capturing and displaying error message and error number information.

> Error: Can't make "forty-two" into type integer.
> Number: −1700
>
> You must enter a number!
>
> OK

MONITORING APPLESCRIPT EXECUTION

If there is one certainty in programming, it is that errors are going to happen. When they do, it is your job as the programmer to track down and eliminate the errors, or *bugs*, that prevent your AppleScript from running correctly. One facility provided by many programming languages that is not currently supplied as a built-in part of AppleScript is debugging. By this I mean that there is no ability to set breakpoints, which are location markers within your script code that when reached, temporarily pause the script so that you can use other debugger facilities such as variable monitoring. With variable monitoring, a debugger lets you track the values assigned to variables so that you can verify that their values are being correctly set and managed by the script. In addition, debuggers also include commands that allow programmers to employ step-by-step control over script statements, allowing programmers to execute scripts one line or more at a time.

As this chapter will demonstrate, despite the absence of a debugger, you can still perform some fairly sophisticated debugging using a number of different programming tools and techniques supported by AppleScript and the Script Editor. However, there is no substitute for a good debugger. Therefore, you may want to take a look at the Script Debugger application developed by Late Night Software (www.latenightsw.com). This application provides a complete AppleScript development environment, negating the need to use Apple's Script Editor application. Script Debugger includes a robust set of debugging features, including those just mentioned. However, Script Debugger is not free. As of the publishing of this book, it was available for $199. If you are really serious about investing your time and effort to become a world-class AppleScript programmer, Script Debugger might very well prove a worthwhile investment.

Tracking Script Execution and Variable Values Using Dialog Windows

In order to debug your AppleScript, you need to know what is going on inside it as it executes. One very easy low-tech way of keeping track of things is to use the `display dialog` command. Using the `display dialog` command, you can pause script execution at predefined locations. For example, you might place a `display dialog` command inside each of your AppleScript's handlers at both the beginning and end of the handlers.

TRAP

The downside to adding a lot of extra display dialog commands to your script file is that you must eventually remove them once you have finished testing and debugging your AppleScript. Alternatively, you may instead want to just comment out the display dialog commands so that they will still be there should you have to later return and further debug your AppleScript.

Using display dialog commands allows you to keep track of the overall execution of your scripts, showing you when each handler is called upon to run and when each handler finishes. Using this programming technique, you can ensure that the logical flow within your AppleScript is occurring in the order that you expected. You might also want to modify the display dialog commands to display the values of key variables so that you can keep track of the variable's value assignments and modifications as the script runs.

TRICK

If your AppleScripts already make extensive use of display dialog commands, you may be able to piggyback on top of these commands by simply adding the information you want to track during the testing of your scripts. For example, back in Chapter 8, "Automating Mac OS X Applications," you created the AppleScript Number Guessing game. You may have found it challenging to test the execution of the game because each time you ran it, you had to actually play the game and discover the game's secret number when testing it, which might have taken you numerous guesses.

Since the game is designed so that you cannot terminate it until after you have guessed the game's secret number, this could make testing a time-consuming process. To speed up testing, it would help to know the secret number from the get go, and an easy way of getting this information would be to display it in the title bar of the dialog window that prompts the player to make a guess. This could be accomplished easily by modifying the statement that produces the dialog window, as shown here:

```
set PlayerGuess to text returned of (display dialog ¬
    "Enter a guess between 1 and 100:" default answer ¬
    "" buttons {"OK"} with title GameTitle & " - " & randomNumber)
```

As you can see, the value of the randomNumber variable has been appended to the GameTitle variable to generate a text string that, when displayed in the resulting dialog window, includes both the name of the game and the value of the game's random number. With this information available, you can more efficiently test the execution of the AppleScript and validate that the script is properly analyzing player guesses.

Using Sound to Track Key Events

If you need to keep track of when certain things occur within your AppleScripts, you can insert an occasional beep command to provide an audio signal, letting you know when a particular handler has been called upon or a particular value modified. The beep command's applicability as a debugging tool is admittedly limited; still, it provides an excellent tool for notifying you when a particular event occurs and takes almost no time at all to insert and remove from your program code.

Working with the Event Log

Although you have not been instructed to use it so far, the Script Editor includes an Event Log view for the data page located at the bottom of the Script Editor window. If you click on the Event Log button before running your AppleScript in the Script Editor, the editor will log information about the execution of your script as it executes.

Writing to the Event Log

Figure 9.9 shows an example of the type of information you would see displayed in the Event Log if you ran the AppleScript Number Guessing game.

FIGURE 9.9

Reviewing script data recorded in the Script Editor's Event Log.

Using this information, you can monitor the execution of your AppleScript and also keep an eye on variable values as they are accessed and modified. If you look closely at the information that is recorded in the Event Log, you will see that it includes copies of program statements that have executed, allowing you to observe execution flow. You will also see variable values as well as any data that is returned from dialog windows with which the user has interacted. If you look closer at the data provided in Figure 9.9, you should be able to track the complete interaction the player had with the last execution of the AppleScript.

To make the Event Log even more useful, AppleScript provides you with access to the log command. Using this command, you can write messages directly to the Event Log. The syntax of the log command is outlined here:

```
log message
```

message represents a text string to be written to the Event Log.

The disadvantages of embedding display dialog commands throughout your AppleScript files are that they pause the execution of your AppleScript and have a tendency to slow down the debugging process. Instead of strategically embedding display dialog commands throughout your AppleScript file, you might instead embed log commands. Any text that you write to the Event Log is easily identified because it is placed inside matching parentheses and asterisks (* *), as demonstrated in Figure 9.10.

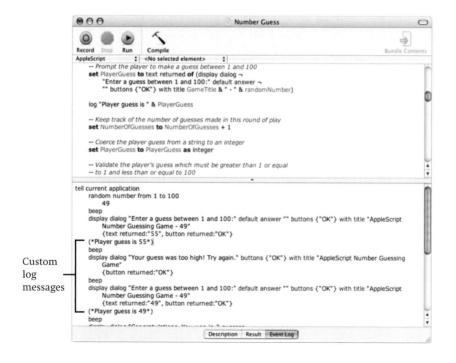

Custom log messages

FIGURE 9.10

Using the log command, you can write anything you want to the Event Log.

As Figure 9.10 shows, data that explicitly identifies the player guesses is now being written to the Event Log. This was accomplished by adding the following statement to the AppleScript.

```
log "Player guess is " * PlayerGuess
```

Working with the Event Log History Window

Event Log data can also be accessed from the Event Log History window, which can be accessed by clicking on the Window menu and selecting Event Log History. When opened, this window displays a list of all Event Log activity that has occurred since you started the Script Editor's current session. For example, in Figure 9.11 you see an example of the Event Log window showing the event history for the current working session. As you can see, so far, the Number Guessing game has been executed four times.

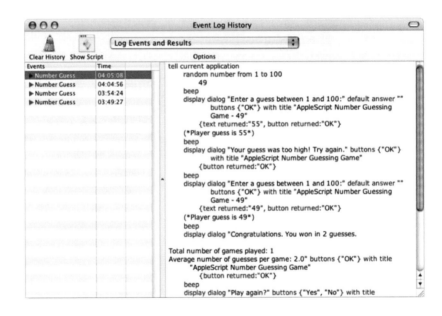

FIGURE 9.11

Viewing event logging information recorded on the Event Log History window.

Unlike the Event Log view in the Script Editor's data pane, the Event Log History window maintains a history of every script executed, allowing programmers to view data recorded from across different executions of an AppleScript. The window is organized into two panes. On the left-hand pane, you will find a listing of every AppleScript that has been executed. The right-hand side shows the data that has been logged for the selected entry in the left-hand pane.

If you want, you can drill down into any entry in the left-hand pane to view additional detail, as demonstrated in Figure 9.12. As you drill down further in the left-hand pane, the information displayed in the right-hand pane changes to show you the output that was logged for that that particular item.

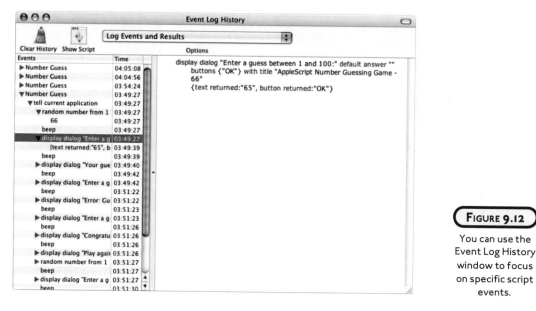

FIGURE 9.12

You can use the Event Log History window to focus on specific script events.

As you can see, the Event Log History window and the Event Log provide you with powerful tools that you can use to monitor the internal operation of your AppleScripts as they execute. By examining the information recorded in these logs, you can track down and identify just about any AppleScript error.

BACK TO THE ROCK, PAPER, SCISSORS GAME

Now it is time to turn your attention back to the development of the Rock, Paper, Scissors game. This version of the game pits the player against the computer, whose moves are generated randomly.

Designing the Game

The development of the Rock, Paper, Scissors game will be accomplished in 12 steps, as outlined here:

1. Create a new AppleScript and save it with a name of RockPaperScissors.
2. Document the script and its purpose.
3. Declare the game's global variables.
4. Develop the overall controlling programming logic for the game.

5. Display the game's closing window.
6. Visually separate control logic from the script's handlers.
7. Create the `GetComputerMove()` handler.
8. Create the `GetPlayerMove()` handler.
9. Create the `EvaluateResults()` handler.
10. Create the `DisplayResults()` handler.
11. Create the `PlayAgain()` handler.
12. Create the `DisplaySplashScreen()` handler.

Step 1: Creating a New AppleScript File

The first step in the development of the Rock, Paper, Scissors game is to open the Script Editor and create a new AppleScript file named RockPaperScissors, as outlined in the following steps.

1. Open the Script Editor application.
2. Click on the File menu and select the Save As option.
3. In the sheet window that appears, enter **RockPaperScissors** in the Save As field and specify the location where you want to save the script file using the Where drop-down menu.
4. Click on the Save button.

Step 2: Providing High-Level Script Documentation

The next step in the development of the Rock, Paper, Scissors game is to provide some basic documentation describing the script's name and its overall purpose. This documentation will include comments embedded inside the script file as well as descriptive text written to the data view of the Script Editor application's Description tab.

Adding External Descriptive Text

The text shown next documents the name of the game and describes its overall purpose. Key this information into the Script Editor's data pane after selecting the Description tab.

```
The Rock, Paper, Scissors Game  v1.0


This AppleScript game pits the player against the computer in a game of Rock, Paper,
Scissors.


Developed by Jerry Lee Ford, Jr.
Copyright 2007
```

To make this text more visually appealing, highlight the game's name and select the Bold menu item located on the Font menu. This will instruct the Script Editor to display the game's name in a bold font.

Embedding Comments Inside the Script

Next, add the following comment statements to the beginning of the Rock, Paper, Scissors AppleScript file to document the script's name, its version, author name, and creation date and to provide a brief description of the script.

```
-------------------------------------------------------------------------
--
-- Script Name: Rock, Paper, Scissors (RockPaperScissors.scpt)
-- Version: 1.0
-- Author: Jerry Lee Ford, Jr.
-- Date: August 2007
--
-- Description: This AppleScript challenges the player to compete
-- against the computer in a game of Rock, Paper, Scissors
--
-------------------------------------------------------------------------
```

Step 3: Declaring Global Variables

Now it is time to define variables that will be used globally throughout the AppleScript and to control the overall execution of the script. This is accomplished by adding the following statements to the end of the script file.

```
-- Declare the following variable as having a global scope
global GameTitle

-- Define variables used by the statements that control the AppleScript's
-- overall controlling logic

set GameTitle to "Rock, Paper, Scissors" -- Stores the game's name

set GameOver to false -- Used to control loop execution

set ValidSelection to false -- Used to control loop execution
```

These statements begin by declaring a variable named GameTitle as global in scope. Next the GameTitle variable is assigned a text string containing the game's name. This variable will be referenced in all `display dialog` commands used in the script to ensure the consistent display of the game's name in all dialog windows. Next, a variable named `GameOver` is assigned a value of `false`. This variable will be used to manage the operation of a `repeat` loop used later in the script to control the game's main programming logic. Next, a variable named `ValidSelection` is assigned a value of `false`. This variable will be used to manage the operation of a second `repeat` loop that will be used when validating player input.

Step 4: Developing the Script's Overall Controlling Logic

With the game's global variables now defined, it is time to focus on the development of the program statements that are responsible for managing the overall execution of the game. This is accomplished by adding the following statements to the end of the script file.

```
-- This loop controls overall game play, calling on handlers as necessary
-- to perform specific functions
repeat until GameOver = true -- Iterate until the player decides to quit

     -- Call the handler that generates the computer move
     set ComputerMove to GetComputerMove()

     -- Repeat until the player has made a valid selection
     repeat until ValidSelection = true

          --Call the handler responsible for collecting the player's move
          set PlayerMove to GetPlayerMove()

          -- Validate the player's move
          if PlayerMove = 1 or PlayerMove = 2 or PlayerMove = 3 then

               -- Set variable value to terminate loop
               set ValidSelection to true

          end if

     end repeat

     -- Call the handler responsible for evaluating the results of the
     -- current round of play
     set result to EvaluateResults(ComputerMove, PlayerMove)
```

```
    --Call the handler responsible for displaying the results of the current
    -- round of play
DisplayResults(ComputerMove, PlayerMove, result)

    -- Call on the handler that is responsible for prompting the player
    -- to play a new round
set KeepPlaying to PlayAgain()

    -- Evaluate the player's response
if KeepPlaying = "No" then -- The player has decided to quit playing

        -- Set variable value to terminate loop
        set GameOver to true

    else -- The player wants to play another round

        --Set variable value to keep the loop iterating
        set ValidSelection to false

    end if

end repeat
```

As you can see, a repeat statement code block has been set up to manage overall control of the game. The code block's execution is based on the value assigned to a variable named GameOver. This variable's value was set to false earlier in this script and will remain that way until the player decides to stop playing the game, at which time the variable's value will be set to true.

Next, the GetComputerMove() handler is executed. This handler is responsible for generating a number from 1 to 3, representing the computer's move. A value of 1 equates to rock. A value of 2 equates to paper, and a value of 3 equates to scissors. The value that is returned is assigned to the ComputerMove variable.

An embedded repeat statement code block is executed next. Its job is to execute until the player has made a valid move, at which time the value assigned to ValidSelection is set equal to true. Within this loop, the GetPlayerMove() handler is executed. This handler displays a dialog window that prompts the player to make her move. The value returned by the handler is stored in a variable named PlayerMove, which is then evaluated to ensure that it's valid. If it is, the value of ValidSelection is set to true, terminating the loop's execution. However, the player's move might not be valid, which would be the case if the player clicked on the dialog window's Cancel button instead of selecting Rock, Paper, or Scissors as a move. If the player's move is invalid, the value assigned to `ValidSelection` remains unchanged and the loop will execute again, prompting the player to again make a move.

Next, the `EvaluateResults` handler is called on to execute and pass the values of `ComputerMove` and `PlayerMove` as arguments. This handler determines whether the player won, lost, or tied the computer. The handler returns a string representing the result of its analysis, which is stored in the variable named `result`. The `DisplayResults()` handler is called on to execute next. This handler is passed the values assigned to `ComputerMove`, `PlayerMove`, and `result` as arguments and is responsible for displaying a dialog window that tells the player the results of the current round of play.

Now that the current round of play has been completed, it is time to find out if the player would like to play more. To accomplish this, the `PlayAgain()` handler is executed. This handler returns a value of `"Yes"` or `"No"` based on the player's decision. This value is assigned to a variable named `KeepPlaying`, which is then analyzed by an `if` statement code block. If the player decides to stop playing, the value assigned to the `GameOver` variable is assigned a value of `false`. Otherwise, it is assigned a value of `true`. A value of `true` will result in the termination of the game's controlling `repeat` loop, resulting in the game's immediate termination.

Step 5: Displaying the Closing Window

Once the `repeat` statement code block has finished executing, all that remains is for the AppleScript to display its closing window, thanking the player for playing. This is accomplished by adding the following statements to the end of the script file.

```
-- Before the games ends, call on the following handler to
-- thank the player for playing.
DisplaySplashScreen()
```

As you can see, the `DisplaySplashScreen()` handler is called to perform this task. Once this handler has finished executing, the AppleScript ends.

Step 6: Visually Separating Control Logic from Handlers

To help visually improve the organization of your AppleScript file by separating overall controlling script logic from the supporting custom handlers, add the following comment statement to the end of the script file.

```
-------------------------- HANDLER SECTION ----------------------------
```

Step 7: Creating the GetComputerMove() Handler

The GetComputerMove() handler is responsible for randomly generating a move on behalf of the computer. This is accomplished by adding the following statements to the end of the script file.

```
-- This handler generates random numbers representing the computer's
-- move
on GetComputerMove()

    -- Generate a random number from 1 to 3
    set randomNo to random number from 1 to 3

    return randomNo -- Return the random number to the calling statement

end GetComputerMove
```

This handler accomplishes its job using the random number command to generate a random number from 1 to 3. This value is then returned to the statement that called upon the handler to execute.

Step 8: Creating the GetPlayerMove() Handler

The GetPlayerMove() handler is responsible for prompting the player to select one of three moves as specified inside a dialog window. This is accomplished by adding the following statement to the end of the script file.

```
-- This handler is responsible for prompting the player to make a move
on GetPlayerMove()

    beep -- Make some noise to get the player's attention

    -- Prompt the player to select Rock, Paper, or Scissors
    set PlayerMove to choose from list ¬
        {"Rock", "Paper", "Scissors"} ¬
            with prompt "Select your move." with title GameTitle

    -- Assign and return a number representing the player's move
    if PlayerMove = {"Rock"} then
        return 1
    else if PlayerMove = {"Paper"} then
        return 2
```

```
    else if PlayerMove = {"Scissors"} then
        return 3
    else
        return 0 -- The player clicked on the Cancel button
    end if

end GetPlayerMove
```

The handler begins by executing the beep command to let the player know that the script needs her input. Next, the choose from list command is used to prompt the player to make a move. The player's selection is then analyzed using an if statement code block and a numeric value is returned to the calling statement. In the event that the player clicked on the Cancel button instead of selecting a move, a value of 0 is returned.

Step 9: Creating the EvaluateResults() Handler

The EvaluateResults() handler, shown next, is responsible for comparing the computer's and the player's moves, which are passed to the handler as arguments to determine the results of the game.

```
-- This handler determines whether the current round of play
-- ended in a win, loss, or tie for the player
on EvaluateResults(ComputerMove, PlayerMove)

    -- The computer picked Rock
    if ComputerMove = 1 then

        if PlayerMove = 1 then return "Tie" -- The player picked Rock
        if PlayerMove = 2 then return "Win" -- The player picked Paper
        if PlayerMove = 3 then return "Lose" --The player picked Scissors

    end if

    -- The computer picked Paper
    if ComputerMove = 2 then

        if PlayerMove = 1 then return "Lose" -- The player picked Rock
        if PlayerMove = 2 then return "Tie" -- The player picked Paper
        if PlayerMove = 3 then return "Win" -- The player picked Scissors
```

```
        end if

        -- The computer picked Scissors
        if ComputerMove = 3 then

                if PlayerMove = 1 then return "Win" -- The player picked Rock
                if PlayerMove = 2 then return "Lose" -- The player picked Paper
                if PlayerMove = 3 then return "Tie" -- The player picked Scissors

        end if

end EvaluateResults
```

As you can see, a series of three if statement code blocks are executed in this handler. Each of these code blocks contains three additional if statements. The first code block checks to see if the computer's move is equal to 1 (representing Rock). Assuming that this is the case, the three embedded if statements are used to determine which move the player selected and then specify a result, which is returned as a text string or "Lose", "Tie", or "Win". The next if statement code block evaluates the computer's and the player's moves when the computer's move is equal to 2 (representing Paper). The last if statement code block evaluates the computer's and the player's moves when the computer's move is equal to 3 (representing Scissors).

Step 10: Creating the DisplayResults() Handler

The DisplayResults() handler, shown next, is responsible for informing the player of the results of the current round of play and should be added to the end of the script file. This handler is passed three arguments, the computer's move, the player's move, and the already determined result of the game.

```
-- This handler displays the results of current round of play
on DisplayResults(ComputerMove, PlayerMove, result)

        -- Convert the computer's move into a text string
        if ComputerMove = 1 then set ComputerMove to "Rock"
        if ComputerMove = 2 then set ComputerMove to "Paper"
        if ComputerMove = 3 then set ComputerMove to "Scissors"

        -- Convert the player's move into a text string
        if PlayerMove = 1 then set PlayerMove to "Rock"
```

```
    if PlayerMove = 2 then set PlayerMove to "Paper"
    if PlayerMove = 3 then set PlayerMove to "Scissors"

    -- Select a text string to be displayed in a dialog window
    -- based on the values assigned to the result variable
    if result = "win" then
        set GameStatus to " You win!"
    else if result = "lose" then
        set GameStatus to " You lose!"
    else
        set GameStatus to " Tie!"
    end if

    beep -- Make some noise to get the player's attention

    -- Display the result of the current round of play
    display dialog GameStatus & return & return & ¬
        "----------------------------------------" & return & return & ¬
        "The computer picked: " & ComputerMove & return & return & ¬
        "You picked: " & PlayerMove & return & return & ¬
        "----------------------------------------" & return & return & ¬
        "" buttons {"OK"} ¬
        with title GameTitle

end DisplayResults
```

This handler begins by executing three if statements that convert the number representing the computer's move to an equivalent string representation. Next, three more if statements are executed to convert the number representing the player's move to an equivalent string representation. Next, an if statement code block has been set up to analyze the value of the result variable, and based on that analysis, a text string is assigned to a variable named GameStatus. This value is then used by the display dialog command that follows to inform the player of the results of the game.

Step 11: Creating the PlayAgain() Handler

The PlayAgain() handler is responsible for prompting the player to continue playing the Rock, Paper, Scissors game. Its program statements are shown next and should be added to the end of the script file.

```
-- This handler displays a dialog window that prompts the player
-- for permission to start a new round of play
on PlayAgain()

    beep -- Make some noise to get the player's attention

    -- Prompt the player to play again
    set reply to button returned of (display dialog ¬
        "Would you like to play again?" buttons {"Yes", "No"} ¬
        with title GameTitle)

    return reply -- Return the player's response

end PlayAgain
```

The dialog window displayed by this handler contains two buttons, labeled Yes and No. The handler assigns a string value to a variable named `reply`, representing the button on which the player clicks and then returns this value back to the statement that called upon the handler to execute.

Step 12: Creating the DisplaySplashScreen() Handler

The `DisplaySplashScreen()` handler is responsible for displaying a dialog window at the end of the game that thanks the player for playing the game. The AppleScript statements that make up the `DisplaySplashScreen()` handler are provided next and should be appended to the end of the script file.

```
-- This handler displays a dialog window that thanks the player
-- for playing the game.
on DisplaySplashScreen()

    beep -- Make some noise to get the player's attention

    -- Display the game's final window
    display dialog "Thank you for playing the Rock, Paper, Scissors" & ¬
        " Game. " & return & return & ¬
        "Copyright 2007" buttons {"OK"} with title GameTitle

end DisplaySplashScreen
```

Testing the Execution of the Rock, Paper, Scissors Game

Assuming that you followed along carefully and did not make any typing errors, the Rock, Paper, Scissors game should be ready to go. As you test the execution of your new game, make sure you thoroughly test every part of the game. For example, keep playing long enough to try every possible combination of results and to ensure that the game correctly evaluates them and properly declares wins, losses, and ties.

SUMMARY

In this chapter you learned about the different types of errors that your AppleScripts are susceptible to and how to analyze and interpret AppleScript error messages. This chapter provided you with advice on how to prevent errors from occurring in the first place. You learned different programming techniques that you can use to keep track of the logical program flow of your AppleScripts and to monitor the values assigned to key script variables to ensure that they are being modified as expected. You also learned how to work with the `try` statement to build error handlers that can trap and react to errors.

Before you move on to Chapter 10, "Introducing AppleScript Studio," I suggest you set aside a little more time to improve the Rock, Paper, Scissors game by addressing the following list of challenges.

CHALLENGES

1. As currently written, the Rock, Paper, Scissors game makes the assumption that the player already knows how the game is played. Consider providing the player with instructions that explain how the game is played and how results are evaluated.

2. Consider adding variables and programming logic to your AppleScript that keep track of game statistics, like the total number of games played, won, lost, and tied and then make this information available to the player. You might, for example, display the game's statistics at the end of the round of play or just once at the end of the game.

10

INTRODUCING APPLESCRIPT STUDIO

I n this final chapter of the book, you will learn how to apply your new AppleScript programming skills to a new programming environment, AppleScript Studio. AppleScript Studio supports the development of desktop applications running on Mac OS X 10.1.2 or higher. AppleScript Studio applications are created using a number of technologies that work together to execute applications written using AppleScript. Because it uses AppleScript as its underlying programming language, AppleScript Studio provides a perfect next step for AppleScript programmers looking to learn how to develop full-featured Mac OS X desktop applications. This chapter will provide you with an overview of the different technologies that make up AppleScript Studio and demonstrate how to use these technologies to create the book's final game project, the Tic-Tac-Toe game.

Specifically, you will learn:

- About AppleScript Studio components including Xcode, the Cocoa Framework, and the Interface Builder
- How to work with AppleScript Studio projects
- How to work with the Xcode project editor
- How to build graphical user interfaces
- How to connect interface controls to AppleScript code

PROJECT PREVIEW: THE TIC-TAC-TOE GAME

This chapter's game project is the Tic-Tac-Toe game. Instead of creating the game as an Apple-Script application, you will use AppleScript Studio to build a desktop application, which will consist of a graphical user interface, allowing the user to start the application directly from the desktop and to interact with it using the mouse.

Figure 10.1 shows how the application will look when first started. As you can see, it consists of a game board made up of nine squares—representing a traditional Tic-Tac-Toe game board—and a button labeled Play.

FIGURE 10.1

To begin playing the game, the player must click on the Play button.

Once the Play button has been clicked, the dialog window shown in Figure 10.2 displays, notifying Player X that the game is now ready for her to make the first move.

FIGURE 10.2

Player X always moves first.

Moves are made when the current player clicks on an unselected game board square, at which time a graphical letter representing the player is displayed on the selected square. Any attempt to select a square that has already been assigned to one of the players is ignored, forcing the player to make a valid selection. Game play continues until either Player X or Player O manages to line up three squares in a row (vertically, horizontally, or diagonally) or every game board square has been selected without anybody winning, in which case a tie is declared. Figure 10.3 shows the dialog window that is displayed when Player X wins the game.

FIGURE 10.3

The game displays a dialog window notifying the players when the game has been won.

Figure 10.4 shows an example of a typical game. As you can see, Player X has outmaneuvered Player O.

FIGURE 10.4

Player X has beaten Player O by lining up three squares in a row—vertically in the third column.

Once the game has been won or declared a tie, the game board is frozen, preventing either player from making another move. The players can begin a new round of play by clicking on the Play button or close the game by clicking on the red close button located on the upper-left side of the game window's title bar.

INTRODUCING APPLESCRIPT STUDIO

As has already been stated, AppleScript Studio provides you with all the tools you need to develop robust, full-featured Mac OS X applications, using AppleScript as the underlying programming language. These applications can display complex graphical user interfaces complete with buttons, popup controls, slider controls, progress bars, radio and checkbox controls and just about any other interface control you might want to use.

Using AppleScript, AppleScript Studio applications can interact with and automate the scriptable Mac OS X applications. As such, you might create AppleScript Studio applications that provide customized front ends to other applications. Alternatively, you might create AppleScript Studio applications that produce automated workflows using features provided by two or more Mac OS X applications, while also providing a unifying user interface. Of course, AppleScript Studio can also be used to create entirely new Mac OS X applications, such as computer games.

HINT Sometimes the use of AppleScript Studio to perform a particular task is overkill. Many times all that you need is to develop small AppleScripts. For example, AppleScript is best used in situations where a graphical user interface is not required to facilitate user interaction. AppleScripts are also well suited for performing repetitive tasks that require minimal user interaction.

AppleScript is an integrated system-level technology available on all Mac operating systems starting with Mac OS 7. However, AppleScript Studio only works on Mac OS X 10.1.2 or later. As such, if you need to develop programs that execute on Mac operating systems prior to Mac OS X 10.1.2, you'll need to rely on AppleScript.

AppleScript Studio is made up of a number of different application development technologies, including AppleScript, which together facilitate desktop application development. These technologies include:

- Xcode
- The Cocoa framework
- Interface Builder

Building Mac OS X Applications with Xcode

Xcode is a free Integrated Development Environment, or IDE, provided by Apple. As of the writing of this book, the current version of Xcode is 2.4.1, which could be downloaded from http://developer.apple.com/tools/download/. Xcode provides you with a powerful code editor and advanced built-in debugging facilities. It also provides a complete working environment from which you can manage all aspects of application development, and it tightly integrates with Interface Builder, which facilities the development of graphical user interfaces.

Understanding the Cocoa Framework

Underneath the covers, the Cocoa framework provides AppleScript Studio with access to development resources required to build desktop applications. Cocoa was initially created to support the development of Objective C programs. However, Cocoa was designed as a flexible framework, allowing Apple to integrate with other programming tools, including AppleScript Studio.

AppleScript Studio depends on Cocoa to simplify the development of application graphical user interfaces. Specifically, interface controls like buttons, radio buttons, sliders, etc., are all supplied to AppleScript Studio by the Cocoa framework. Cocoa manages the fundamental operation of the interface controls, ensuring that they operate like they should, eliminating the programmer of this responsibility. For example, Cocoa ensures that when a button control has been added to an application it properly reflects changes in the button's state when the player clicks on it, identifying when the button control has focus, and that it is depressed.

Crafting Graphical User Interfaces Using Interface Builder

Another application development technology used by AppleScript Studio is Interface Builder. Interface Builder is made up of a number of windows, each of which is used to perform a specific purpose when creating graphical user interfaces. Interface Builder's windows include:

- **Window.** Every new AppleScript Studio project is automatically assigned a default window to be used as the basis for developing a graphical user interface.
- **Cocoa-Controls Palette.** A window containing collections of interface controls that can be added to application windows to create graphical user interfaces.
- **MainMenu.nib.** Provides access to the different components that make up an application's user interface, including such things as windows, menus, and image and sound files.
- **MainMenu.nib—MainMenu.** A customizable application menu, representing the application's menu system.

Project Organization

Once installed, you can start Xcode by opening /Developer/Applications/ and clicking on the Xcode icon. You can also open existing AppleScript Studio projects by opening the File menu and selecting the Open option.

AppleScript Studio applications are a type of Xcode application. The primary structure used to organize and manage an Xcode application is a project, which provides a means of storing and interacting with the files and resources that make the application. Xcode projects are stored in folders and assigned an .xcodeproj file extension.

In order to create a new application, you must begin by creating a new Xcode project. This is accomplished by selecting the New Project option located on Xcode's File menu, as demonstrated in Figure 10.5.

After clicking on the New Project menu item, Xcode starts an Assistant that prompts you to specify the type of application you want to create, as demonstrated in Figure 10.6. Xcode supports the creation of many different types of applications, as shown in the figure. Since this chapter is about AppleScript Studio, select AppleScript Application. This tells Xcode what types of files, resources, and framework information is required to create your new application.

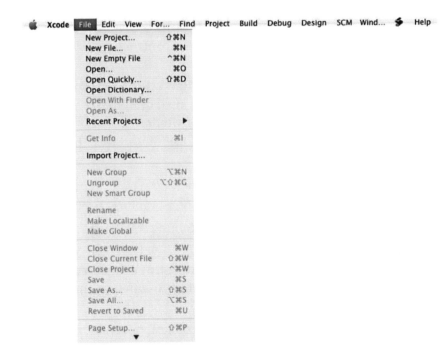

FIGURE 10.5

The Xcode's File menu provides commands for creating and opening application projects.

FIGURE 10.6

Xcode's Assistant prompts you to identify the type of project you want to create.

After specifying that you want to create an AppleScript Application and clicking on the Next button, the Assistant prompts you to supply a name for your new application and the location where you want to save it, as shown in Figure 10.7.

FIGURE 10.7

Naming your new
AppleScript
Studio project.

Once you have specified a name for your project and the location where it is to be saved, the Assistant's Next button changes into a Finish button. Click on this button to close the Assistant and create your new Xcode project. At this point, Xcode's project window will appear. You will use the window to build and test the execution of your new AppleScript application.

GETTING COMFORTABLE WITH THE XCODE PROJECT WINDOW

As has been stated, the Xcode project window is where you will manage the development of your AppleScript Studio applications. Each time you start Xcode and create a new AppleScript Studio project, the Xcode project window is displayed, as demonstrated in Figure 10.8.

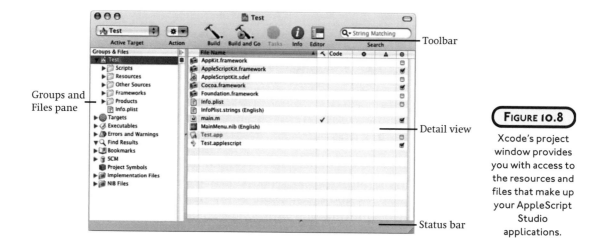

Groups and Files pane

Toolbar

Detail view

Status bar

FIGURE 10.8

Xcode's project
window provides
you with access to
the resources and
files that make up
your AppleScript
Studio
applications.

By default, the Xcode project window is organized into four sections. The Xcode toolbar resides at the top of the window, displaying icons representing commonly used commands. The Groups & Files pane is located on the left-hand side of the window, just under the toolbar, and is responsible for organizing and providing access to the files and resources that make up the project. The Detail view is located just to the right of the Groups & Files pane. Its purpose is to display more information about the currently selected item in the Groups & Files pane. Lastly, the status bar is located at the bottom of the project window and is used by Xcode to display messages as you work with your project.

Examining the Project Window Toolbar

The project window toolbar, shown in Figure 10.9, provides programmers with easy access to the Xcode commands outlined here:

- **Active Target menu.** Lists the active target (e.g., your Xcode project).
- **Action button.** Provides quick access to commands that are applicable to the selected file or resource.
- **Build button.** Compiles your AppleScript Studio application.
- **Build and Go button.** Compiles and executes your AppleScript Studio application.
- **Tasks button.** Halts the execution of any current operation.
- **Info button.** Opens the Info window, which is used to view and interact with group and file items.
- **Editor button.** Displays and hides the display of the Xcode code editor in the Detail View pane.
- **Search field.** Performs a search of the currently displayed file or resource.

FIGURE 10.9

The Xcode toolbar provides access to Xcode commands.

Understanding Groups & Files

Whenever you create a new project, Xcode's Assistant prompts you to identify the type of project you are creating. Based on your selection, Xcode automatically assembles a collection of files and resources required to build and execute your application. The Groups & Files pane, shown in Figure 10.10, displays and provides you with access to all of these files and resources.

FIGURE 10.10

A look at the default set of files and resources that make up a new AppleScript Studio application.

The files and resources displayed in the Groups & Files pane are organized hierarchically into groups and displayed as individual items. Folder icons are used to represent groups. Files and other items are represented by unique icons that visually identify their type. The following list outlines a number of key groups and files that you will need to understand to work effectively with the Xcode project window.

- **Scripts Group.** Stores AppleScript files that you write to make your AppleScript Studio application do what you want it to. By default, this group contains one script that is automatically assigned the same name as your project along with an .applescript file extension. You can add more AppleScripts to this group if required.

- **Resources Group.** This group stores resource files used by the application. If your AppleScript Studio application uses any graphic or sound files, you may want to add them to this group by dragging and dropping into the group. Also included in the Resources group is the MainMenu.nib file, which stores instructions that are used to create the application's graphical user interface. This interface is assembled using Interface Builder, which can be started by double-clicking on MainMenu.nib.

- **Other Sources.** This group contains a file named main.m. This file stores Cocoa code that is used to build the project's AppleScript Studio application.

- **Frameworks.** Contains frameworks required to develop and execute your AppleScript Studio application.

- **Products.** Stores the product specified for each project target. By default, each AppleScript Studio project contains one target that results in the creation of one application. This application is given an .app file extension and is stored in a subgroup called Build. When you are finished developing your AppleScript Studio application, copy the files located in the Build subgroup to distribute your application.

- **Targets.** Targets specify instructions needed to build an application. New AppleScript Studio projects have a single target, assigned the same name as the project, minus a file extension.

- **Errors and Warnings.** This group displays a list of any errors generated when you compile your AppleScript Studio application. If your application fails to compile and execute, you should look here for error messages telling you what went wrong.

Displaying Detailed Project Information

The Xcode project window's Detail view provides detailed information for the currently selected file, resource, or group. By default, it displays the following list of columns.

- File Type
- File Name
- Build Status
- Errors
- Warnings
- Code
- Target

If you want, you can configure the Detail view, adding or removing columns, by selecting or clearing items listed under the Detail View Columns entry located on Xcode's View menu.

Working with Xcode's Code Editor

Xcode also provides you with an advanced code editor loaded with helpful features. These features include:

- Syntax color coding
- Code completion
- Automatic code indentation
- Syntax checking
- Automatic matching of closing brackets and parentheses

Xcode automatically generates an empty AppleScript file with a file extension of .applescript as part of every new AppleScript Studio project. This script is stored in the Scripts folder. If you select this script and then click on the Editor button located in the Xcode project window's toolbar, Xcode will display and allow you to edit the script file in the project window's Detail view, as demonstrated in Figure 10.11.

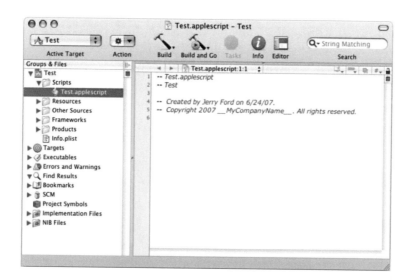

FIGURE 10.11

Viewing the AppleScript file that Xcode has added to your AppleScript Studio project.

TRICK If you prefer, you can double-click on the AppleScript file and Xcode will respond by displaying the script file in a separate code editor window.

At the very top of the code editor, you will see a light gray Editor Navigation Bar. The Navigation Bar has the following features.

- **Previous and Next Arrow Buttons.** Switches between script files when two or more have been opened.
- **Script Icon.** Displays an icon representing the type of code file being edited.
- **File Name Menu.** A popup menu that displays the name of the script file being edited as well as any other open script files. You may display any open script file by clicking on its name.
- **Function Menu.** A popup menu that lists and provides access to every handler in the script file.
- **Bookmarks Menu.** Provides access to bookmarks saved for the current file.
- **Breakpoints Menu.** Provides access to breakpoints set for the current file.

- **Go To Counterpart Button.** This option does not apply to AppleScript files.
- **Included Files Menu.** This option does not apply to AppleScript files.
- **Lock Status Button.** Allows you to lock and unlock the script file's edit status.

Examining the Info Window

Xcode's Info window gives you the ability to view and modify items located in the project window. To open this window, click on the Info button located on the Xcode Project window's toolbar. The Info window displays information about the currently selected item. Based on the type of item that is selected, the Info window typically organizes item data in different views. You can switch between these views by clicking on one of the buttons located at the top of the window. For example, Figure 10.12 shows the information that is displayed on the General view of the Info window for an AppleScript file.

FIGURE 10.12

Examining the
General view for
an AppleScript
file.

As you can see, in addition to displaying all kinds of information about the selected item, the Info window also lets you modify all kinds of item properties.

OTHER KEY APPLESCRIPT STUDIO COMPONENTS

In addition to Xcode Code Editor, the Cocoa framework and Interface Builder, there are a number of other Xcode components that, while there is insufficient room to cover in this chapter, you should at least be aware of. These windows include the Inspector window, Terminology Browser, and Debugger windows.

HINT The information provided in this chapter only scratches the surface of AppleScript Studio programming. To better understand AppleScript Programming, I recommend you read *AppleScript Studio Programming for the Absolute Beginner* (ISBN: 1598633031), the only comprehensive book available that addresses all aspects of AppleScript Studio programming.

The Inspector Window

Another Xcode window that you will work with a lot is the Inspector window. Using this window, you will configure interface control properties and set up event handler connections. Generally, you will work with Interface Builder first to create your application's graphical user interface and then use the Inspector window to further configure interface controls and event handler connections. To open the Inspector window, click on the Show Inspector option located in the Interface Builder's Tools menu.

The Inspector window is organized into a number of different views, which vary based on the item being configured. You can switch between these views by clicking on the popup list control located at the top of the Inspector window and selecting the view you want to work with. Figure 10.13 shows the Inspector window's Attributes view.

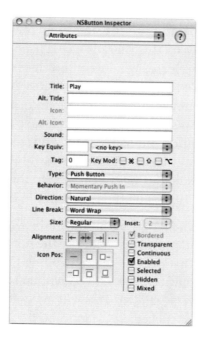

FIGURE 10.13

Accessing property attributes associated with an interface control.

By modifying attribute properties for windows and interface controls, you can change their appearance and functionality. For example, in Figure 10.13, you can see the attributes for a button control. This control has been assigned a Title of Play. Title represents the text that is displayed on top of the button control as its caption or label. If you look at the bottom of the window, you will see that the button control's Enabled property is selected. This tells Xcode to make the button control accessible when the application is started. If necessary you could clear this attribute and the button would go into a disabled state, in which case it would be up to you to programmatically enable it at a later point during the application's execution.

Another important Inspector window view that you need to be familiar with is the AppleScript view, as demonstrated in Figure 10.14. From this view you can assign a name to the selected window or interface control. Doing so allows you to programmatically reference the control in the AppleScript portion of your application, which is key to being able to manipulate windows and interface controls.

Windows and controls are designed to interact with specific events. For example, events associated within button controls include the clicked event. This event is triggered whenever the user clicks on a button control. Since most applications use buttons to allow the user to initiate some sort of action when clicked, it is necessary to configure the button control's clicked event handler to respond to this event. This is accomplished by opening Interface Builder, selecting the control, then opening the Inspector window, and switching to its AppleScript view. The Event Handler area on this view displays a list of all the event handlers that you can configure for the currently selected window or interface control. Event handlers are grouped into different categories. The button control's clicked event handler is located in the Action group. To enable it, drill down into the Action group and select it. Next, you must associate the event handler that was just enabled with a specific AppleScript. All the AppleScripts that make up your application are listed at the bottom of the AppleScript. By default, a new AppleScript is automatically created for each new AppleScript Studio application. All you have to do is click on the radio button control just to the left of the application AppleScript, as demonstrated in Figure 10.14, and then click on the Edit button.

In response, Xcode will display the specified AppleScript file in the Xcode code editor, which now includes the clicked event handler that was just added to the AppleScript file. When you are ready to write the code statements that provide the controlling program logic that actually makes your AppleScript Studio applications work, you will do so by adding the appropriate programming logic inside this event handler. This will make the application respond appropriately when the button control is clicked.

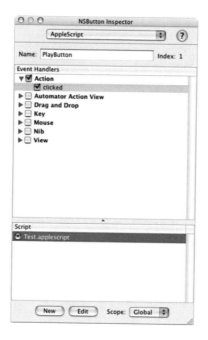

FIGURE 10.14

Configuring the
clicked event
handler for a
button control.

You will typically need to set up at least one event handler connection for every interface control with which the user can interact. For controls like button controls, they all share a common event handler, meaning that while, for example, you must individually configure each button control event handler's clicked event to programmatically respond when the user clicks on one of the application's buttons, only one on clicked event handler is added to your AppleScript file. To determine which button control the user has clicked, it is critical that you remember to assign a name to each button control. This will allow you to programmatically identify which button control was clicked and then execute the appropriate AppleScript statements based on that determination.

The Terminology Browser

Like the Script Editor application, Xcode also provides you with easy access to a terminology browser window, from which you can view different scriptable applications' terminology. You can display the Dictionary window, shown in Figure 10.15, by clicking on the Open Dictionary option located on the Xcode File menu.

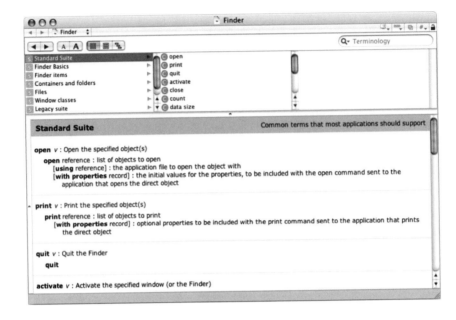

FIGURE 10.15

Xcode provides easy access to its own terminology browser.

Xcode's Debugger

Although there is insufficient space in this chapter to cover it in any detail, it is important that you be aware of Xcode's built-in debugger, shown in Figure 10.16.

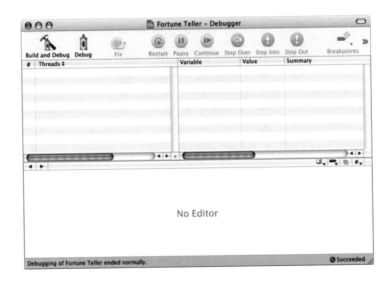

FIGURE 10.16

Xcode's integrated debugger gives you detailed control over the execution of script statements.

Using Xcode's built-in debugger, you can control, step by step, when script statements are executed, pausing execution whenever you want to check on the values of your variables.

This finite level of control makes it possible to keep track of the overall execution of your AppleScript and facilitates the identification of errors. Xcode even supports a Fix and Continue feature, allowing you to modify your script statements and then to recompile your application without having to terminate the current debug session.

CREATING GRAPHICAL USER INTERFACES USING INTERFACE BUILDER

AppleScript Studio is a desktop application development tool, meaning that its applications can interact with the user by means of graphical user interfaces or GUIs. To create these GUIs, you use Interface Builder. Interface Builder helps you do this by providing access to a large collection of predefined interface controls that you can add to application windows using drag and drop. Once added to a window, Interface Builder allows you to move and change the size of interface controls. Using the Inspector window, you can modify the interface control's properties and connect controls to AppleScript event handlers.

You will find Interface Builder located in the /Developer/Applications folder. However, most programmers start it from within Xcode by double-clicking on the MainMenu.nib file located in the Xcode project window's Files & Groups pane. As Figure 10.17 shows, Interface Builder consists of a number of different windows.

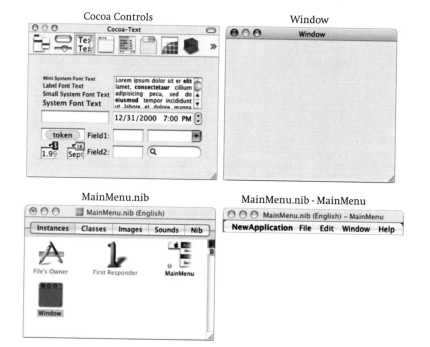

FIGURE 10.17

Interface Builder is made up of a number of interrelated windows.

Every AppleScript Studio application is assigned a default nib file named MainMenu.nib, which stores instructions that are later used to build the application windows when your AppleScript Studio application is compiled.

Working with Cocoa Controls

The Interface Builder window that displays all sorts of interface controls is referred to as the Cocoa Controls palette. This window organizes interface controls into groups that are accessed by clicking on icons located at the top of the window. To add a particular control to an application window, all you have to do is drag and drop it onto the window.

 You can also add new windows to your AppleScript Studio applications by dragging and dropping the appropriate type of window from the Cocoa Controls palette onto the MainMenu.nib window.

Interface Builder helps you align interface controls by providing visual indicators. Once you have placed an interface control onto an application window, you can change its size and location by clicking on it and using the control's resizing handles to grab hold of it. When working with a control, Interface Builder displays visual indicators to assist you in aligning the control with other controls that you may have already added to the window, as demonstrated in Figure 10.18.

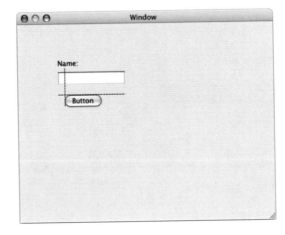

FIGURE 10.18

Interface Builder
provides visual
indicators to assist
you in aligning
interface controls.

Cocoa is the Xcode component that provides AppleScript Studio applications with access to interface elements like menus, interface controls, and windows. Most application GUIs consist of one or more windows filled with various interface controls. Examples of these controls include button and bevel button controls. A button control is an application button that is used to initiate an immediate action. Button controls have rounded edges and can display limited amounts of text. A bevel button is another type of button control. In addition to displaying text, bevel button controls can also be used to display graphics. Bevel buttons have a three-dimensional look and can have square or rounded edges.

MainMenu.nib Contents

Interface Builder's MainMenu.nib window is organized into different views. The default view, the Instances view, is the view that you will need to use most often. It displays the following icons.

- **File's Owner.** An object outside of the nib file that facilitates communication between objects defined within the nib.

- **First Responder.** Sets the interface control that initially receives focus when the GUI is initially displayed.

- **MainMenu.** Stores instructions that define the contents of the application's menus.

- **Window.** Represents the application's default window.

 Focus is a term that identifies the interface control that is the target for keystrokes. Focus is set selecting a window control.

You do not need to worry about the File Owner object. Xcode takes care of it for you. Nor will you usually need to do anything with First Responder. Since most Mac OS X applications have some sort of menus, you will need to learn how to work with MainMenu window, which is used to add and remove menus and menu items. Window represents the default windows for your AppleScript Studio application. Additional windows can be added to your applications if necessary.

BACK TO THE TIC-TAC-TOE GAME

Okay, now let's turn our attention back to this chapter's game project, the Tic-Tac-Toe game. This version of the Tic-Tac-Toe game is a two-player version, in which Player X and Player O take turns clicking on unselected game board squares in an effort to line up three squares in a row (horizontally, vertically, or diagonally). To create this game, you will need to learn how to work with AppleScript Studio, which you will do by carefully following the instructions provided in the sections that follow.

The Tic-Tac-Toe application will be created in five steps, as outlined here:

1. Start Xcode and create a new AppleScript Studio application.
2. Create the game's graphical user interface.

3. Configure menu, window, and control properties and set up connections between interface controls and AppleScript event handlers.
4. Add the script statements required to operate the game.
5. Compile and execute the Tic-Tac-Toe application.

Step 1: Creating a New Project

If it is not already started, open Xcode and then create a new AppleScript Studio application using the steps outlined here:

1. Open the /Developer/Applications/ folder and double-click on the Xcode icon.
2. Once Xcode starts, click on the New Project option located on the File menu. In response, Xcode will start an Assistant, which displays a list of application templates.
3. Select the AppleScript Application template and click on the Next button.
4. Type **Tic-Tac-Toe** as the filename of your new Mac OS X application and then specify the location where you want to store your new application.
5. Click on the Finish button.

Step 2: Creating the User Interface

Now it is time to set up the graphical user interface for the Tic-Tac-Toe game, as outlined in the following procedure.

1. Double-click on the MainMenu.nib file located in the Resources group. This will start the Interface Builder.
2. Using the resize handle located in the lower-right corner of the application window, resize the window until it is approximately 2.5 inches wide and 3 inches tall.
3. Drag and drop nine instances of the bevel button control onto the window. Resize each bevel button so that together they take up most of the available display area, leaving only a small area at the bottom of the window, approximately 1/3 of an inch in height.
4. Drag and drop an instance of the button control onto the bottom portion of the window and center it. Double-click on the button control and type **Play** as the button control's caption, as demonstrated in Figure 10.19.

FIGURE 10.19

Examining the design of the Tic-Tac-Toe game's graphical user interface.

During the play of this game, Player X and Player O will take turns clicking on different game board squares (bevel button controls) to make moves. When first started, the game will load a blank image file into each game board square. To visually indicate which squares have been selected, the game will load graphic files representing the letter X or O onto each square. For this to work, you must add copies of these three graphic files to your AppleScript Studio project. You will find copies of these files on this book's companion website located at http://www.courseptr.com/downloads/. Once you have downloaded the images to your computer, drag and drop each of these jpeg files onto the Images view of Interface Builder's MainMenu.nib window.

Step 3: Setting Control Properties

Now that you have created a new AppleScript Studio project and designed the graphical user interface for your application, it is time to modify property settings belonging to the application's menus, windows, and interface controls. In addition, you need to configure an association between the application's interface controls and the program code that you will soon place in the application's on clicked event handler.

Customizing the Application's Menus

Let's begin the customization of application properties by modifying the menu system. To do this, you will need to double-click on the MainMenu icon location on the Instances pane of the MainMenu.nib window. In response, the Interface Builder will display the application menus. By default, new AppleScript Studio applications are automatically assigned a number of default menus, most of which are not needed by this application. As a result, the first thing you should do is select and delete the Edit menu by selecting it and pressing the Delete key. Do the same thing for the Help menu. Next, click on the Window menu and then delete each menu item located under that menu—except for Minimize—by selecting each menu item and pressing the Delete key. Next, select the File menu and delete each of its menu items, except for Close.

At this point, the only thing left to do is customize the contents of the Application menu. For starters, double-click on the Application menu and rename it Tic-Tac-Toe. Then double-click on the About Application menu item and rename it About Tic-Tac-Toe. Next, rename the Hide Application menu item to Hide Tic-Tac-Toe. Finally, rename the Quit Application menu item to Quit Tic-Tac-Toe. When done, the MainMenu.nib window should look like the example shown in Figure 10.20.

●○○ MainMenu.nib (English) – …
New Tic-Tac-Toe File Window
About Tic-Tac-Toe

Preferences…   ⌘,

Services   ▶

Hide Tic-Tac-Toe   ⌘H
Hide Others   ⌥⌘H
Show All

Quit Tic-Tac-Toe   ⌘Q

FIGURE 10.20

Examining the
layout of the
game's Tic-Tac-
Toe menu.

Specifying Window and Control Properties

Now it is time to modify properties belonging to window and interface controls. These modifications include assigning a name to each control, so that the control can be programmatically identified when the application is run, and setting property values that affect the appearance and behavior of the window and its interface controls. For starters, click on an open portion of the application window and then open the Inspector window by clicking on the Show Inspector menu item located on Xcode's Tools menu. At the top of the Inspector window is a popup button control that, when selected, displays a listing showing the different views that can be displayed by the Inspector window. Select the Attributes option. This view displays several window properties that affect the look and operation of the application window. Type **Tic-Tac-Toe** in the Window Title field to display the name of the game in the window's title bar. Next, clear the Zoom (and resize) option. This will prevent the players from being able to modify the size of the Tic-Tac-Toe game board window at runtime. At this point, the Inspector window should look like the example shown in Figure 10.21.

Now, select the popup menu located at the top of the Inspector window and select the AppleScript option. From here you can assign a name to a window so that it can be programmatically referenced. To do this, type **main** in the Name field. At this point, the Inspector window should look like the example shown in Figure 10.22.

At this point, you have made all of the required modifications to the game's window. Now it is time to modify properties belonging to each of the game's nine bevel button controls and its button control. Begin by selecting the first bevel button control, located on the first column of the first row of the application window, and then select the Attributes view of the Inspector window. Next, type **Tink** into the Sound field. Tink is a sound file installed by default on every Mac OS X computer. The Tink sound file will play whenever the player clicks on the first bevel button control. Click on the Type popup control and select the `Square Button` property, configuring the overall shape of the bevel button control.

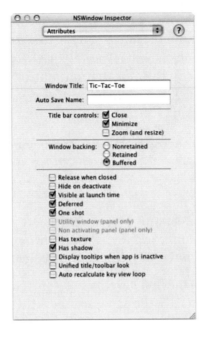

FIGURE 10.21

Examining window
attributes.

FIGURE 10.22

Assigning a name
to the application
window.

As players make moves by clicking on game board squares (bevel buttons), the game will
display graphic images representing player moves (images of the letter X and O). Selecting

one of the six Icon Pos buttons located at the bottom of the Inspector window determines how the image is displayed. Click on the middle button on the first row to center any image that is displayed on this bevel button control. Next, clear the Enabled property. This will prevent the players from being able to click on the bevel button control when the game is first started. You will programmatically control the availability of the game's bevel button and button controls.

 There are six buttons to choose from when specifying the Icon Pos property. Each of these buttons represents a different configuration, with different combinations of text and graphics.

At this point, the only configuration task remaining for the bevel button is to assign it a name, which is accomplished by selecting the AppleScript view from the popup control located at the top of the Inspector window and then typing **A1** in the Name field.

Now that you have seen how to configure the first bevel button control, you need to configure the remaining eight bevel buttons in exactly the same manner—the only difference is the names that you assign to each button. The names that you should assign to each of the game's bevel button controls are shown next and are identified by their physical position on the game board.

```
A1 A2 A3
B1 B2 B3
C1 C2 C3
```

Once you have finished configuring the bevel buttons, you need to modify the Name property belonging to the game's lone button control, assigning it a name of PlayButton.

Setting Up the Application's Event Handler

Once a new game has started, players take turns making moves by selecting game board squares (bevel buttons). Each time a player clicks on an unassigned square, the game displays a graphic image representing the current player on that square and then checks on the status of the game to see if it has been won, lost, or tied or if game play should continue.

To set this series of steps into motion, you will have to add an event handler to the game's AppleScript that executes whenever one of the bevel button's controls is clicked. This is done by configuring each of the bevel button controls, as well as the game's button control, to trigger the clicked event handler. This is accomplished by selecting one of these controls and then opening the Inspector window and switching to its AppleScript view. The button and bevel button control's clicked event handler is located in the Action group in the Event Handler area. To enable it, drill down into the Action group and select it, as demonstrated in

Figure 10.23. You also need to select the radio button located just to the left of the application's AppleScript name, located in the script area at the bottom of the Inspector window.

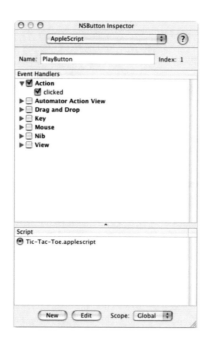

FIGURE 10.23

Enabling the clicked event handler for a bevel button control.

Make sure that you configure the clicked event handler for each of the application's button and bevel button controls. If you fail to configure the clicked event handler for a given control, that control will not be able to initiate any action when clicked. Once you have configured clicked event handlers for the last button or bevel button control, you need to perform one additional step for that button. Specifically, you need to click on the Edit button located at the bottom of the Inspector window. In response, Xcode will display your application's AppleScript file, which will now include an entry for the clicked event handler. This event handler will automatically be executed any time one of the button or bevel button controls is clicked.

Step 4: Adding a Little Programming Logic

Now that you have set up the clicked event for the button control and each of the bevel button controls, it is time to get back to something a little more familiar—writing AppleScript code. At this point, the contents of your AppleScript Studio application's AppleScript should look similar to this:

```
-- TicTacToe.applescript
-- TicTacToe

--  Created by Jerry Ford on 6/21/07.
--  Copyright 2007 __MyCompanyName__. All rights reserved.

on clicked theObject
    (*Add your script here*)

end clicked
```

The Tic-Tac-Toe game will use a number of different global variables to store data that will be accessed throughout the AppleScript file. The variables represent each of the game board squares (bevel button controls) as well as the name of the current player (Player X or Player O) and a count of the total number of moves made by both players. So, the first statements that you add to your AppleScript file will declare these variables as global. When you add these script statements, shown next, to the script file, make sure that you insert them after the script file's opening comments but before the `on clicked` event handler.

```
-- Define global variables used throughout the script
global a1, a2, a3, b1, b2, b3, c1, c2, c3
global Player, Moves
```

The next step in the development of your AppleScript is to add the script statements that are responsible for controlling the overall execution of the game. This is accomplished by inserting the following AppleScript statement into the `clicked` event handler, as shown here:

```
-- The on clicked event handler controls the overall execution of the game
on clicked theObject

    -- Determine if the player clicked on the Play button
    if name of theObject is "PlayButton" then

        ClearBoard() -- Clear out all previous moves

        StartGame() -- Reset global values

    else -- One of the nine bevel buttons (game board squares) was clicked

        AssignMove(name of theObject) -- Assign square to the player
```

```
        set BoardStatus to AnalyzeBoard() -- Analyze the game board

        set GameStatus to IsGameOver(BoardStatus) -- See if game is over

        if GameStatus = "GameOver" then
            DisableBoard() -- The game is over so disable the game board
        else
            SwitchTurn() -- Toggle player turns
        end if

    end if

end clicked
```

Take note of the `theObject` parameter that Xcode added to the beginning of the event handler. Xcode will automatically pass the name of the button or bevel button control that is clicked as an argument to this handler. As such, by inspecting the value assigned to `theObject`, you can programmatically determine which button or bevel button the player clicked.

The statements that make up the `clicked` event handler are organized into an `if` statement code block. The first two statements are executed if the user clicks on the button control named `PlayButton`. If this is the case, the `ClearBoard()` handler is executed. This handler is responsible for preparing the game board for a new round of play. Also the `StartGame()` handler is called. This handler resets the game's global variables back to their initial values.

If, on the other hand, one of the game's bevel button controls was clicked, the code statements located in the `else` portion of the code block will execute instead. These script statements call upon a number of custom handlers. For starters, the `AssignMove()` handler is called. This handler is responsible for assigning a graphical letter X or 0 to the square, depending on whose turn it is. The `AnalyzeBoard()` handler is executed next. This handler is responsible for determining if either player has managed to line up three squares in a row and returns a value of X or 0 if one of the players has done so or an empty string to indicate that neither has won.

The value returned by the `AnalyzeBoard()` handler is assigned to a variable named `BoardStatus`, which is then passed to the `IsGameOver()` handler. This handler checks to see which player, if any, has won the game or if the game has ended in a tie. The handler returns either a value of `GameOver`, in the case of a win or a tie, or an empty string, indicating that the game is not over yet. If the game has been won or tied, the `DisableBoard()` handler is called. This handler disables all of the bevel button controls that make up the game board, preventing either player from being able to make another move. If the game has not been won or tied, the SwitchTurn() handler is called. This handler is responsible for toggling between Player X and Player O's turn.

The remainder of the AppleScript file is made up of the custom handlers mentioned above, all of which will be discussed in the sections that follow.

Creating the ClearBoard() Handler

The ClearBoard() handler, shown next, is responsible for preparing the game board for a new round of play.

```
--This handler is responsible for resetting the game board
on ClearBoard()

    tell window "main" -- Send commands to the "main" window

        -- Display blank game board squares
        set image of button "A1" to load image "_.jpg"
        set image of button "A2" to load image "_.jpg"
        set image of button "A3" to load image "_.jpg"
        set image of button "B1" to load image "_.jpg"
        set image of button "B2" to load image "_.jpg"
        set image of button "B3" to load image "_.jpg"
        set image of button "C1" to load image "_.jpg"
        set image of button "C2" to load image "_.jpg"
        set image of button "C3" to load image "_.jpg"

        -- Enable each square
        set enabled of button "A1" to true
        set enabled of button "A2" to true
        set enabled of button "A3" to true
        set enabled of button "B1" to true
        set enabled of button "B2" to true
        set enabled of button "B3" to true
        set enabled of button "C1" to true
        set enabled of button "C2" to true
        set enabled of button "C3" to true

        -- Disable the Play button
```

```
            set enabled of button "PlayButton" to false

        end tell

    end ClearBoard
```

The handler begins with the `tell` statement, which directs all remaining statements to the application's main window.

 In addition to directing AppleScript statements at scriptable Mac OS X applications, the `tell` command can be used to direct commands to specific AppleScript Studio application windows, provided those windows have been assigned a name. Assigning names to your application windows is important since many applications consist of multiple windows.

The first set of statements inside this handler is responsible for displaying a blank image file named _.jpg file on each of the game's bevel button controls. The next set of statements in the handler enable each of the bevel button controls. Finally, the last statement disables the `PlayButton` control, preventing a new game from being started until the current game is finished.

Creating the StartGame() Handler

The code statements that make up the `StartGame()` handler are shown next and should be added to the end of the script file. This handler is responsible for resetting each of the game's global variables to their default values, readying the game for a new round of play.

```
-- This handler is responsible for resetting global variables to their
-- default values
on StartGame()

    tell window "main" -- Send commands to the "main" window

        -- Reset variable values representing game board squares
        set a1 to ""
        set a2 to ""
        set a3 to ""
        set b1 to ""
        set b2 to ""
        set b3 to ""
        set c1 to ""
```

```
    set c2 to ""
    set c3 to ""

    -- Reset variables representing the current play and the
    -- number of moves made
    set Player to "X"
    set Moves to 0

    -- Player X always goes first
    display dialog "Player X's Turn" buttons {"OK"}

  end tell

end StartGame
```

Creating the AssignMove() Handler

The code statements that comprise the AssignMove() handler are shown next and should be added to the end of the script file. This handler takes as an argument a value representing the square selected by the current player.

```
-- This handler is responsible for assigning the selected square to the
-- current player
on AssignMove(Square)

    tell window "main" -- Send commands to the "main" window

        -- Assign the selected square to the current player
        if Square = "A1" then set a1 to Player
        if Square = "A2" then set a2 to Player
        if Square = "A3" then set a3 to Player
        if Square = "B1" then set b1 to Player
        if Square = "B2" then set b2 to Player
        if Square = "B3" then set b3 to Player
        if Square = "C1" then set c1 to Player
        if Square = "C2" then set c2 to Player
        if Square = "C3" then set c3 to Player

        -- Assign an X image when it is Player X's turn
        if Player = "X" then set image of button (Square as string) ¬
```

```
            to load image "x.jpg"

    -- Assign an O image when it is Player O's turn
    if Player = "O" then set image of button (Square as string) ¬
            to load image "o.jpg"

    set Moves to Moves + 1 -- Keep track of the number of moves made

    --Disable the selected square so that it cannot be selected again
    set enabled of button (Square as string) to false

end tell


end AssignMove
```

This handler begins by executing a series of if statements to determine which game board square was selected. Next, two if statements are executed to determine whether to display a graphic X or O on the selected game board square (bevel button control). Next, the value assigned to Moves is incremented by 1 to keep track of the total number of moves made during the current round of play.

Creating the AnalyzeBoard() Handler

The AnalyzeBoard() handler, shown next, is responsible for determining whether the current player has managed to line up three consecutive game board squares.

```
-- This handler is responsible for determining if the current player
-- has managed to line up three consecutive squares
on AnalyzeBoard()

    tell window "main" -- Send commands to the "main" window

        -- Look horizontally
        if a1 = Player and a2 = Player and a3 = Player then return Player
        if b1 = Player and b2 = Player and b3 = Player then return Player
        if c1 = Player and c2 = Player and c3 = Player then return Player

        -- Look vertically
        if a1 = Player and b1 = Player and c1 = Player then return Player
        if a2 = Player and b2 = Player and c2 = Player then return Player
```

```
    if a3 = Player and b3 = Player and c3 = Player then return Player

    -- Look diagonally
    if a1 = Player and b2 = Player and c3 = Player then return Player
    if a3 = Player and b2 = Player and c1 = Player then return Player

    return "" -- Return an empty string

  end tell

end AnalyzeBoard
```

If the current player has managed to line up three consecutive squares, the player's name (Player X or Player O) is returned. Otherwise, an empty string is returned.

Creating the SwitchTurn() Handler

The script statements that make up the SwitchTurn() handler are shown next and should be added to the end of the script file.

```
-- This handler is responsible for toggling between player turns
on SwitchTurn()

    tell window "main" -- Send commands to the "main" window

        if Player = "X" then -- Switch to Player O if Player X went
            set Player to "O" -- Set Player O as the current player
        else -- Switch to Player X if Player O went
            set Player to "X" -- Set Player X as the current player
        end if

        -- Inform the players of the switch
        display dialog "Player " & Player & "'s Turn" buttons {"OK"}

    end tell

end SwitchTurn
```

When called, the SwitchTurn() handler manages the process of switching player turns. Each time the game switches player turns, a display dialog command is used to inform the players whose turn it is.

Creating the IsGameOver() Handler

The script statements that comprise the IsGameOver() handler are shown next and should be added to the end of the script file. This handler processes an argument that either specifies whether one of the players has won the game or consists of an empty string, indicating that neither player has won the game.

```
-- This handler is responsible for determining if the current round of play
-- has ended
on IsGameOver(Winner)

    tell window "main" -- Send commands to the "main" window

        if Winner = "X" then -- Player X has won

            display dialog "Player X wins!" buttons {"OK"} -- Display results
            set enabled of button "PlayButton" to true -- Enable Play button
            return "GameOver" -- Return a string indicated the end of the game

        else if Winner = "O" then -- Player O has won

            display dialog "Player O wins!" buttons {"OK"} -- Display results
            set enabled of button "PlayButton" to true -- Enable Play button
            return "GameOver" -- Return a string indicating the end of the game

        else

            if Moves = 9 then -- The game has ended in a tie

                display dialog "Tie." buttons {"OK"} -- Display results
                set enabled of button "PlayButton" to true --Enable Play button
                -- Return a string indicating the end of the game
                return "GameOver"

            end if

        end if
```

```
      return "" -- Return an empty string indicating the game is not over

   end tell

end IsGameOver
```

This handler is organized using an `if` statement code block wrapped inside a `tell` statement code block. The `if` statement checks to see if the player has won the game. If this is the case, the `PlayButton` button control is enabled, and a value of `GameOver` is returned. If `Player X` has not won the game, an `else if` statement checks to see if `Player O` has won. If neither player has won, the value of `Moves` is analyzed to see if it equals 9, in which case all game board squares have been selected and the game has ended in a tie.

Creating the DisableBoard() Handler

The last handler to be added to the AppleScript is the `DisableBoard()` handler, whose script statements are shown next. This handler disables all game board squares, preventing the players from interacting with them until a new game is started.

```
-- This handler is responsible for disabling the game board when the game
-- is over
on DisableBoard()

    tell window "main" -- Send commands to the "main" window

        --Disable all game board squares
        set enabled of button "A1" to false
        set enabled of button "A2" to false
        set enabled of button "A3" to false
        set enabled of button "B1" to false
        set enabled of button "B2" to false
        set enabled of button "B3" to false
        set enabled of button "C1" to false
        set enabled of button "C2" to false
        set enabled of button "C3" to false

    end tell

end DisableBoard
```

Step 5: Testing the Tic-Tac-Toe Game

All right! At this point, your copy of the Tic-Tac-Toe game should be complete and ready for testing. Assuming that you carefully followed the steps outlined in the previous sections and you did not make any typos, everything should work as described earlier in the chapter. To compile and run your AppleScript Studio project, click on the `Build and Go` button located on the Xcode code editor's toolbar. If all goes as it should, your application should start running within a few moments. If this does not happen, then an error has occurred, as indicated by the presence of a red X located in the lower-right corner of the Xcode code editor's status bar. Double-click on this red X to view information about any errors that may have occurred. More than likely, any errors are going to be the result of either forgetting to assign a name to one of the interface controls that makes up the application user interface or a typo somewhere in the script file.

As with your AppleScripts, remember to thoroughly test your AppleScript Studio applications, making sure that the game properly recognizes when Player X or Player O wins the game and when ties occur. Also, make sure that the game board is properly reset before the start of each new round of play.

SUMMARY

In this chapter, you learned how to create Mac OS X desktop applications using AppleScript Studio. In doing so, you learned how to leverage your investment in AppleScript programming. You learned how to work with a number of different AppleScript Studio technologies, including Xcode, the Cocoa framework, and Interface Builder. This included learning how to work with Xcode's code editor and how to create complex graphical user interfaces. You also learned how to use the Inspector window to configure interface controls and to connect script code to interface controls.

Now, before you put this book down and move on to other things, I suggest you spend a few additional minutes improving the Tic-Tac-Toe game by addressing the following list of challenges.

CHALLENGES

1. As currently written, the Tic-Tac-Toe game assumes that the player knows how to play the game. Consider modifying the game so that in addition to the game board, it displays a dialog window displaying basic instructions for playing the game.

2. Consider displaying a dialog window at the end of each round of play that provides players with statistics like the number of games won by each player, the number of games resulting in a tie, and the total number of games played.

3. Consider improving the game by modifying the dialog window that informs the player when a game has been won. For example, in addition to identifying which player has won, you might also state how (diagonally, vertically, or horizontally).

WHAT'S ON THE
COMPANION WEBSITE?

I n order to become a proficient AppleScript programmer, you will need to spend time developing new AppleScripts. This may mean creating new AppleScript games like the ones covered in this book. However, more than likely, you'll end up developing all kinds of different scripts. For example, you may have a list of tasks that you want to automate or a list of applications that you would like to tie together in order to develop new workflows that result in capabilities that none of the applications alone are capable of performing.

As you learn and experiment with AppleScript and explore its many different capabilities, it helps to have a good collection of AppleScripts from which you can draw upon and find working examples of how to perform various types of tasks. This book provides you with hundreds of small examples and code snippets that you can use as templates when adding functionality to your own AppleScripts. In addition, each chapter ends by demonstrating how to build a complete AppleScript game, giving you step-by-step instructions on how to develop each game.

If you have been creating all of the game scripts presented in this book as you have gone along, then you already have access to a good collection of source code. Inside these AppleScripts, you will find examples of how to work with loops and apply conditional logic. You will also find examples of how to work with variables, lists, event handlers and a host of other AppleScript programming language structures. You will also see examples of how to interact with and control Mac OS X applications.

However, if you have chosen to skip around when reading this book, then you may have missed out on some of this book's game scripts. Not to worry, you have easy access to every game developed in this book from its companion website located at www.courseptr.com/downloads. Table A.1 provides a brief overview of each of the games presented in this book.

TABLE A.1	APPLESCRIPT FILES AVAILABLE ON THE COMPANION WEBSITE	
Chapter	**Application**	**Description**
Chapter 1	AppleScript Humor Script	This script provides your initial introduction to AppleScript programming and offers a good overview of the steps involved in creating and executing AppleScripts.
Chapter 2	AppleScript Story Teller	This script demonstrates how to interact with the player and collect user input as well as how to programmatically interact with and control Mac OS X's built-in speech synthesizer.
Chapter 3	AppleScript Fortune Teller	This AppleScript demonstrates how to store and retrieve data in variables through the creation of a fortune teller game that provides randomly generated answers to player questions.
Chapter 4	AppleScript Typing Test	This AppleScript demonstrates how to apply conditional logic through the creation of a typing game that challenges the player to type in a series of sentences without errors.
Chapter 5	Godfather Trivia Quiz	This AppleScript demonstrates how to work with strings and lists through the creation of a computer game that presents the player with a multiple choice trivia quiz that tests the player's familiarity with the Godfather movie trilogy.
Chapter 6	AppleScript Shell Game	This AppleScript demonstrates how to improve script organization through the implementation of custom handlers as a means of grouping related program statements.

Chapter	Application	Description
Chapter 7	AppleScript Lottery Picker	This AppleScript demonstrates how to write data to a text file and then automate the printing of that file through the creation of a game that generates lottery ticket numbers.
Chapter 8	AppleScript Number Guessing Game	This is a number guessing game that challenges the player to attempt to guess a number between 1 and 100 in as few guesses as possible, guided by hints provided by the game after each guess is processed and analyzed.
Chapter 9	Rock, Paper, Scissors	This AppleScript game is an implementation of the classic Rock, Paper, Scissors game that pits the player against the computer.
Chapter 10	Tic-Tac-Toe	This AppleScript ties together all of the programming concepts and techniques covered in this book through the development of a two-player Tic-Tac-Toe computer game.

WHAT NEXT?

A s you have no doubt realized by completing this book, there is a lot to learn about AppleScript. Hopefully you have found this book to be a good beginning and a worthy first step. However, you should not view the completion of this book as the end of your programming education, but rather as just the beginning. When it comes to learning how to use AppleScript to develop scripts that automate your computer and its many applications, this book has really only scratched the surface. There is so much out there to discover and learn.

To become an effective and accomplished AppleScript programmer, you need to continue to read and keep up with the latest happenings in the AppleScript programming community. To help you along your way, this appendix provides you with a list of additional reading sources, websites, mailing lists, and forums where you can go to interact with other AppleScript programmers and stay on top of things as you learn to become an AppleScript guru.

RECOMMENDED READING

Now that you have completed this book, you may want to consider moving onto books that are focused on providing a more advanced level of discussion of AppleScript. Two such books are shown below. Each will serve as an excellent follow-up to this book.

AppleScript: The Definitive Guide

by Matt Neuburg

ISBN: 0596102119, O'Reilly Media, 2006

This book provides an excellent technical discussion on AppleScript programming, and it is a good resource for advanced AppleScript programmers.

AppleScript: The Comprehensive Guide to Scripting and Automation on Mac OS X

by Hanaan Rosenthal

ISBN: 1590596536, Apress, 2006

This book provides experienced programmers with information needed to take AppleScript programming to the next level.

If, on the other hand, you want to use your new AppleScript programming knowledge and apply it to the development of Mac OS X desktop applications, then I strongly recommend you consider reading the following book.

AppleScript Studio Programming for the Absolute Beginner

by Jerry Lee Ford, Jr.

ISBN: 1598633031, Course Technology PTR, 2006

This book provides complete nuts-and-bolts coverage of AppleScript Studio programming and provides an excellent resource for AppleScript programmers looking to make the jump to desktop application development on Mac OS X.

Locating AppleScript Studio Resources Online

There are other ways to learn about AppleScript than just through books. For example, you can find really good articles posted on websites belonging to online magazines such as www.macworld.com and www.mactech.com. As with any major programming language, there is no shortage of websites that you can visit to learn more about AppleScript. However, some are more useful than others. To help you hone in on some of the better websites, I have provided you with a list of sites that I consider to be most worth visiting.

Apple's AppleScript Web Pages

Apple provides an abundance of AppleScript information on its AppleScript web page located at http://www.apple.com/macosx/features/applescript/, as shown in Figure B.1. Here you will find links to online documentation, development tools, and third-party websites.

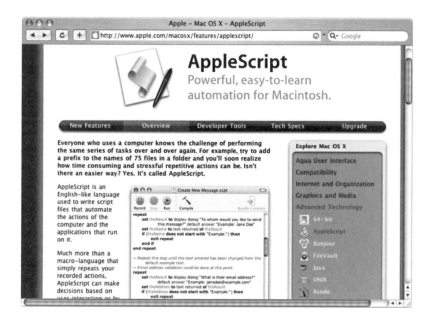

AppleScript Reference Library

Apple provides you with free access to a large collection of AppleScript documentation, which you can find at the AppleScript Reference Library located at http://developer.apple.com/referencelibrary/AppleScript/. The documentation that you find here includes both introductory and advanced materials, as shown in Figure B.2.

FIGURE B.2

Accessing free
AppleScript
documentation
provided by Apple.

MacScripter.net

MacScripter.net, located at www.macscripter.net, provides you with access to free articles, sample scripts, tutorials, and a bunch of other AppleScript goodies, as shown in Figure B.3.

FIGURE B.3

MacScripter.net
provides you with
access to tons of
sample scripts.

Apple's AppleScript Studio Web Pages

Apple's AppleScript Studio web page, located at http://www.apple.com/applescript/studio/, is an excellent resource for learning more about AppleScript Studio. From this website, shown in Figure B.4, you can download and install Xcode, which includes AppleScript Studio, as well as a host of free sample projects. You will also find links to tons of AppleScript Studio information, including online documentation provided by Apple.

FIGURE B.4

Visit Apple's AppleScript Studio web page to stay up to date with the latest developments in AppleScript Studio.

APPLESCRIPT MAILING LISTS

One of the best ways to learn about any programming language is to meet and exchange thoughts and information with other programmers. One excellent way of accomplishing this is to participate in mailing lists and forums dedicated to talking about AppleScript. Mailing lists allow you to post questions and get answers to your questions from other programmers. In addition, you can view other people's discussions and learn from them as well. Best of all, mailing lists provide you with a way to introduce yourself to the AppleScript community and to become a participating member. As you'd expect, there are a number of mailing lists dedicated to AppleScript. To help you find some of the better ones, I have provided a starter list in the sections that follow.

Apple's AppleScript-Users Mailing List

A good place to begin is with Apple's AppleScript-Users list located at http://lists.apple.com/ mailman/listinfo/applescript-users, as shown in Figure B.5. This mailing list facilitates discussion among programmers working on developing AppleScripts that automate the operations system and its applications.

FIGURE B.5

AppleScript-Users is an Apple-sponsored mailing list set up to facilitate discussions among AppleScript programmers.

Yahoo! Groups: AppleScript Mailing List

Yahoo is a sponsor of thousands of online discussion forums. As you would expect, they have one dedicated to AppleScript, which you can find at http://groups.yahoo.com/group/ applescript/, as shown in Figure B.6.

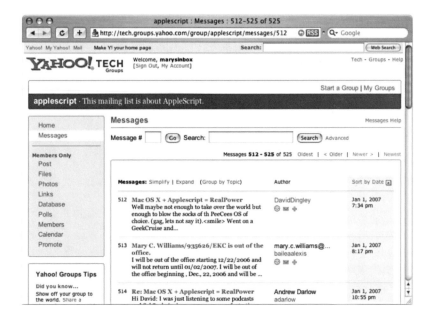

FIGURE B.6

Yahoo's AppleScript discussion forum was started in 1998 and has hundreds of participating members.

MacScripter's AppleScript Forum

Another excellent source of AppleScript information can be found at MacScripter's AppleScript Forum, which is located at http://bbs.applescript.net/, as shown in Figure B.7.

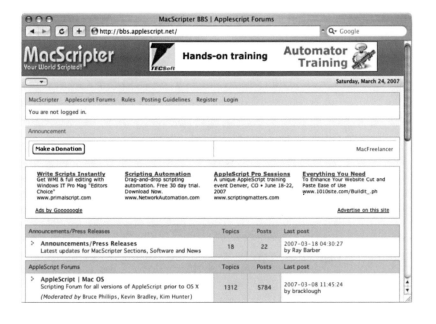

FIGURE B.7

MacScripter's AppleScript forum sponsors discussions on both Mac Classic and Mac OS X as well as AppleScript Studio.

GLOSSARY

Absolute Path. A path that specifies the complete disk and folder structure required to identify the location of a file or folder.

Alias. A direct reference to an object (as opposed to a copy of the object).

Append. The process of adding one value to the end of another value.

Apple Events. Messages sent between AppleScripts and Mac OS X applications in order to facilitate inter-application communications.

Apple Menu. A special menu created by Mac OS X that provides access to computer information, system preferences, and commands that shutdown the system and put it into a sleep.

AppleScript. An English-like scripting language that runs on Max OS X.

AppleScript Studio. A collection of technologies that support the creation of native Mac OS X desktop applications complete with graphical user interfaces.

Applet. A term used to refer to AppleScripts set up to run like a regular application.

Application. Generates a self-contained AppleScript application, sometimes referred to as an applet, which can be executed like any other Mac OS X application.

Application Bundle. A script distribution package that allows programmers to include text, images, movies, or other types of files as part of an AppleScript application.

Argument. A value passed to a script or handler as input for processing.

Array. An indexed list of values stored and managed as a unit (analogous to a list in AppleScript).

Assistant. An AppleScript Studio utility that is designed to guide users through the steps required to begin creating an AppleScript Studio desktop application.

Attribute. A property associated with an object that describes some aspect of the object.

Boolean Class. An AppleScript class that represents a value that is either true or false.

Breakpoint. A marker that identifies a point in a script file where a program debugger pauses when executing the script.

Bugs. A term used to reference application errors.

Bundle. A folder configured to look like an individual file but that can be used to package resources required by an application or script for execution.

Character. An individual character within a string.

Class. Scriptable objects (nouns) that you can programmatically interact with in the application.

Cocoa. A collection of technologies and resources that work together to support the development of AppleScript Studio applications.

Cocoa Controls. Controls that can be used to create graphical user interfaces in AppleScript Studio applications using a simple drag and drop approach.

Code Block. A group of statements that are executed as a unit.

Coercion. The process of converting data from one type to another.

Command. A language keyword that performs a specific task when executed as part of a script statement.

Comment. A statement embedded within a script file for the purpose of documenting the program statements that make up that script file.

Compiling. The process of converting script statements into an executable format that can be processed by the operating system.

Concatenation. The process of merging two or more strings to create a new string.

Constant. A value that is known at development time and does not change during script execution.

Current Working Directory. The folder in which an AppleScript will look as the default location for any files or resources whose paths have not been specified.

Date Class. An AppleScript class used to store date and time data.

Debugger. An application that provides programmers with explicit control over the execution of script statements, allowing script execution to be paused to inspect the value of variables and to trace the order in which statements have executed.

Dialog Window. A popup window that displays text and retrieves user input.

Dictionary. A repository in which Mac OS X applications record the terminology that they support.

Dictionary Browser. A Script Editor window that displays the terminology exposed by scriptable applications.

Droplet. An AppleScript that executes whenever a file or folder is dropped onto it, allowing the file or the contents of the folder to be processed in some manner.

DVD Player. A Mac OS X application that plays DVDs.

Embedded. A statement that has been inserted inside or nested within a code block.

Endless Loop. A loop that runs forever without a programmatic way of terminating its execution.

Escape Character. A special sequence of characters that begins with the \ character followed by a letter that AppleScript recognizes and replaces with an equivalent ASCII character.

Event. An action, such as the starting of an AppleScript or the dropping of a file or folder onto an AppleScript, that triggers execution of statements that respond to the event.

Event Handlers. A special type of control block that is called upon to execute when an associated event occurs.

Explicit Coercion. The programmatic conversion of data from one type to another, as specified by the programmer.

File Class. An AppleScript class that defines an object reference to a specified file, which can then be used to programmatically refer back to the file.

Finder. A Mac OS X application that can be used to manage disks, folders, and files.

Folder Action. An AppleScript that is automatically executed whenever a change occurs in a specified folder.

Function. A term, roughly analogous to a handler, used in other programming languages to create modular and reusable program code.

Global Variable. A variable that is accessible from anywhere within a script file.

Handler. A subroutine that defines a group of script statements that can be called upon as a unit from any location within a script.

Help Viewer. A Mac OS X application that performs a search of the Mac OS X Help system.

Home Directory. A folder assigned to every user with an account on a Mac OS X computer where personal files can be stored.

HyperTalk. A precursor language to AppleScript created in the late 1980s by Bill Atkinson.

Implicit Coercion. The automatic conversion of data from one type to another based on the context in which that data is referenced.

Inspector Window. An Xcode window that can be used to view and modify properties belonging to AppleScript Studio object attributes and associate control events with specific event handlers.

Integer Class. A numeric data type representing a whole number (without a decimal point).

Interapplication Communication. The underlying architecture on Mac OS X that facilitates the sending of messages between applications.

Interface Builder. A software application used as part of AppleScript Studio to assist in the development of graphical user interfaces.

Interface Element. A control that provides AppleScript Studio applications with access to predefined classes, including controls and windows.

Iterate. The process of repeating the execution of a loop.

iTunes. A Mac OS X music application designed to manage and play music and audio files.

JavaScript OSA. A special version of the JavaScript programming language that has been modified to execute directly on the operating system.

Library Palette. A Script Editor window that provides access to commonly used application dictionaries.

List. An ordered collection of values, which can then be referenced and managed as a unit.

Local Variable. A variable accessible only within the scope in which it is defined.

Logical Error. An error generated because of a logical mistake made by the programmer in the design of an application.

Looping. The process of repeating the execution of script statements.

Mail. A Mac OS X application that can be used to send and receive e-mail messages.

MainMenu.nib. A file used to stored information regarding the state of components that make up an AppleScript Studio application's user interface (windows, controls, menus, etc.).

Nested. A statement that has been placed in a code block.

Noun. A resource, such as a file, folder, or disk drive, which is controlled or acted upon.

Null String. An empty string ("").

Object. Any resource to which AppleScript can submit an Apple event message.

Paragraph. A set of characters demarcated by a return or new line character.

POSIX. A UNIX standard that defines a standard means of identifying the location of files and folders.

Property. A specialized type of variable that remains accessible during and after script execution.

Pseudocode. The English-like outline of the logic required to design all or part of an AppleScript.

Real Class. An AppleScript class that represents a real number (may include a decimal point).

Real Number. A number that includes a decimal point.

Record. An unordered collection of data stored in key-value pairs.

Relative Path. A means of specifying the location of a file or folder relative to the current working directory.

Root. The top-most level of a computer's file system.

Runtime Error. An error that occurs because of an illegal action during script execution.

Safari. A scriptable Mac OS X web browser application that can be used to surf the Internet.

Scope. A term that refers to the location within a script where a variable can be accessed.

Scriptable Application. An application that receives and processes Apple events.

Script Assistant. An optional Script Editor feature that, when enabled, assists programmers in the formulation of script statements by offering suggestions for completing the typing of keywords and statements.

Script Bundle. A script distribution package that allows programmers to include text, images, movies, or other types of files as part of an AppleScript.

Script Debugger. An AppleScript editor developed by Late Night Software that provides advanced AppleScript debugging facilities.

Script Editor. A free script editor supplied as part of Mac OS X that can be used to develop and execute AppleScripts.

Script File. A collection of programming statements, often referred to as a script, that is contained within an executable file.

Smile. A free AppleScript editor developed by Satimage.

String class. An AppleScript class that represents a string value.

Suite. A collection of related classes and commands defined in application dictionaries.

Syntax Error. An error that occurs if a programmer does not follow AppleScript's rules when writing AppleScript statements.

System Events. A Mac OS X application that is responsible for starting the operating system and for managing the execution of other applications.

Terminal Application. A Mac OS X application that provides command-line access to the UNIX command shell.

Terminology. The classes, commands, and properties exposed by a scriptable Mac OS X application.

TextEdit. A scriptable Mac OS X word processing application.

Undefined Variable. A variable to which a value has not been assigned.

Variable. A pointer to a location in memory where data can be stored and retrieved.

Verb. An action performed on a noun.

Word. A contiguous set of characters within a text string, separated from other characters by a blank space or other delimiter.

Workflow. An AppleScript that automates the execution of one or more applications in order to perform a process or task.

Xcode. A Mac OS X application development tool that provides many of the underlying technologies required to create AppleScript Studio applications.

INDEX